GANGSTERS AND GOLD DIGGERS

GANGSTERS AND GOLD DIGGERS
OLD NEW YORK, THE JAZZ AGE, AND
THE BIRTH OF BROADWAY

JEROME CHARYN

Four Walls Eight Windows
New York / London

Published in the United States by
Four Walls Eight Windows
39 West 14th Street
New York, NY 10011

U.K. offices:
Four Walls Eight Windows/Turnaround
Unit 3, Olympia Trading Estate
Coburg Road, Wood Green
London N22 6TZ, England

http://www.4w8w.com

First printing December 2003.

Library of Congress Cataloging-in-Publication Data

Charyn, Jerome.
    Gangsters & gold diggers : old New York, the Jazz Age, and
the birth of Broadway / Jerome Charyn.
        p. cm.
Includes bibliographical references (p.) and index.
ISBN 1-56858-278-1 (cloth)
    1. Broadway (New York, N.Y.)—History. 2. New York
(N.Y.)—History—1898–1951. 3. New York (N.Y.)—Social life
and customs—20th century. 4. New York (N.Y.)—Biography.
I. Title: Gangsters and gold diggers. II. Title.

F128.67.B7C47 2003
974.7′1—dc21
                                                                                2003052473

Book design by Dr. Prepress, Inc.

10 9 8 7 6 5 4 3 2 1

Printed in the United States

To my own bestiary:
Bert Williams, Louise Brooks, and "Owney the Killer" Madden

CONTENTS

CHAPTER ONE
THE GREY GHOST

1.

He wasn't a great writer, only a good one. He didn't have Fitzgerald's flair or Hemingway's ability to seize a word, to live within the empty spaces of a text. He was no modernist, just a chronicler of the Big Street. Carpers and cavilers would accuse him of falsifying Broadway, of turning it into a gilded country, and perhaps he did. But he's the least understood of writers, the least explored. His tales of Broadway are largely out of print, like half-forgotten dinosaurs, but we remember his name, *Runyon*, and the argot he introduced, *Runyonese*, and the musical it inspired, *Guys and Dolls*. He was the Jack Dempsey of journalists, the "heaviest hitter" among William Randolph Hearst's stable of star reporters. He'd been hired by Hearst in 1911, and by 1919 his columns were syndicated all over the world. His series on Dempsey in the *New York American* was the most widely read profile ever written. In 1929 he published his first Broadway story, "Romance in the Roaring Forties," in Hearst's *Cosmopolitan* magazine. It was like a minor earthquake. Editors quickly discovered that a Runyon story could increase their circulation by sixty thousand souls. Characters such as Dave the Dude, a benevolent bootlegger, and Miss Missouri Martin, hard-boiled owner of the Sixteen Hundred Club, were becoming almost a common currency.

"I took one little section of New York and made half a million dollars writing about it," Runyon boasted. His popularity had already eclipsed that of Hemingway and Fitzgerald. He was the rage of London. Reporters marveled at his Runyonese, how he was "enriching" the language, and feared that he might change it forever. Feared or not, his echo was profound. It reached other writers, like Anthony Burgess, whose futuristic slang in *A Clockwork Orange* was influenced by Runyon's Broadway, where it was always four o'clock in the morning and Dave the Dude was marching up and down the Big Street, rescuing some chorus doll in distress.

Novelist and newspaperman Jimmy Breslin, one of Runyon's most recent biographers, doesn't buy into the myth of Broadway. "Damon Runyon invented the Broadway of *Guys and Dolls* and the Roaring Twenties, neither of which existed." Runyon's "good guy gangsters," like Dave the Dude, weren't good guys at all. Yet columnist Heywood Broun, who traveled the same streets as Runyon did, wrote in his introduction to Runyon's first collection of stories: "I recognize the various characters concerned as actual people who are at this moment living and loving, fighting and scuttling no more than a quarter of a mile from the place where I live."

I'm suspicious of both Breslin *and* Broun. Breslin was born in 1930, and couldn't have encountered Dave the Dude, real or imagined, on the Big Street, couldn't have known any of Runyon's chorus dolls from the Ziegfeld Follies (the Follies disappeared after 1931). Even if he'd rehearsed for his entire life, he'd never have stumbled upon the feel of Runyon's Street. No one could. "For writers and others who were tracking it, Broadway was always a moving target," notes historian William R. Taylor in "Broadway: The Place That Words Built." And during the 1920s, that target was almost impossible to find, as the fabric of Broadway was shifting so fast. It's as if a brand-new America had appeared in the form of gangsters and gold-digging chorus girls, the archetypes of Runyon's stories. And these archetypes were even less real to Heywood Broun, who was searching for "actual people" in Runyon's private bestiary. Thus he diminishes Runyon to a local colorist, a kind of sentimental voyeur. And Runyon was much more ambiguous than that, even if his stories were reductive, and the gangsters were always good. . . .

In "Madame La Gimp," Dave the Dude, capturer of "beauties," stands in a doorway talking to a "busted-down Spanish doll," who was once a "big shot on Broadway," a Spanish dancer who had to give up "the dancing dodge" on account of an accident. And Dave, who listens to no one, listens to Madame La Gimp. Intrigued, he tells her story to Runyon's nameless narrator.

"The old doll is in a tough spot. It seems that she once has a baby which she calls by the name of Eulalie, being it's a baby girl, and she ships the baby off to her sister in a little town in Spain to raise up, because Madame La Gimp figures a baby is not apt to get much raising-up off of her as long as she is on Broadway."

But this little maneuver becomes her downfall. She works as a cleaning woman at an apartment hotel on Park Avenue called the Marberry, and has been using the hotel's stationery to send letters to her baby, who is now eighteen, pretending that she lives at the hotel. But Madame's baby is about to marry the son of a Spanish count; the count's entire family is touring the world and will stop in Manhattan to meet Madame La Gimp, who lives in a cellar on Tenth Avenue.

Total catastrophe! Except that being a former dancing doll entitles her to catch the ear of Dave the Dude, who has no limits or boundaries on Broadway, and is prepared to move the planet for Madame. He's the official bootlegger at the Marberry, provider of champagne, and he has a customer in the building lend his apartment to Madame. Then he asks Miss Missouri Martin and his own "ever-loving wife," Billy Perry, a former tap dancer at the Sixteen Hundred Club, to "remake" Madame and restore a bit of her beauty.

The Dude triumphs, of course. The count's people fall in love with Madame, and Dave decides to have a party at the hotel. To impress the count, he invites Manhattan's biggest celebrities: Al Jolson, Mayor Jimmy Walker, and Otto Kahn, Broadway's own banker—that is, he invites their stand-ins, such as Tony Bertazzola of the Chicken Club, Skeets Bolivar, Rochester Red . . . and chorus girls from the Sixteen Hundred Club who pretend to be torch singers Sophie Tucker and Helen Morgan, and actress Jeanne Eagels (a heroin addict who died of an overdose in 1929).

The party's a walloping success, but the Dude is in a rage. His fellow gangsters, who were Madame's guests, have stolen articles from different apartments at the Marberry. "I am greatly mortified," says the Dude, particularly about "the baby grand that is removed from Apartment 9-D."

Runyon's story was filmed twice, by Frank Capra in 1933 as *Lady for a Day*, and by Capra again in *Pocketful of Miracles* (1961), with Glenn Ford as Dave the Dude and Bette Davis as Apple Annie, a bittersweet version of Madame La Gimp. It was Capra's last film. By 1961 Runyon's guys and dolls had already lost their bite. But that doesn't diminish "Madame La Gimp." The story has a kind of primitive power that comes from two sources: Dave the Dude's monumental, almost manic largesse, which Heywood Broun could never have witnessed, because it could only have happened in Runyon's imagined, Breughel-like Broadway, where people dance and drink champagne and steal baby grands . . . and from the narrator, who is unlike any other narrator we have ever seen.

It's William R. Taylor who helps pinpoint this uniqueness. "To read Runyon's Broadway stories today is to enter . . . a world that is almost entirely voice. . . .There is little description of any kind." And even Runyon's slang is "fused into the narrative voice," without which we would have cuteness and chaos. Because the narrator never initiates the action, never falls in love, it's difficult to grasp that he alone drives the stories, labels and "relabels the human goods of the Broadway world." The most obvious tag of his narration is the total use of the "historical" or "perpetual" present tense, which Taylor sees as a controlling device. But it's more than that. It freezes time, locks us into the landscape. The vocabulary never changes, even if another character assumes the narration, tells a tale within the tale—like Pincus the busboy in "Little Pinks," who wheels a crippled "chorus Judy" all the way to Florida on foot. When Little Pinks narrates to us *and* the narrator, we lose our bearings, as if the narrative itself were a disembodied voice. And we begin to suspect that the tropes and tricks of the narration is not to reveal, but to hide things, that in spite of the story's manic edge, there is an undercurrent of isolation.

The narrator seems to be a citizen of Broadway, like the other citizens he writes about. His identity isn't challenged. He can argue with Dave the Dude, be present at a burglary, bring a dying gambler home to his wife (who won't take the gambler in because she's giving a party and can't be bothered with all the blood), but the narrator himself is a visible invisible man, *of* the stories, trapped within their landscapes, yet psychically apart, like Runyon himself, wounded, deeply flawed, an outsider longing to create a skin for himself, the skin of Broadway.

2.

He'd always been an outsider, looking to get in. His destiny was sealed at birth. The chronicler of Broadway was born in *Manhattan*, Kansas, on October 8, 1880. His father was an itinerant journalist and typesetter. His mother died when he was nine, and both the boy and his father became eternal wanderers. They would often take turns sleeping in the same single bed, according to Jimmy Breslin. And the boy would become a child reporter at twelve, after finishing elementary school. One of his heroes was gunman-sheriff Bat Masterson, whom Runyon would later meet in Colorado, after Bat himself had become a journalist, writing about "man-killers" in the Wild West. . . .

He was a soldier during the Spanish-American War, a drifter, a sports writer for the *San Francisco Post* and the *Rocky Mountain News,* and began to report on politics and crime. He moved to Manhattan—New York, not Kansas—in 1910 and joined Hearst's *American.* In 1911 he married Ellen Egan, society editor on the *Rocky Mountain News,* and published *The Tents of Trouble,* a book of poems. He was fast becoming a denizen of Broadway, where he bumped into Bat Masterson, now an alcoholic sports columnist who lived on West 49th Street.

Runyon parked his wife, his daughter Mary Ellen (born in 1914), and his son Damon Jr. (born in 1918) on Broadway and 95th Street and kept a penthouse apartment at the Forrest Hotel on West 49th. He lived by his own particular rules, "a peacock who spent an hour each day dressing himself" and had "dozens of suits color-coordinated not only down to his socks but even to his typewriters." He wore suspenders decorated with his own profile and "more jewelry than a bride." He drank forty cups of coffee a day, a cigarette with each cup. He was a nighthawk who went to bed at dawn and rarely woke before three in the afternoon. He estranged himself from his wife and kids, spending as little time with them as he could. He hated the rich—Park Avenue and polite society—and politicians, except for Jimmy Walker, who was a nighthawk like himself.

He preferred the company of gangsters, gamblers, tough Broadway detectives like Johnny Broderick, chorus girls, boxers, and baseball players. But in spite of his tomcatting, he had few intimate friends, and "in his personal relationships he appears to have been aloof, even cold." As a transplanted Kansan and Coloradan, he would always feel like a man of the West in the curious Wild West of Manhattan, where he could seek outlaws and an outlaw culture. His "friends" were Al Capone (lately of Chicago), gambler Arnold Rothstein, and bootlegger Owney Madden. Their sort of turmoil seemed to comfort him. A teetotaler, he never touched champagne or Madden's beer. He would write about jokesters, but hated dirty jokes. He was a lonely, enigmatic man.

In 1921 a Jewish delicatessen, Lindy's, opened on Broadway between 49th and 50th. It was a modest hole in the wall that would become world-famous for its cheesecake (comedienne Fanny Brice had it flown or wheeled in to her wherever she performed). During this "delicatessen decade," Lindy's would soon become *the* delicatessen on Broadway. *Everybody* ate there. Harpo Marx, who hung out at Lindy's, remembers "cardplayers, horseplayers, bookies, song pluggers, agents, actors out of work and actors playing the Palace, Al Jolson with his mob of fans, and Arnold Rothstein with his mob of runners and flunkies."

Much of the allure of Lindy's was Leo Lindemann, the owner-manager who was always around. He was delirious about Broadway; as soon as dusk approached, signboards on the Big Street turned "into a crater of light. I never get used to it." Lindy's own signboard was modest, lit with 25-watt bulbs. But it wasn't Lindy's lights that his best customers sought out. It was the coziness, the small comforts, a home away from home, where Harpo could be "back with my own people, who spoke my language, with my accent"—the accent and language of Broadway.

Mrs. Lindemann, who helped manage the deli, was a bit of a schoolmarm. She preferred the company of young actors and old vaudevillians rather than the gamblers and gangsters, who, she felt, gave Lindy's a bad name. But her husband had a much shrewder nose for business *and* democracy. Jolson, Runyon, Walter Winchell, and Rothstein all had their particular tables, and pulled in other customers. Rothstein's table was sacrosanct. It was right near the cashier's booth, and after 9 P.M. no one else was allowed to occupy it but Rothstein himself. He conducted business over cups of coffee and a Danish. . . .

Jolson may have been the king of Broadway, with his name lit in forty-foot letters on top of the Winter Garden, but he wasn't much of a king at Lindy's. It was Rothstein who ruled, in spite of Mrs. Lindemann (he was always involved in secretive deals and might have been Leo's silent partner). Lindy's was his permanent address, his private telephone exchange, his office, his kibitzer's corner. Lucky Luciano, Legs Diamond, and Frank Costello (Runyon's principal model for Dave the Dude) would all play court to him. Diamond, both cowardly and vicious, was one of his bodyguards and enforcers. Costello was his protégé. He taught Dave the Dude and Luciano how to dress. He financed their enterprises. He was banker to the underworld. And he never sought notoriety. Lindy's was enough for A. R.—The Brain, as Runyon began to call him. He understood the power that Runyon had. "They"—the printing presses—"do not stop. You are not fighting a man with a pen. You can kill a man with a pen, but the presses keep rolling. So you really are fighting a printing press. That fight cannot be won."

Lindy's would become Mindy's Restaurant in the Broadway tales, a cafeteria and delicatessen nonpareil, the locus and defining point of Runyon's imagination.

One night The Brain is walking me up and down Broadway in front of Mindy's Restaurant, and speaking of this and that. . . .

The action often starts and ends in Mindy's. It's almost as if no other place exists or has much importance on the Big Street. In *The Crack-Up*, Scott Fitzgerald wrote about Broadway and his own fall from grace, when he lived in a kind of alcoholic stupor, trembling, having to take care of his mad wife, the once-beautiful Zelda, with rashes all over her body, her mind ablaze, while in his "dark night of the soul it is always three o'clock in the morning, day after day."

But dark nights of the soul were outlawed at Mindy's Restaurant. Three o'clock in the morning was when all the fun began. And four o'clock was the magic hour, when the chorus dolls from Missouri Martin's Sixteen Hundred Club or the Midnight Frolic on Ziegfeld's roof would appear at Mindy's, have an early-morning snack, and play with whatever gambler was promising them "a diamond ring as big as a cough drop."

Mindy's was more than a delicatessen; it was a desideratum, like Hemingway's ideal of a clean, well-lighted place. But it wasn't clean or well-lit. In fact, it's as nondescript as the few other points on Runyon's private compass, the Hot Box or the Sixteen Hundred Club. . . .

Runyon's is a very narrowed universe, and his argot is just as narrow; it's the patois of racetracks, boxing arenas, gambling dens, bordellos, night clubs, speakeasies, cafeterias, with a sprinkle of Yiddishisms, because Yiddish had become the unofficial language of the Street. Runyon's guys and dolls weren't necessarily Jewish, but Mindy's, with its gefilte fish, was a Jewish haven, and Yiddish had become one of the coded signs of an outlaw culture.

Runyon's "slanguage" was a counterattack against white Protestant America, its idea of racial purity, its dislike of gamblers and chorus girls, who were poisoning the country with alcohol and sex. And so scraps of Yiddish were like a secret tongue—a *finnif* was a five-dollar bill—but Runyon's patois was already old-fashioned, even as he wrote his stories. He talks of a gangster's "moxie," or pluck, "a tough gorill," a disheartened gambler who "scrags himself," a "chorus Judy" who looks "wiser than a treeful of owls."

Hardly a revolution!

We have a chorus of colorful characters, colorful names, in Runyon's bestiary: Saul the Soldier, Hot Horse Herbie, Frankie Ferocious, Germany Schwartz and Joey Uptown (who are outsiders and don't belong to the Big Street), Bad Basil, Handsome Jack, Benny the Blond Jew, "The Seldom Seen Kid who is called The Seldom Seen," and Madame La Gimp, of course. But Runyon's Broadway is irrevocably white. There are no piano ticklers or honky-tonk men on the Big Street. Harlem is absent; it does not even appear on Runyon's map.

William R. Taylor also reads a good deal of misogyny into Runyon. "Runyon's world is preeminently a world of men. Women figure in it as obsessions, as hostages, as prizes. . . . They are stolen or hustled [like cattle]. They provoke violence in men and they seldom talk." They are, he continues, "dumbbells, dumb blondes," or "dumb wives who outsmart their husbands. . . ."

Taylor accurately describes the tone and mood of the stories, and Runyon's underlying fear of women. Mindy's is a men's club, with a couple of decorative dolls. Yet there is an erotic engine that drives Broadway. And if women are often "obsessions" and "prizes," it's these obsessions that give the stories their juice, take them outside the bondage of a dated and often dead argot. The blondes aren't as dumb as Taylor believes; they might be gold diggers, but it's their beauty that defines them, not their greed. A woman is either a "beauty" or a "red-headed raggedy doll." A "beauty" can stop the action, destroy the narrative frame, bring havoc to Broadway. Runyon admits that "even a guy like Dave the Dude may go daffy over a doll." Almost all the dolls on Broadway are chorus girls from the Ziegfeld Follies, Earl Carroll's "Vanities," or Missouri Martin's Sixteen Hundred Club. They're young, with lightning legs, and nervous, narrow hips.

In "A Very Honorable Guy," gambler Feet Samuels is in love with Hortense Hathaway, a showgirl in "Georgie White's 'Scandals,'" and "all she has to do is to walk around and about Georgie White's stage with only a few light bandages on and everybody considers her very beautiful, especially from the neck down. . . ."

Feet Samuels is broke. Dave the Dude has offered him a job "riding rum between here and Philly," but Feet turns it down because he can't tolerate being away from Mindy's. And he can't declare his love, because if he does, Hortense "will expect me to buy her some diamond bracelets," as any gold-digging doll would do.

So with The Brain vouching for him he sells his body to a certain Park Avenue doctor, promising to "scrag himself" in a month. And with the money he gets he goes on a big gambling spree; whatever crap game he's in, he has it "all crippled up." He buys Hortense her diamond bracelets, but soon the month is up, and Doc Bodeeker comes after him with a butcher knife.

Feet runs away, and while running he declares his love.

"I love you too, Feet," says Hortense, "because nobody ever makes such a sacrifice as to hock their body for me."

It turns out that Doc Bodeeker is just as daffy about Hortense. "I am in love with her from the night I see her playing the part of a sunflower in 'Scandals.'"

To keep him from killing Feet, Hortense hits him over the head with a ham. The narrator brings the doc into Mindy's and revives him with a cup of coffee and a Bismarck herring. The delicatessen listens to the doc's tales of woe. "I am broken-hearted. I also seem to have a large bump on my head."

"Do not worry," says The Brain. "I will make everything good, because I am the guy who okays Feet Samuels with you. . . . His credit is ruined forever on Broadway."

But Feet and Hortense don't give a damn. They disappear to Newark, "raising chickens and children right and left," and "all of Hortense's bracelets are now in Newark municipal bonds, which," the narrator assures us, "are not bad bonds, at that."

It's Hortense who empowers the story, holding sway over the men who watch her dance. And this entitlement is what Broadway was about. *The chorus girl.* She was much more coveted than any star. And Runyon captures this to perfection. Hortense's hypnotic charm lasts much longer than the lingo, and like all good gold diggers, she's transformed into an "ever-loving wife."

Runyon's best story, "Little Pinks," doesn't seem so *Runyonesque*, because it reaches beyond the cynical flora and fauna of Broadway and forces us into the territory of a modern fairy tale, with magic and emotion. Once again, the action unfolds around a "chorus Judy," Your Highness, who "plays the frost for all who are not well established as practically zillionaires, and she makes no bones of stating that her angle is to find a character of means who is not entirely repulsive and marry him." She is perhaps "the most beautiful Judy that ever hits Broadway."

She's heartless, of course. And Mindy's agrees that "Your Highness will sooner or later marry the United States Mint, or maybe the Bank of England." But another fate befalls her. A bookmaker, Case Ables, slaps her down the stairs of the Canary

Club, after she refuses to go out with him, and she's crippled for life. A busboy at the Canary Club, Little Pinks, a half-pint with a big nose, is her secret admirer. Whenever she goes to work at a nightclub, Pinks follows her there. She doesn't even know he's alive. And the consensus at Mindy's is that "a bus boy has no right to admire anybody and consequently Little Pinks is in great disfavor with one and all." No matter. He takes the crippled Judy to his cellar apartment and looks after her. Your Highness still doesn't know he's alive. She wants to go to Florida, sit in the sun, and meet some zillionaire. . . .

Pinks remains loyal to her, and the narrator wonders why he is "slaving for a cold, selfish little broad. . . . What is your percentage?"

Pinks has no percentage. "I love her," he says.

And he gets her to Florida in her wheelchair, stealing food along the way, running into bank robbers and convicts, who are instantly under her spell. Your Highness still isn't satisfied. Pinks continues to slave for her. But no matter how hard she flirts, she can't attract a fly, rich or poor. Your Highness has lost her looks and is "so thin she is almost a shadow."

She's convinced she knows the cure. "Pinks, I must have a lot of jewelry. I must, I must, I must."

Pinks becomes a cat burglar for her, steals "a whole hatful of jewelry," which pleases her for a little while. Pinks is arrested, but a certain Dr. Quincey of Chicago acts as his angel. The doctor had bought the jewels for his own ever-loving wife, but as soon as he sees Your Highness wearing them, he can tell that she is dying. He asks the cops to let Pinks remain at liberty until the little busboy can finish caring for her. And Pinks does care for her. Suddenly her eyes "are as big as dinner plates." And she no longer has an appetite for zillionaires.

"Kiss me, Little Pinks," she says.

And he kisses her for the only time in his life.

"Little Pinks, I love you," she says and slips away into paradise.

He goes to jail and tells his story to the narrator.

"I am indeed sorry for you," the narrator says.

"Sorry for me? . . . I am sorry for you. You never kiss Your Highness and hear her say she loves you."

But the story ends on a much more bitter note. Case Ables comes to Florida, and Pinks cripples him with a baseball bat. He goes back to jail. And a guy in the sheriff's office, who is very indignant, says that "we can't have our winter tourists treated like Mr. Ables."

And we know that, except in the narrator's mind, Little Pinks is already forgotten. The narrator's role in the narration becomes a bit clearer: he's no voyeur or spy. His function is to keep the myth of Broadway alive, to remember a culture that will disappear with the same lightning as a chorus girl's legs. That's why the narrator has such a devotion to the present tense. It isn't simply gangster talk, the argot of ill-educated men. It's the obsessive, almost delusional, need to clutch the moment, immortalize it, and that's why there's so much exaggeration: "Bad Basil can scarcely sleep good any night he does not kill some guy."

If Basil is really bad, as grandiose as Al Capone, he might not fall into oblivion. And so Broadway, with Mindy's as its cradle of warmth, becomes the capital of night. "If there's one thing I hate and despise," says the narrator, "it is the daylight." Daylight is the actual, the specific, the mundane, the territory of wives and electric bills. It's when the citizens and the chorus dolls have to sleep, whereas "everybody knows that at four o'clock in the morning the torch is hotter than at any other time of the day."

But the Street didn't only live for love. T͟
kinds of tumult: "If a guy is looking for troub͟
along toward four o'clock in the morning any͟
that the right address is nowhere else but Mindy͟ s.

Nowhere else but Mindy's, where Runyon must have hoped his
guys and dolls would sit and sit until there was no more sun.

3.

In "The Idyll of Miss Sarah Brown" we meet Obadiah Masterson, otherwise known as The Sky. The Sky is Runyon's homage to his boyhood idol, Bat Masterson, a citizen of Broadway
when he died on October 25, 1921. The Sky isn't a gunman, he's
a gambler from Colorado and a wanderer who lives in hotel
rooms. He's thirty years old, "a tall guy with a round kisser, and
big blue eyes." He carries a lot of cash, and one extra suit of
clothes. He doesn't have a house, a car, a watch, or a piece of jewelry. And wanderer as he is, he falls in love with a mission worker
on Broadway, Miss Sarah Brown. "And after a couple of ganders
at the young doll, The Sky was a goner."

The story twists here and there to tell us how Miss Sarah
becomes Mrs. Sky, how Sky joins her mission, after letting her
win his soul in a crooked game of dice. It's romance à la Runyon,
and would become the backbone of a Broadway musical that
doomed the stories themselves, made them antiquated. How
could Runyon's modest words compete with guys and dolls who
could dance and sing, with the chiaroscuro of a stage set, a floating crap game, a glimpse of Havana, and a sanitized Mindy's
without The Brain?

But it's The Sky who disturbs our dreams and not his Broadway double, who belts, "I've Never Been in Love Before." By

ɔ0, when *Guys and Dolls* opened, Runyon's Broadway was long
gone, with the bootleggers, the gold diggers, and a busboy who
would have wheeled a crippled chorus Judy to China. But Runyon had invested so much of himself in his portrait of The Sky,
and the man behind the portrait, Bat Masterson. Runyon may
have dressed like a dandy, but he lived out of a suitcase, like The
Sky. Broadway was a bachelor's refuge, even if most of the bachelors were married men.

What about Bartholomew Masterson, the Bat? So much has
been written about him that it's hard to separate Bat from all the
ballyhoo, particularly when a good deal of the writing was done
by Masterson himself. He was a "man-killer" who may only have
killed one man, a cavalry sergeant, Melvin A. King, after the sergeant found Bat in bed with his girl, Molly Brennan, a prostitute
in Sweetwater, Texas. In one of the legends surrounding "the
Sweetwater duel," Molly tossed herself in front of Masterson,
protecting him from the sergeant's bullets. She herself was killed,
and using her body as a shield, Masterson managed to kill Melvin
A. King.

It's almost a tale that could have been told in Mindy's.

The sergeant had wounded him in the leg, and Masterson
had to walk with a cane. He was almost a gimp. He went to work
in Dodge City as one of Wyatt Earp's deputies and would bop
lawbreakers over the head with his cane, or "bat." And that's how
Bat Masterson was born.

He ran for sheriff of Ford County, Texas, and won. He also
owned part interest in a Dodge City dance hall. Later he was a
U.S. marshal, but he lost his job after a local paper accused him
of being a crook, so he had to earn his keep playing cards. He
joined Wyatt Earp in Tombstone, helped him clean up the town,

while he himself continued to gamble. In 1882 he was marshal of Trinidad, Colorado, where he also opened a gambling house and saloon. Then he began to drift, dealing cards in different towns. He bought a variety theatre in Denver, where he met Emma Walker, an actress and former saloon girl, and married her in 1891. He began writing a weekly sports column in one of the Denver papers, and that's how he and Runyon met.

In 1902 he moved to Manhattan with Emma. President Theodore Roosevelt appointed him a deputy marshal. He also wrote a sports column for the *New York Morning Telegraph*. He was a fixture on Broadway, gambling, watching illegal prize fights, drinking hard, brawling, visiting bordellos, attending the Follies, running after chorus girls, writing. . . .

And it's no miracle that Runyon metamorphosed him into The Sky. Bat was the ideal man of the West who'd settled in the new Dodge City. Manhattan was its own frontier town, and Mindy's was a saloon that served seltzer and cream soda. Its desperadoes were called Bad Basil and Dave the Dude. Its saloon girls danced for Ziegfeld or Earl Carroll and Miss Missouri Martin—aka Texas Guinan, queen of Broadway's nightclub hostesses, who befriended Runyon; Missouri Martin could just as well have been a hostess at a dance hall in Dodge.

More than one critic has noted the resemblance between Dodge and the Big Street. According to Patricia Ward D'Itri, Runyon's Broadway "extend[s] the mystique of the Western cowboy and gunslinger." And William R. Taylor sees Runyon as part of "a common tradition of Western storytelling." But I'm not convinced. Broadway was a no-man's-land, neither of the East nor the West. It ate up your past and your tradition. The Big Street was where you went when you had nowhere to go. It didn't really function during the day; sunlight exposed the drabness of yet another cowtown, another main drag, which served as a mirror of your own insignificance.

Like the Big Street's other citizens, Runyon needed Broadway. He was a man with few inner resources, like so many of his fictional characters who flocked to Mindy's; his sole existence had become a kind of performance, a puppet show, a single song—about a sad, insatiable want.

He abandoned his family. His first wife died in 1931, and Runyon married again, this time to Patrice Amati, whom he advertised as a Spanish countess. She was a waif he'd met in Mexico when she was still a child. He'd "adopted" her at a distance, helped send her to school. She was twenty-six years younger than Damon. He loved the countess as much as he could. She divorced him in 1946, the same year he died of throat cancer.

His larynx had been removed in 1944. He lost his voice, had to scribble his commands on a piece of paper, and he spent his last days in the company of Walter Winchell, with whom he'd had many a spat (Walter battled with everybody). But these two bitter, lonely men were now reconciled. Walter admired the Broadway tales, and even appeared in several of them as Waldo Winchester. And now Runyon sat at Winchell's private table inside the Stork Club, and then they would prowl Manhattan like a couple of nighthawks in Winchell's roadster, which had a police radio, and they would arrive at the scene of a crime, often before the police. "Finally after a nightcap of ice-cream sodas, I would drop him off at his hotel," Walter remembered. Nighthawking with Winchell had become Runyon's last pleasure in life. . . .

They were like a vaudeville act: "one unable to speak, the other unable to stop talking." Walter and Damon. Winchell had popularized Broadway in his gossip column long before Runyon ever did. He scribbled and spoke like a machine gun, and captured all the brashness of Broadway. Yet little remains but the chatter. The heartbreak isn't there. There were no columns about a crippled chorus Judy and Little Pinks. As Stanley Walker reminds us in *The Night Club Era*: "Winchell, the ex-hoofer, caught the tempo [of Broadway]. That tempo was brittle, cheap, garish, loud, and full of wild dissonances," like Walter himself. "Broadway is a street of synthetic romance, of phony titillation." And Winchell uncovered that synthetic romance. Damon uncovered something else. Winchell understood this, and perhaps that's why he welcomed Runyon into his private little club of prowlers.

Winchell called him "the Grey Ghost of Broadway," and a ghost he was, but that ghost, sitting at the top of the Forrest Hotel, had found a particular way to fit his persona into a fleshless, nameless narrator who, according to Jimmy Breslin, "revealed nothing of himself. . . . A narrator hiding behind a false voice was the closest he would ever come to allowing his life to be seen and felt by others." But Breslin is wrong. Runyon's lack of syncopation, his deliberate flatness, his numbing argot, were part of an elegiac tone. He was *giving* us Broadway, without Fitzgerald's stunning music, without the romance of Jay Gatsby, the bootlegger who'd gone to "Oggsford" and sought Daisy Buchanan's moneyed voice. The closest to Gatsby that Runyon would ever get was Sky Masterson, and The Sky didn't have a million shirts in his closet and a touch of mystery. Mystery and complication weren't what Runyon was about.

We revere Fitzgerald and hardly read Runyon at all. We dismiss him and his cartoon characters as cannon fodder for a musical comedy. Yet we ought to look again. There's an hysteria underlying Runyon's monochromes, a desperate desire to block out the sunlight, to limit the landscape of Broadway to four o'clock in the morning at Mindy's. And if we do look, we might find a whole dominion, a hunger that marked Broadway, where bootleggers and chorus dolls, slumming Park Avenue matrons and scribes like Waldo Winchester mingled for one brief moment in a Broadway delicatessen and lived on cold borscht and gefilte fish and strawberries washed with Mindy's own hands.

When the Grey Ghost was dying, Mr. and Mrs. "Lindy" Lindemann would bring him a bowl of crushed strawberries and clotted cream. Broadway itself seemed to reside in that bowl. It didn't have the power of Proust's magic cake. Nothing does. But it could soothe a man who had lost his larynx.

CHAPTER TWO
Fast and Furious

1.

There was a boisterous, maddening Broadway long before Runyon. Looking up and down the crooked lanes of lower Manhattan in 1774, John Adams, future president of the United States, wrote: "I have not seen one real gentleman, one well-bred man, since I came to town. At their entertainments there is not conversation that is agreeable; there is not modesty, no attention to one another. They talk very loud, very fast and altogether. If they ask you a question, before you can utter three words of your answer, they will break out upon you again, and talk away."

They talk very loud, very fast and altogether.

One can almost conjure up an eighteenth-century counterpart to Mindy's gang of gamblers on Broadway. . . .

It started as an old Indian trail that cut a swath across Manhattan and continued through the Bronx. The Dutch called it *Heere Straat* (High Street) and then *Breede Wegh* (Broadway). It was the main road of New Amsterdam, a town that was almost an illusion. The Dutch hadn't come to America to escape persecution or start a sect. They'd come to trade. They were factotums, farmers, and commissioners of the Dutch West India Company, which wanted to fatten itself in the New World. The earliest maps were pieces of fiction, with the houses of Manhattan's wealthiest merchants peering toward Europe. One map, made in 1672, was almost a replica of Lisbon. The mapmakers were *dreaming* Europe when they landed in the harbor, with its "wild worldly" men.

For architect Rem Koolhaas, these early maps are European, "but kidnapped from their context and transplanted to a mythical island," where they recreate "a utopian Europe, the product of compression and destiny," the very lineaments of modern Broadway.

Koolhaas reads Manhattan "as the product of an unformulated theory, *Manhattanism*," whose program was "to exist in a world totally fabricated by man, i.e. to live *inside* fantasy," like Mindy's and the Main Stem.

Yet it was fantasy quickened with commerce. The uniqueness of *Manna-hata* (an old Indian word with a double meaning: "island of hills" and "drunken homeland") was that even after the British seized it and the American colonists rid themselves of the British yoke, Manhattan would remain Dutch, with a love of business and brawling. Just a decade after New Amsterdam was founded in the spring of 1624, "a startling percentage" of its population "seemed to be smugglers, pirates, prostitutes, and drunks."

As one observer noted in 1653: "They all drink here, from the moment they are able to lick a spoon. . . . The women of the neighborhood entertain each other with a pipe and brazier; young and old, they smoke."

And *Breede Wegh* would widen under Dutch and British rule. It had its own hanging tree, where unfortunate pirates, highwaymen, pilgrims, and slaves would swing in the sun. It had an equestrian statue of King George III at Bowling Green and the foot of Broadway, which the rebels would destroy in 1776, by separating the king from his horse. It had bands of roving players who would perform in the streets at modest little theatres on or near Broadway. The first professional performance was of *Richard III*, in 1750. How appropriate that Manhattan's emblematic entertainer would be a murderous hunchback with a poet's tongue. And theatergoing itself would become a long, long march up the ribs of Manhattan, with Broadway as its spine. . . .

Minstrel shows arrived like a storm in 1832, with Thomas D. Rice dancing and singing his blackface routine, "Jumping Jim Crow"—the archetypical white man in black paint. Other white performers copied from him, and soon the city had an avalanche of Jim Crows, all babbling in an invented Negro dialect. It's difficult for us to imagine the ferocity of these "coon shows," which had the curious effect of making blacks invisible and omnipresent at the same time. Blacks were almost never written about in nineteenth-century New York, according to Luc Sante in *Low Life*. They had their own districts, such as Gay Street in Greenwich Village, even their own "Little Africa" within the Tenderloin, that ghetto of whorehouses, dance halls and saloons on Manhattan's West Side, below Fortieth Street. But they couldn't walk into any theatre or saloon that wasn't reserved for blacks, except certain hovels called black-and-tans, where they could mingle with "white trash."

The minstrel show "introduced an imagined world of blacks without whites," a world which audiences seemed to adore, because it gave blackface comedians the liberty to poke fun at white people and their ways, while pretending to be "coons." It was racist rigamarole, appalling *and* as popular as "naked drama," or burlesque, which began to monopolize Manhattan theatres by the end of the Civil War. Both blackface and burlesque would become part of the variety show in working-class concert halls and saloons. "Variety" was strictly for males. Raucous and vulgar, it was the specialty of "Satan's Circus," as reformers liked to call the Tenderloin.

The Tenderloin got its name from a police captain, Alexander S. Williams, who in 1876 was transferred to the old Twenty-ninth Precinct, which covered the wicked West Side. He would stroll along Broadway with a grin and wink at his friends. "I've had nothing but chuck steak for a long time, and now I'm going to get a little of the tenderloin."

Every concert hall, every saloon, every brothel, every street-walker in Satan's Circus fatted the pockets of Clubber Williams, who collected bribes while he twirled his nightstick. Clubber was having the time of his life in the Tenderloin, whose streets were packed with brothels. "There is more law in the end of a police-man's nightstick than in the Supreme Court," he loved to brag. Meanwhile he amassed a fortune. Clubber had a mansion in Cos Cob, Connecticut, holdings in Manhattan real estate, and various bank accounts, large and small. He'd fattened himself so fast that streetwalkers and brothelkeepers complained about his greed. But the Board of Police Commissioners acquitted him of any and all charges. And Clubber continued to roam the Tenderloin and collect his due. He adored burlesque and the rough company of variety halls. The chorus girls who frolicked on stage in flesh-colored tights were little more than prostitutes who fell under the protection of Clubber Williams. He took his pleasure with the girls and parceled them out to his clientele.

And then Clubber lost his paradise. Reformers such as Charles Parkhurst, the fiery minister at Madison Square Presbyterian Church and head of the New York Society for the Prevention of Crime, sampled the brothels and saloons of Satan's Circus in disguise, forced Clubber Williams to retire, and sent shivers through the Tenderloin as police shut the most notorious brothels. But chorus girls got rid of their flesh-colored tights and moved from variety and burlesque to vaudeville, a brand-new art form, perfected by Tony Pastor, who had once been a variety performer in his own saloon, and now took the wickedness and a touch of chaos out of variety and turned it into an entertainment that would dominate the theatre for over thirty years.

What made vaudeville unique was this: "Audiences felt that each show was being invented just for them." And it probably was. The separate acts that composed a complete bill would often change from night to night. There was minstrelsy, a bit of burlesque, musical numbers leading toward the eighth act—where the star performed alone on stage, minus the busyness of clowns and jugglers—and the ninth and closing act, a piece of fluff that might include "trick animals or trapeze artists," something to calm the audience after the disappearance of the star.

As one fan remembers: "I loved it—miss it—neither film nor tv has the warmth, the excitement, or the life of vaudeville—it reached and touched *you*, individually."

Almost all the great stars of Broadway in the twenties—Al Jolson, Fanny Brice, Mae West, W. C. Fields, Sophie Tucker, Eddie Cantor, Fred and Adele Astaire, and the Marx Brothers— started in vaudeville, as did Charlie Chaplin, Fatty Arbuckle, and Buster Keaton. Walter Winchell was also an ex-vaudevillian; much of his nervous rat-a-tat style came from a song-and-dance man's rapid-fire delivery.

Vaudeville grew into chains, or circuits, "which radiated from New York City in the East and Chicago in the West, like an octopus with a brain [on Broadway] and tentacles reaching far into the country." When they were *debutants*, Jolson, Fields, and the

Marx Brothers were constantly on the road, living out of suit-
cases, from boardinghouse to boardinghouse, chasing chorus
girls, chorus girls with or without pink tights.

2.

The myth of the chorus girl was already in place at the beginning of the twentieth century. How could it not have been
when a particular chorus girl, Evelyn Nesbit, was the muse
behind the murder of America's most celebrated architect, Stanford White. Stanny was addicted to showgirls. He kept a tower
apartment in the old Madison Square Garden, and inside the
tower was a red velvet swing. . . .

One night he discovered a fifteen-year-old with copper hair
in the chorus of *Florodora*. It was 1901. He brought Evelyn to his
tower, sat her on his swing, drugged her . . . and offered to have
his dentist fix her teeth. The Florodora Girl became White's mistress, but he had a wandering eye. Evelyn matured into Manhattan's most glorious "mermaid." She married Harry Kendall Thaw,
a morbid millionaire from Pittsburgh, who was jealous of White.

In the summer of 1906, at the premiere of *Mamzelle Champagne* on the roof of Madison Square Garden, Thaw shot Stanford White in the head. Evelyn would testify at the murder trial,
discuss in intimate detail her rides on the red velvet swing. The
whole country was enthralled. Chaste *and* lascivious in the high
collar she wore on the witness stand, Evelyn had become "the
first sex goddess in American history," according to E. L. Doc-
torow in *Ragtime*—Cleopatra with red velvet rather than an asp.
It was White who was really on trial, White and his harem of
chorus girls. Thaw was declared incompetent and sent to Matteawan State Hospital for the Criminally Insane. He rode to the

asylum in a private railway car, with crowds waving to him along the tracks while he drank champagne with his friends.

Evelyn wasn't invited on the ride to Matteawan. Dime novels were written about her. Readers participated in her "ruin." She went on the vaudeville circuit, billed as Mrs. Harry K. Thaw. By the beginning of the twenties, "she was a tired, nervous little woman trying to make a go of a tearoom" near Broadway.

The person who would profit most from the chorus girl and her new cult was Florenz Ziegfeld, or Flo. He was an impresario who started out with strongmen, not chorus girls, exhibiting Eugene Sandow, the most muscular male on the planet. At the Chicago World's Fair (1893), Flo discovered that he couldn't sell a strongman to the crowd. No one cared how many chains Sandow could break with his chest, so Ziggy stood him inside a black booth, covered his body with powder and chalk, and created a marble man. People flocked to the black booth with all their friends. Flo's "statue" was the sensation of the fair.

But Ziggy tired of Sandow and attached himself to Hannele Held, a *choristka* with a Yiddish troupe that happened to be touring London at the time. Flo was irresistible. He had a "Mephistophelian look." He brought Hannele back to New York in 1896 and made her his common-law wife, she who was born in Warsaw and had once been with the Folies Bergères. Flo disguised his wife's Jewish origins and little Hannele became Anna Held, the French beauty from the Folies Bergères with "bad brown eyes." He pinched her waist with whalebone until she was like a voluptuous flower, "fashionable and filthy," a shorter, fatter, foreign prototype of the all-American Ziegfeld Follies Girl. She was no longer a *choristka* and she couldn't be fondled like the chorus girls from Satan's Circus. She was sultry and aloof, and she didn't have to wear chalk, like Eugene Sandow. Flo sculpted her body inside a corset. She would whirl in front of an audience, sing "Won't You Come and Play Wiz Me?" or her signature song, "I Just Can't Make My Eyes Behave."

She's forgotten now, but princes and presidents fell in love with Anna Held. *Ragtime* is wrong. Anna Held was once a much bigger sex bomb than the Girl in the Red Velvet Swing. Ziggy starred her in seven shows, including *Higgedly-Piggedly* and *Papa's Wife*. He began a national craze when he pretended that Anna Held guarded her complexion by bathing in gallons of milk. He was shameless in his search for publicity stunts. His whole life was "consumed by superficiality in both his personal and professional affairs. He had nothing else. Appearances were his only reality."

Flo and Anna Held dined every night at Rector's, the Main Stem's premier restaurant and cabaret, a long yellow building at Broadway and 44th. It was at the edge of Longacre Square, a district of carriage-repair shops a little north of the Tenderloin. Manhattan's theatres and music halls had inched up from Park Row to the Bowery and Union Square and began to cluster around the "Deuce"—42nd Street and Broadway. Rector's became the locale of this exodus uptown. It didn't need a sign to announce itself. Rector's only marking was an "illuminated griffin suspended from its façade." Its décor was green and gold, with crystal chandeliers and mirrors that went up each wall. It had a hundred tables on the ground floor, reserved for its usual clientele, and seventy-five tables upstairs for customers who came in off the street. But these upstairs tables were invisible, like the customers themselves.

Everybody came to Rector's, including Stanford White, Evelyn Nesbit, and Harry Thaw. But the restaurant had a particular darling: Anna Held. "A hush fell on Rector's as soon as Anna

Held made her entrance" in a plumed hat and a gown that was deliciously décolleté. She might even surrender herself and sing a number from her latest musical, if Ziggy allowed it. She had to compete with homegrown beauties, like Lillian Russell, with her blue eyes and blonde, blonde hair. Anna was a tiny girl—five feet tall—but within her whalebone she had the classic hourglass figure of her era, with a bird's waist. And when she rolled her bad brown eyes, the celebrities at Rector's couldn't concentrate on their lobster or their soup. . . .

It was Anna who gave Flo the idea for his Ziegfeld Follies, "nagging him into producing a revue" that would promote "young, beautiful girls in lavish but abbreviated costumes," like the Folies Bergères. It was 1907, and a bit of the modern had crept onto the Big Street. The Follies would accurately mirror the preoccupations of their time, like a slightly surreal never-never land of New York and the nation. Ziggy would provide his own atmosphere. Dubbing the roof of the New York Theater the "Jardin de Paris," he cobbled together a variety show that was four hours long, with a fanciful theme—Captain John Smith and Pocahontas Visit Ziegfeld's Manhattan. The hit song of the 1907 Follies was "If a Table at Rector's Could Talk." But Ziggy didn't include his own common-law wife. He wanted taller, leggier girls who didn't have the look of an hourglass and wouldn't roll their eyes. They could be a *little* dirty, but they also had to be decorative: he preferred silence to song in a Ziegfeld Girl. Others could sing, or juggle, or tell jokes, but the Ziegfeld Girl had to hypnotize the audience with her hauteur.

It had never happened on Broadway. Ziggy had reinvented the notion of a chorus girl. He realized that the chorus girl "played to a vast cultural imagination and to that imagination's confusion . . . about female sexuality and about women as workers in a mixed-sex world." The chorus girl had achieved her semi-independent status before Flo arrived. Millionaires sought her out, whether Stanford White or William Randolph Hearst, who preferred the demimonde of chorus girls and gamblers to heiresses and high society.

The chorus girl could excite, because she lived at the edge of whoredom. Her "supposed freedom and independence masked the actual economic dependence of most women on men." Ziggy pounced on this and made *his* girls visible and unavailable, beyond the machinations of any man but himself. The sportsmen at the old concert halls had grabbed at the girls, devoured them; Ziggy's audience could only devour with their eyes. Desire was suddenly safe. Hearst, who would appear and reappear in the second row at the Follies, his hat in an empty seat beside him, was always mesmerized. As Marion Davies, herself a former Follies Girl, remembers: "[H]e had the most penetrating eyes—honest, but penetrating eyes. He didn't have a harmful bone in his body. He just liked to be by himself and just look at the girls on the stage while they were dancing. I think he was a very lonesome man."

The upscale audience of the Follies no longer consisted of predators from Satan's Circus. They were men who liked to watch, who took their delight from the act of watching. Yet that didn't prevent them from pursuing romance. But it was much more ritualized; they would leave boxes of candy and a note for their favorite chorus girl. And there was often something infantile about these pursuits, almost delirious, as if they were chasing icons in their dreams.

And what about the women—mistresses and wives—who often accompanied these men to the Follies? Were they there to marvel at the décor, the "living curtain" of chorines, the "expensive frivolity" of show after show? Or did they find something more engaging and erotic, a lifeline they could grasp? As Dixie Dugan, the comic-strip character and star of the "Zigfold Follies," loved to say: "All there is to this Follies racket is to be cool and look hot."

The Follies caught on like a house on fire, and soon Ziegfeld was as famous as the Follies itself. Everyone wanted to be a "Zigfold Girl," including Dixie Dugan and the ten thousand unemployed chorus girls who flocked to New York. No one could compare with each new idol of the Follies, like Nora Bayes, aka Lenora Goldberg, a Cleveland girl, or Lillian Lorraine, Ziggy's alcoholic mistress, or Olive Thomas, who committed suicide in a Paris hotel before she was twenty. Life was dangerous and swift for Ziggy's girls—most of them wouldn't survive their twenties on or off the stage. There were other divas around, other choruses, other revues, "but the most modern and daring of all female occupations was that of the Follies Girl. . . ."

3.

Ziggy alone couldn't have carried Broadway on his back, or built the strange, dreamlike village that clustered around the "Deuce." The *New York Times* had moved uptown from Park Row in 1904 and built a terra-cotta tower on Longacre Square. When New York's first subway opened the same year, with a stop at 42nd Street and Broadway, Adolph Ochs, the *Times'* magisterial publisher, insisted that the subway stop be called "Times Square," and that Longacre Square itself be renamed in honor of the *Times*. He would celebrate this renaming with a New Year's Eve spectacular in 1905, midnight fireworks that metamorphosed a few years later into a lit ball traveling down the length of the tower like a mysterious but controllable comet. Ochs dreamt that such a tower, with its midnight comet, "would preside over the square as a civic presence, a kind of journalistic *hôtel de ville* or *rathaus* rather than as a center of misrule," which of course it would soon become, with a language that was much racier than the *New York Times*, an underworld that was more elaborate and magical than a terra-cotta tower, and a whole army of chorus girls and clowns.

Nineteen hundred and five would bring another unpredictable element to the birth of modern Broadway: Sime Silverman and *Variety*. Silverman, a 32-year-old newspaper "veteran," borrowed twenty-five hundred dollars from his father-in-law and took a real gamble in starting a weekly devoted to vaudeville when there were half a dozen other entertainment weeklies in town, including *Billboard*. He nearly went bankrupt in his first year, "as sheriffs parked out in the office so often that everyone assumed they were employees." But the sheriffs weren't parked there very long. Silverman was too much of a genius, in spite of his rough, ravelly look. He transformed *Variety* from a typical trade rag into an original, idiosyncratic "voice" that not only found a lexicon for vaudeville but for other forms of pleasure and play. In 1910, while Jack Johnson ruled as the first black heavyweight champion and was about to fight former champion Jim Jeffries, Silverman scooped every other paper on the planet by appointing Al Jolson as *Variety*'s correspondent to cover the match. Jolson, who adored boxing and followed it religiously, wrote that Johnson toyed with Jeffries like a cat would toy with some domesticated mouse.

It was Silverman who invented the term "slanguage" to describe the new idiom of the Street; much of that idiom had come from vaudeville itself, and it was *Variety* that mapped its boundaries, creating a kind of shorthand that could discuss indi-

vidual acts. A "bundle actor" was someone who, like most vaudevillians, traveled light, without any baggage; "the Death Trail" was
a string of cheap hotels that spun out from Chicago to the last web
of deserted towns on the Pacific Coast; the "disappointment act"
was a last-minute replacement for some act that had never
showed; "shtick" was a performer's own stylish bag of tricks; an
actor who "took the veil" was one who retired from the circuit; "out
of town" was anywhere but the Main Stem; "the stix" were the
boondocks, any little bump of backcountry; "playing to haircuts"
was the last act on a bill, when performers had to glance at the
back of each head, as the audience was about to disappear. . . .

There would have been no Runyon or his Broadway tales
without Sime Silverman, who understood that Broadway was a
constant volcano—a landscape that couldn't complete itself. And
like some masterful urban anthropologist, he was there to catch
the visible and invisible lava. "By the twenties, *Variety*, intended
as the medium for communicating within the Broadway world,
itself became the message." It was *Variety*, and not the *New York
Times*, that had the boldness and wit to announce the crash of
1929 with WALL STREET LAYS AN EGG.

Silverman would remain a citizen of Broadway for most of
his life, a fan of the Follies who might wander into Rector's back
room and watch Ziegfeld at one of Arnold Rothstein's marathon
card games, with judges, police chiefs, and John McGraw, manager of the New York Giants; or perhaps he would visit
McGraw's poolroom, a little lower down on Broadway, beside
Herald Square. McGraw was a roustabout who was constantly
getting into drunken brawls, and some guy would have to shove
him into a cab and send him home to his apartment at Broadway
and 109th. That guy might be Damon Runyon, who adored him,
or A. R. himself, who was a silent partner in the poolroom.

"Muggsy" McGraw and his Giants were the real kings of New York. The most successful team in baseball, McGraw's Giants won the first World Series (1905), against the Philadelphia Athletics. They were written about, mimicked, and reviled with their manager, "Black John," who was often accused of taking bribes, with or without the assistance of his silent partner, A. R. Flo would pay homage to McGraw, having his girls glide around in baseball caps and little else at the Follies. In 1919, McGraw would become part owner of the Giants in a deal brokered by The Brain. Rothstein himself received shares in the team, under the table, of course. He and Black John would roam the Roaring Forties, where most of the gambling houses were situated in sumptuous brownstones, east and west of Broadway. They might stop at Rector's or Shanley's, Bat Masterson's favorite haunt. Masterson was a Giant fan, like everybody else in New York.

Something happened in 1920. The Yankees, New York's *other* team, stole Babe Ruth, a boisterous left-handed pitcher and outfielder, from the Boston Red Sox. Ruth was a phenomenon. In his maiden year with the Yanks, he hit more home runs, fifty-four, than the whole Giant team. But the Giants still owned New York. They beat the Yanks and Babe Ruth in the World Series of 1921 and '22. Then Black John did a stupid thing. The Yanks were tenants at the Polo Grounds, the Giants' playing field in Harlem Heights; but with Babe Ruth the Yanks broke all attendance records, and out of jealousy or spite, McGraw wouldn't renew their lease.

The Yanks built their own "palace," Yankee Stadium, across the river from the Polo Grounds, and on opening day in April 1923, they filled the rafters, with an overflow of twenty-five thousand fans who couldn't get in to watch the Babe. It was the ruin of McGraw and his Giants, who were no longer the darlings of Broadway. Nineteen twenty-three was another Subway Series—New York vs. New York—and Babe Ruth hit three home runs that helped destroy the Giants. Black John's brand of "inside" ball, where the batter would scratch out a single and try to score, was rendered obsolete by Ruth's home runs.

McGraw was part of an older era—Rector's, Delmonico's, and Shanley's would all vanish during the twenties, as Prohibition ate into the profits. Delmonico's would reappear, but not with Diamond Jim Brady and John McGraw. The speakeasy, the nightclub, the Automat, and the delicatessen would come into fashion. Lindy's opened in 1921, and it would become Rothstein's lair until the day he died. It didn't have mirrors wall to wall, or a griffin and four full orchestras. It was a dump, but Arnold, who didn't drink anything stronger than a tall glass of milk, preferred boiled potatoes and borscht to lobster Newburg. And the Babe preferred hot dogs *and* women, often three at a time. As baseball historian Lee Allen notes: Ruth was "a large man in a camel's hair coat and camel's hair cap, standing in front of a hotel, his broad nostrils sniffing at the promise of the night."

He lived at the Ansonia Hotel on Broadway and 73rd, a beaux-arts palace built in 1904 as the premier residence of successful artists, actors, writers, musicians, and Broadway impresarios. Ziegfeld had a thirteen-room suite, arriving with Anna Held soon as the Ansonia opened; after the Follies began, Ziggy moved Lillian Lorraine into a much smaller suite one floor above his own and shuffled between his mistress and his wife. But Ruth was the first baseball player who could afford the Ansonia's extravagant price. He would practice his swing on the landings, drop baseballs down the stairwell, like a mischievous boy.

He was "bigger than the President," bigger than any movie star or prince. If he was banned from baseball for part of a season because of his pranks, he would go on the vaudeville circuit with a primitive mind-reading act, sing a couple of songs in baritone, and earn more than he ever could with a baseball bat. He was a continual clown who loved to pose in front of a camera. He'd become the bad boy of baseball, fighting with managers, players, fans. When the Giants taunted him during the 1922 World Series, calling him "nigger" and other names, he burst into the Giant clubhouse, challenged the entire team, and said: "I don't mind being called a prick or a cocksucker or things like that. I expect that. But lay off the personal stuff."

He'd participated in the birth of an era, the 1920s and its "main stem," Manhattan, where Ruth reigned, "driving down Broadway in a low-slung convertible, wearing a coonskin coat." But it wasn't all about a city of "beautiful nonsense," of hectic, hysterical fun, starring Scott Fitzgerald's flappers and philosophers. Modern Broadway wasn't simply an electric playground, a vaudevillian's dream, where no one had to go "out of town" and everyone could have his own private "shtick." The Babe was about vaudeville, about showmanship, but he was also about a kind of stunning performance that had never been seen before: "In Charleston he swung so hard striking out that as he spun around, his spikes caught in the hard clay of the batter's box and he wrenched an ankle. He was carried off the field writhing with pain. No one in Carolina could recall seeing a man swing so hard he hurt himself when he missed."

And it was more than that. Most of all, the Babe was a sexy beast. "Everything about him reflected sexuality—the restless, roving energy; the aggressive skills; fastball pitching; home run hitting; the speed with which he drove cars; the loud, rich voice; the insatiable appetite. . . ."

Appetite defined the new Broadway—an endless hunger, an almost childlike innocence *and* cruelty. Al Jolson, the hungriest of singers, who lived in a constant state of want, loved to piss on people. Whether it was his own accompanist or golf partner, that was the price you had to pay: being pissed on by "Jolie." Like Ziegfeld, like Rothstein, like the Babe himself, he couldn't bear being alone. He would have liked to swallow all of Broadway, including the Winter Garden and Lindy's. Rothstein had much of the same rootless longing. When asked what it was he wanted, he would mutter, "Maybe—maybe to be king of the world."

Ruth was already the Sultan of Swat, the man whose ferocious swing had redesigned baseball, turned it from an old-fashioned pitchers' duel into a feast of home runs, with fans clamoring for further exploits. "He ate a hat once. He did. A straw hat. Took a bite out of it and ate it."

But it was the danger that marked him, a swing like a hurricane that could hurt itself, a sexual greed that could take him through an entire bordello in one night. "He was the noisiest fucker in North America."

Would he have become the hero of his time if he'd remained with the Red Sox? I'm not convinced. The nation cottoned to him because he was outsized, the greatest, most flamboyant gargoyle in a city of gargoyles—fast and furious, like Broadway itself. The twenties crystallized around the Babe. He was a *new* player in a *new* stadium in the *new* baseball of livelier balls, in the *new* language of sportswriting that seemed to have been invented just for him. *Bambino*, or "Babe" in Italian, soon became BAM, and that's how he appeared in headlines, whether it was Silverman's *Variety* or the *Daily News*.

It's no accident that the first successful tabloid in America was started in Manhattan by Chicago tycoon Joseph M. Patterson, in 1919. Patterson's rag was a perfect vehicle for Ruth: with a picture or two it could chart his bellyaches, his banishments, his feuds; his farcical poses in a wig and a woman's costume; his mock campaigning for presidential candidate Al Smith, a cigar in his mouth and a black derby on his head; his second marriage, to a former Follies Girl; his fishing trips with teammate Lou Gehrig; his home runs and heroic strikeouts, his body coiled like a corkscrew; his golfing tours in Florida with Al Smith, both of them wearing fashionable knickerbockers; his hijinks with Yankee batboy Eddie Bennett, a benevolent hunchback who fed the Babe bicarbonate of soda to relieve the heartburn that accompanied his diet of hot dogs; his trips to orphanages and hospitals, which readers followed with devotion, because the Babe himself was some kind of orphan. . . .

The *Daily News* was about exaggeration, and so was Ruth. He was called "ape" and "gorilla" before there ever was a King Kong. And if Ruth didn't have the Empire State Building to play with (it wasn't opened until 1931), he did have Broadway, where he might listen to jazz and drink bootleg whiskey with another bad boy, cornetist Bix Beiderbecke. The Babe had grown up at a bad boys' school in Baltimore, St. Mary's, which housed a lot of orphans, and would give the illusion that the Babe himself was an orphan, though his parents were very much alive and wanted to tame his wildness. St. Mary's would become his dormitory for life. He didn't leave until he was twenty, and perhaps he didn't leave at all. His jibes, his pranks, his cruel taunts were like the antics of an orphan who was let loose in the world, and somehow in his psyche he had to return there every night. That's why he was such a partner to Broadway, that picaresque home for the homeless, charged with a sexual pull, an urgency that was made for "foundlings" like Ruth.

4.

Ruth may have come to the Yanks almost by chance (and the suicidal tendencies of the Red Sox), but if 1920 marked his initiation into the culture of Broadway, then there were other initiations that form a kind of cultural calendar, a pictorial history of Manhattan's metamorphosis and movement toward the modern.

1881

—The first electric signboard arrives on lower Broadway with the message, *MANHATTAN BEACH* (in south Brooklyn) *SWEPT BY OCEAN BREEZES*. The sign is instant vaudeville. Viewers in the street are startled and amazed; some of them sit for hours and blink, haunted by this new electric life, as if letters could become glowworms.

1883

—The Brooklyn Bridge, one of the marvels of the Western World, opens with its miles of steel cord, and Coney Island soon becomes the nation's densest summer resort, reachable to all Manhattanites. Coney Island is "a foetal Manhattan," according to Rem Koolhaas, and an infant Broadway, where the "false daytime" of electric light will produce an endless cycle of fun. . . .

1893

—The Anti-Saloon League is founded in Oberlin, Ohio. It will grow into the most powerful lobby in Washington, and will become the single most effective force in the fight for national

Prohibition, campaigning ruthlessly against "wet" candidates in Congress and waging war against big cities like New York, with its Satan's Circus.

1900

—The new century will "anoint" the career of Carrie Nation as a saloon-breaker. She's a female Paul Bunyan, six feet tall, with a hatchet in her hand. An evangelist for the Women's Christian Temperance Union, she begins to hear voices, like Joan of Arc, and one particular "voice" beckons her to attack the saloons in Kiowa, Kansas. She crosses the country on a rampage, carrying cobblestones, a billiard ball, and a hatchet, which will become her war sign. "Part fraud, part fanatic," she's arrested many times. She describes herself as "a bulldog running along at the feet of Jesus." Her fame will spread throughout the planet as she's shot at and beaten up by customers in different saloons. But she's as much a brawler as any of these men. And when she shows up in New York City at the saloon of former heavyweight champion John L. Sullivan, she can't seem to find the great John L. He'd rather not "mix" with Carrie Nation. To help pay for her hospital bills, she enters vaudeville. Not content with her "hatchetings," she campaigns to get rid of tobacco, corsets, and portraits of nudes. . . .

1904

—In the seventeenth century, Dutch explorers name Coney Island after wild rabbits, or *konijn*, that cover the area. Wild rabbits are still found in 1904, but the exploration of Coney is complete. The "island of rabbits" is all booked up. Visionaries such as George C. Tilyou, Frederic Thompson, and William H. Reynolds, who would also develop properties in the heart of Manhattan (it's Reynolds who is responsible for the Chrysler's silver crown), create three little metropolises along Surf Avenue: Steeplechase Park (1897), where rubes from Manhattan, Brooklyn, and the Bronx can ride mechanical horses attached to undulating iron rails, some as high as thirty-five feet, and get paddled by clowns at the end of the race; Luna Park (1903), where the same rubes can transport themselves to a mindscape modeled on the symmetrical bumps of the moon, with a telegraph office, minarets, and more than a million incandescent bulbs; and Dreamland (1904), the most ambitious, which longs to forever end the notion of travel in ordinary, mundane time, offering popcorn vendors dressed as little devils, an entire town of midgets, an incubator that's more innovative than any hospital and can protect premature babies until they "hatch," a circus with animals that are utterly trainable and as alert as human beings, a dome of creation near a cellar that's supposed to signal the end of the world, a replica of Venice and a voyage through Switzerland, with the vistas of Mt. Blanc on a huge wall. Even more sensational is the burning hotel, a little "passion play" on one of Dreamland's blocks, where guests inside the hotel are rescued from oblivion by a band of acrobatic angels in fire hats, who ride impossible ladders while smoke is sucked out of the hotel "and the city block prepared for the next performance." What other playland could ever compete with this? Had Dreamland remained intact, there might never have been the need for an amusement park in the middle of Manhattan.

1911

—The man-made devils that guard Dreamland's End of the World catch fire, and Dreamland burns to the ground. For once the acrobatic angels and their ladders are unable to help. "The most pathetic victims" of the fire are the overeducated circus animals, whose very humanness destroys a good number of them, as they wait for their masters' signals, signals that never come. "For many years after the holocaust, surviving animals are sighted on Coney, deep in Brooklyn even, still performing their former tricks. . . ."

1913

—Modern art suddenly comes to Manhattan at the 69th Regiment Armory. This "Armory Show" will be reviled by almost everyone but the artists themselves. Teddy Roosevelt, former Roughrider and president, condemns these modernists as maniacs. Sixteen hundred paintings and pieces of sculpture by American and European artists are on exhibition, including the work of Picasso, Matisse, Brancusi, and Duchamp. Caruso comes to the show, "delightedly d[raws] caricatures of cubist art and scatter[s] them to a boisterous crowd." But it's one painting, Duchamp's *Nude Descending a Staircase* (1912)—with its sense of seizing motion in time and space so that a single nude becomes several—that the critics pounce upon, calling it "Explosion in a Shingle Factory." Yet there's a curious relationship between Duchamp's multifaceted nude and the Follies. But no one, not Ziegfeld, not Anna Held, nor Lillian Lorraine can quite fathom the lyrical force of the Follies—many nudes descending a staircase, like a cubist tableau. "Chorus girls, dressed in playful and glorious attire . . . boldly presenting themselves as consumer objects, as symbols of adornment and success, advertising the body as a locus of desire and personal transformation."

—The Palace opens on Broadway and 47th. It will soon become the mecca of vaudeville and the "home" of Fanny Brice when she isn't at the Follies, appearing like an ugly swan between musical numbers, as if she's mocking the haughty, unapproachable glamour of Ziggy's girls. She has her own glamour at the Palace, where she's *almost* beautiful, as she clowns and sings a sad song. Everyone wants to play at the Palace, whether it's the Marx Brothers, Will Rogers, or W. C. Fields; you couldn't "exist" without the Palace, couldn't find a national audience. Performers would gather outside on the sidewalk, waiting to be discovered. There was no audience as perceptive or as critical as a Palace audience, one that could "mirror the theater's design—smart, elegant, and sophisticated."

—The original "Great White Way" was much further down on the Big Street, next to Union Square, the territory of Tony Pasteur, Evelyn Nesbit, and Theodore Dreiser's Sister Carrie. It was master signbuilder O. J. Gude who invented the phrase. Gude's great success didn't just come from his accumulation of power and the signboards he built. He was a much more complicated pharaoh. He grasped the psychology of his own time and was prepared to shape the future. "Signboards are so placed that everybody must read them, and absorb them, and absorb the advertiser's lesson willingly or unwillingly." But by 1913 Gude's signboard culture has crept uptown. Times Square may still be called the Tenderloin by journalist Julian Street, may still be surrounded by zones of gambling and prostitution, but it's also the new "Great White Way," land of electric light and permanent, drifting crowds, the new Coney Island of the nation, with a feast of signs "that allowed merchants to change reading matter every day and to move it rapidly along the boards from right to left."

—Ragtime conquers Broadway and starts a dance craze that will continue right up to the eve of America's entry into the Great War. Of course, ragtime had been around for years, and had been brought to Manhattan by piano ticklers in the Tenderloin's own Black Bohemia. But in 1911 Irving Berlin, aka Israel Baline, a former singing waiter from the Lower East Side, writes "Alexander's Ragtime Band," about a nameless confidence man who invites listeners of the song to meet Alexander, "the leader man," a black pied piper, at some campfire revival. But the listeners never meet Alexander and his "coon band." White audiences can't get enough of Berlin. And in 1913 Berlin boldly declares in his "International Rag" that America "started somethin'," that the whole world is "jumpin' all around" and has become "ragtime crazy." Suddenly the Big Street is crowded with *thé dansants* and cabarets, where unescorted middle-class white women can spend the afternoon sipping tea and dancing with gigolos like George Raft, a graduate of Owney Madden's Gopher Gang who would later move to Hollywood. Even restaurants like Rector's couldn't remain aloof and had to build a special cabaret where customers could dance. Owner George Rector later admits: "Nobody went into Rector's to dine. We had a kitchen, but the chefs were all out on the dance floor with the customers." And by the end of the year even the Vatican gets into the act, attacking the deviltry of ragtime. But it hardly matters: the waiters are still out on the dance floor. . . .

—Cass Gilbert's Woolworth Building rises on lower Broadway and Park Place. A kind of Gothic cupcake, sixty stories high, it's the tallest building in the world until Chrysler is completed in 1929. Woolworth is called "the cathedral of commerce," a hymn to capitalism. The brashness of its lobby, with vaulted ceilings that depict an earthly paradise *and* playful gargoyles—Cass Gilbert himself appears, clutching a replica of Woolworth—is very much like the Main Stem, which loves to salute the biggest, the boldest, and the best.

—The Follies move to another house, the Amsterdam, on 42nd Street, where Ziggy creates a second, smaller version of the Follies—the Midnight Frolic—on the Amsterdam's roof. Customers can attend the Follies and then ride upstairs to the roof and catch a more intimate show, with a "see-through" runway that brings them much, much closer to the girls. The Midnight Frolic is also a training ground for new chorines and comics, like Will Rogers. The Frolic is racier than the Follies, and customers can literally watch nudes descending a metal staircase that's right over their heads.

—The father of public relations, Edward I. Bernays, a nephew of Sigmund Freud, gets a job as a theatrical press agent and revolutionizes Broadway. The boy is twenty-three. Like a celestial puppeteer, he surrounds the performers and plays he's promoting with mock events. He does for an entire stable of actors what Ziegfeld once did for Anna Held—thrusts them into the public eye and keeps them there. And the motor that drives Bernays, the secret of his success? It's simple. He's star-struck. "I hobnobbed with actors and actresses whose names shone on marquees. I went backstage whenever I wanted to. . . . Life was one thrill after another."

—Anna Held divorces the great Flo. Tired of having Lillian Lorraine as an upstairs neighbor, she moves out of the Ansonia and into the Savoy. Once the biggest star on Broadway, with her "bad brown eyes" beckoning from billboards and cigar boxes, she's succumbed to the Follies, to Ziggy's avalanche of girls. When reporters ask whether there will be a reconciliation with Flo, she smiles and says, "One does not relight a dead cigarette." Without Ziggy to produce her shows, Anna flops. But she still has things to say about feminine charm. "I don't care at all who is President, if the lace on my bodice is put on right."

1915

—Born in Vienna in 1872, Joseph Urban, an impoverished architect, illustrator, and theatrical man, arrives from Boston and becomes stage designer for both the Follies and the Midnight Frolic. The Follies might have evaporated, been utterly forgotten, without his designs. Urban develops a sense of movement in deep space, a geometric dream machine, like Duchamp's *Nude Descending a Staircase*. He offers the Follies his own gift of architecture, wants to capture time, "celebrate the present moment rather than reform it." The erotic can always sit snugly inside his stylized atmosphere and motifs that soften the chaotic character of any revue. For his first Follies he invents a blue sky that never varies from scene to scene and has an hypnotic effect. Urban loves to sculpt in space, transforming Ziggy's girls into a kind of living architecture—bodies are sensational props for Urban, pieces of an elaborate picture puzzle that can't be found anywhere else on the Main Stem.

—Frenchman Georges Claude invents neon light, which will ultimately transform the Big Street into a blaze of green and blue that can't be swallowed up by the sun. Neon "seemed to glow in intensity from a distance . . . it could be seen in the day, at night, through fog and rain." It will create the illusion of perpetual, shimmering night that Broadway will need to become the modern Babylon.

1916

—The Broadway Association and the Fifth Avenue Association—collections of combative merchants—battle it out over where projecting signboards can and cannot be placed. Broadway wants unlimited access. But the Fifth Avenue merchants, who are wealthier and more aggressive, insist that projecting signs be banished from Washington Square to 110th, along Fifth Avenue. Fifth Avenue wins the war. Its long elegant vista will be unharmed. Broadway fights back. A new zoning law grants the unlimited use of giant billboards, but only on the Main Stem. One of the peculiarities of American capitalism is to "concentrate and confine such activity [billboards] to a limited space, while at the same time *liberating* it to an unparalleled degree."

—Anna Held has been overseas, entertaining French troops at the front. When she returns to America, she's almost in a state of shock. Frightened of the lights on Broadway, she starts to scream, "Put out the lights! The Zeppelins will get you!"

1917

—America enters the Great War on April 6. The theatre season is curtailed, as the government orders a blackout on Broadway.

1918

—August 12, Anna Held dies of multiple myeloma, cancer of the bone marrow. She will be buried twice—first in White Plains and then at Mount Pleasant—where Babe Ruth and Dutch Schultz will also be buried.

—November 11, Armistice Day; without wartime restrictions, the Big Street "reopens" in a rush of light.

1919

—Irving Berlin writes "A Pretty Girl Is Like a Melody" for the 1919 Follies, which stars Eddie Cantor and Bert Williams, both of them in blackface. Williams, a black comedian, steals the show as he plays a black man playing a white man who pretends to be black. He parodies Cantor, without Cantor ever knowing it. Williams is the first black to appear in the Follies, but he's almost never on stage with Ziggy's girls. Like Fanny Brice, he's the "ugly swan" who provides the comic relief and a form of parody that attacks the Follies—an anti-show within the show itself. Only Ziegfeld would ever allow it, and it marks the Follies' modernity, that sense of pure play. "A Pretty Girl Is Like a Melody," staged on one of Urban's sculpted staircases, with the Ziegfeld Girls' outlandish walk while wearing six-foot headdresses, will become the theme song of all future Follies, as Ziegfeld attempts to "glorify" an American girl who can never really be captured. To emphasize this in later revues, Ziegfeld will supply his devoted patrons "with balloons for playing 'catch' with the coyly elusive chorus girls or lariats to 'rope' them."

—*The Gold Diggers*, by Avery Hopwood, is the great success of the season. Hopwood owns the Big Street. He writes hit after hit after hit. His plays are packed with chorus girls and backstage romance, farce, and melodrama. It's Hopwood who invents the term *gold digger*, gives it an ironic twist—the gold digger is a grasping, greedy girl who "digs" for success and a big fat marriage, but still has a heart of gold.

—F. Scott Fitzgerald, a penniless writer, arrives in Manhattan without many prospects. He has holes in his shoes, like James Gatz, his fellow Midwesterner who transformed himself into Jay Gatsby. Like Gatz, he's hopelessly in love with a Southern girl who has the sound of money in her voice. Critics (and private detectives) keep searching for the historical counterpart of Fitzgerald's mythic bootlegger, but they ought to give up the search. The James Gatz who exploded into Gatsby bears a striking resemblance to Scott Fitzgerald, who kept a ledger, like Gatz, and who exploded into fame in 1920, at the very beginning of the Jazz Age, when his novel, *This Side of Paradise*, was published. "Within weeks, the blond midwesterner—with the eerily ravishing looks, one man said, of an archangel—had become a national celebrity, and the most poignantly meteoric career in the history of American letters had begun."

—October 2, after campaigning for a peace treaty that a reluctant Congress won't ratify, President Wilson suffers a stroke that paralyzes the left side of his body.

1920

—January 16, the Eighteenth Amendment, ratified in 1919, goes into effect, banning the sale and distribution of alcohol, and the Prohibition era begins. White Protestant Americans had declared war on Catholics, immigrants, and big cities like Chicago and New York. It was rural America's last stand. It broke the saloon and created the speakeasy and the bootlegger, who will run the 1920s more than any president or police chief.

—April 3, Scott Fitzgerald recaptures his Southern belle, Zelda Sayre, and marries her in the rectory of St. Patrick's Cathedral. They will have a "honeymoon" at the Biltmore, in Suite 2109. She's much too wild for him. Scott can neither live with nor without Zelda. She will dive into the fountain at Union Square, dance on a kitchen table at the Waldorf. "And I don't want to be famous and fêted—all I want is to be very young always," says Zelda, one of the very first flappers. During the 1920s, she and Scott will spend less than two years within the "walls" of Manhattan, but they will remain the quintessential Broadway couple . . . until both of them start to unravel.

—August 18, the Nineteenth Amendment is ratified, giving women the right to vote in *all* elections, national and local. But women's suffrage will hardly change the contours and complexion of the twenties. It was not an age of politics. The disillusion and fatigue of the war had helped create the flapper, the girl who didn't give a damn, who wore open galoshes and would dance on a table, like Zelda Sayre. It also created the gangster, often an ex-soldier unable to adjust to the blandness of civilian life.

—November 2, the first radio broadcast station is opened in East Pittsburgh to cover the presidential election returns. Radio will counter the silent ghosts of the movies, with the clatter, fury, and chaos of a world that's like the Big Street. It will also spread Broadway's fast talk and bouncy music to the rest of America. Soon half the country will speak *Broadway*.

—In December, Woodrow Wilson, who helped establish the League of Nations, is awarded the 1919 Nobel Peace Prize. But he can't go to Europe to collect his prize. He sits inside a darkened White House, his windows shuttered, the gates locked. The country falls into a kind of dream state. Wilson's second wife, Edith Galt, serves as his "regent." It could almost be a Broadway melodrama. But Edith Galt isn't a gold digger; she's trying to free her husband from the pain of the presidency.

1921

—March 4, Wilson's "reign" ends. He and Edith Galt will move into a house on S Street, where he broods like a living dead man.

1923

—Owen "Owney" Madden, former head of the Gopher Gang, is released from Sing Sing after spending nine years within its walls. He will soon become the most successful bootlegger Manhattan ever had.

1924

—May 1, Missouri Martin, aka Texas Guinan, opens the El Fey, one of the first nightclubs in Manhattan, at 105 West 54th. Tex has little money of her own. The club is backed by Madden and another ex-member of the Gopher Gang, Larry Fay, a horse-faced hoodlum. It's at the El Fey that café society is born, that curious mingling of high and low—sophomores from Yale, chorus girls, crime and sports reporters, impresarios, white jazz singers, bootleggers, millionaires, movie stars, playboys, heiresses, gamblers, politicians, composers, and playwrights. At the El Fey one could find Fanny Brice, Al Jolson, Eddie Cantor, George Gershwin, Gloria Swanson, Mae West, Harry Thaw, who'd been released from his insane asylum and continued to chase young girls, Arnold Rothstein, Avery Hopwood, Damon Runyon, Walter Winchell (one of Tex's protégés), Sime Silverman, Ellin Mackay, the richest girl in America, "Bunny" Wilson, America's greatest literary critic, Jimmy Walker, the future mayor of New York, and girls from the

Follies—the Midnight Frolic would close shortly after Prohibition began—who might dance for Tex. "You had to go there, dance every night," said Ben Finney, one of Tex's friends. She would arrive at two in the morning, a bleached blonde wearing diamonds and a salmon-colored dress, climb on a chair, blow a police whistle, shout "Hello, suckers!" and the fun would begin.

—Tabloid fever continues as William Randolph Hearst launches the *Daily Mirror*, in direct competition with the *News*. Both papers "presented American life not as a political and economic struggle, but as a three-ring circus of sport, crime, and sex," almost as if humanity had become a great big vaudeville show, with each new edition of the *News* or the *Mirror* providing eight acts on a bill that might change three times a day, depending on the number of editions. The gangster has seized the front page as readers follow the exploits of Legs Diamond, who dresses like a duke and keeps dancing around a barrage of bullets. "He was dangerous and senseless. And yet the truth is that for a time Diamond was feared above all other gunmen." His mistress, Kiki Roberts, is a chorus girl with the hottest legs in town. He has his own "speak," the Hotsy Totsy Club, on Broadway and 54th, with bullet holes in every wall. With his wide-brimmed white hat and haunted eyes, he's captured the public's imagination: mean and lean, a savage killer with a sense of style.

1925

—Another lean and dapper man, who looks like Legs and loves to be seen with chorus girls, is elected mayor of New York. He's Jimmy Walker, the man Broadway has been waiting for. The scion of a corrupt political machine, he dances in and out of City Hall when he isn't being chauffeured around in his Duesenberg or attending the Follies. Ziggy and other producers always reserve two seats on the aisle for Beau James, the Jazz Mayor. Like Irving Berlin, he's also a songwriter, but with only one hit, "Will You Love Me in December As You Do in May?" It's played wherever he goes. . . .

—Broadway has become "a staggering machine of desire," unequaled anywhere. And it's not the invention of one man, Damon Runyon, or the machine-gun hype of another, Walter Winchell, or the "slanguage" of Sime Silverman and the constant vaudeville of the *Daily News*. These are only reflections in a mirror that constantly distorts itself. Runyon will come the closest to describing Broadway's vagabondage, its outlaw culture, its own self-absorption, its terrible need of the night. It will become capitalism's crazy horse, where everything goes, and nothing could compete with its lights. "Bottles of beer appear and transform themselves into dwarfs drinking; showers of gold peanuts fall from the skies, dragons breathing smoke become a film title; cigarettes are ignited, automobiles materialize. Mountains, towns, lamaseries, men with top hats, nude women with teeth, spring into existence and are wiped off into oblivion." "The machine is here," writes investment banker Paul Mazur in 1925 for the *Harvard Business Review*. "It has an appetite of its own which must be satisfied." By 1925 Runyon's Broadway "flowed as a central capitalist space . . . as an immoral space, as a 'liberated' realm of fantasy wherein . . . no limits were placed on what could be bought or sold." But equally important, it was a great big nightclub and delicatessen that lived in the dark.

—Pundits loved to call Harlem the Black Broadway, but it isn't true. Harlem was more like the Tenderloin. It may have had the Cotton Club on 142nd and Lenox, with its chorines who are "tall, tan, and terrific," but listen to a Ziegfeld Girl: "America in

the twenties was exclusively Anglo-Saxon in its ideas of beauty,"
says Louise Brooks, who was her own kind of sexual outlaw.
Blackness wasn't celebrated at the Cotton Club, whose chorines
were *almost* white. It was a phony, sentimental glimpse of an
imagined South, like Bert Williams' cakewalk, only Bert was
aware of the phoniness and drew upon it in his repertoire of
tricks. The Cotton Club was a "jungle" where whites could go
and dream of a primitive sexuality, like good little voyeurs. But
practically all the clubs in Harlem were run by white gangsters,
such as Madden and "Big Frenchy" DeMange, who kept the
chorines away from customers. Whites controlled the whiskey
and the prostitutes. By 1925 Harlem had replaced Broadway "as
New York's underworld entrepôt."

1926

—January 4, Irving Berlin elopes with heiress Ellin Mackay.
Her father, Clarence Mackay, the telegraph tycoon, disinherits
his daughter and she's erased from the Social Register. But America's foremost disinherited girl isn't worried. She's wild about
Berlin. Their names are constantly in the news as they dance at
different cabarets. "It is not because fashionable young ladies are
picturesquely depraved that they go to cabarets. They go to find
privacy," Ellin writes in *The New Yorker*. And we realize that café
society has "buried" the Social Register. Ellin is the baroness of
Broadway, and Irving is her baron.

1927

—The Bambino hits sixty home runs, and fans expect him to
hit a hundred next season, like a rocket to the moon. He's become

part of Broadway's "weather," with his own publicist, Christy Walsh. Ruth is "the first sports figure to be packaged like a product," as he licenses "his name and face." He's a human billboard, towering over everything, everything in sight.

—A banner year on Broadway, as 264 new plays and musicals open. It wouldn't startle anyone if Broadway's Jazz Mayor had gone to every single opening with his permanent escort, Betty Compton, a gorgeous ex–Follies Girl. At the Follies he seems part of the spectacle, as he gets up from his seat to chat with Eddie Cantor, while Cantor is in the middle of singing a song . . . about the Jazz Mayor himself. Cantor carries the entire show on his back, together with a menagerie of live ostriches and cobras. But the Follies doesn't feel that modern anymore. The idea of glorifying the American girl is a bit old-fashioned in a nation of flappers, where every other grandma is bobbing her hair. But Ziggy hasn't lost his touch. He produces *Show Boat*, a musical by Jerome Kern and Oscar Hammerstein II that actually has some content in a *contentless* Broadway that never takes a chance. Paul Robeson, as a black stevedore, stops the show every night, freezes time on Broadway, with his rendering of "Ol' Man River" . . . and Helen Morgan as the doomed mulatto, Julie La Verne, will solidify her career as a torch singer right on stage as she sings "Bill" and "Can't Help Lovin' Dat Man." Urban himself has designed a set that allows Robeson and Morgan to "literally step out of the action, to leave the stage set" and sing directly to the audience on a tight little "island" called an apron. It was like a strange electric shock that jolted you and left you there to dream. There were very few blacks in the audience, but at least well-fed white America could have a little history lesson. "It was like nothing ever seen before on Broadway, a daring and darkly romantic musical saga, set on a nineteenth-century Mississippi riverboat, that took as its subject the mixing of races and the subjugation of blacks in American life."

—Another jolt would be *The Jazz Singer*, a silent film with several tinny-sounding songs and a few syncopated sentences spoken by Al Jolson, half of them ad-libbed. But when Jolson, at the piano with his mama in her Orchard Street flat, tickles the keys and talks about moving up to the Bronx, where there's "the Ginsbergs, the Guttenbergs, and the Goldbergs—oh, a whole lot of bergs," it's almost as if he's right in your lap. "The effect was not so much of *hearing* Jolson speak as of *overhearing* him . . . and it thrilled audiences bored with the conventions of silent cinema." It also marked a momentary marriage between Hollywood and the Big Street. *The Jazz Singer* is a Broadway melody—the cantor's boy who makes good, who can chant at the synagogue on Yom Kippur and still keep his career.

—Jimmy Walker, who attended all of Texas Guinan's nightclubs, may have kept Prohibition bloodhounds at bay, but a war was going on between New York and the United States. Prohibition "drove nightlife underground" and "reinforced the belief that nightlife was an outlaw in the United States and that New York was not America." As Billy Rose, one of the nightclub owners, observed: "All dressed up, [the bootlegger] needed a place to glow. And the only place where he was welcome was Broadway." This was the heart of Runyon's Broadway, where the bootlegger (or the gambler) was the main "capitalist." And it's not so surprising that Dave the Dude (Frank Costello) was obliged to play Robin Hood. Bootlegging had made him almost as rich as Kublai Khan. And Robin Hood had to have a hangout. Why not Mindy's or Missouri Martin's Sixteen Hundred Club, where he could "glow." And his natural ally was the gold-digging chorus girl, who was as much of an outlaw in the eyes of white Protestant America, as much of a mongrel, even if Ziegfeld, another mongrel, tried to "glorify" her, make her whiter than white.

1928

—It was the beginning of the end, *before* Black Tuesday (October 29, 1929), when the market crashed, and the Great Depression pinched everyone's pocketbook, crippled the theatre and nightclubs, ravaged the billboards and chased whatever capitalists there were away, because suddenly their playground had grown grim. Instead of a consumer culture there was chaos . . . and products that nobody could afford to buy. And what single event precipitated Broadway's fall? The murder of Arnold Rothstein, lord of Lindy's, banker to the underworld, the man who held the fabric of Broadway in his fist. He was the knot between gangsters, politicians, and the police. He owned a piece of everything—nightclubs like the Silver Slipper, the New York Giants, Broadway musicals (even though theatre bored him to death), racehorses, bootleg whiskey, and protection rackets, where he'd use Legs Diamond or another one of his bodyguards to shake down businessmen on Broadway. Nothing moved, nothing flowed without The Brain, who had half of Broadway inside his head. But he'd gone into narcotics, was short of cash, and welshed on a big gambling debt. And one night in early November he's found on the back stairs of the Park Central Hotel with a bullet in his groin. Walker's with Betty Compton at a club in Westchester when he hears the news. He speeds back to Manhattan in his silver-trimmed Duesenberg like a bullet of his own. It's the worst news of his political life. A. R., who's into everything else, is a secret part of Walker's administration. Rothstein dies on election day. If the cops really have to dig, the Jazz Mayor will be out of a job. And so his police commissioner, Grover Whalen, appointed in December, keeps himself busy by chasing Communists and closing nightclubs that New York had never bothered to close.

1929

—Texas Guinan is caught in the shuffle. Prohibition agents padlock club after club, federal prosecutors put her on trial, and now Grover Whalen calls Tex's protégées—the Guinan Graduates—a little gang of prostitutes. Tex counterattacks, asks Whalen why his police haven't been able to find Rothstein's killer. Whalen forces her out of the Club Intime at the Hotel Harding, and Tex has to get onto the vaudeville circuit with her troupe of girls. She will become a wanderer from now on, find it harder and harder to open a new club. And Tex's exile from the nightclub scene is like a kiss of death. Each of her clubs, however unstable, had been even more of a haven than Mindy's. She livened up Broadway like no other hostess, but she was much more than a hostess, "this formidable woman, with her pearls, her prodigious gleaming bosom, her abundant and gleaming beautifully bleached yellow coiffure, her bear-trap of shining white teeth." She kept falling in love with *nogoodniks*, gamblers and confidence men, who would manage her affairs and rob her blind. She had "a gangster aura," according to Ann Douglas. She traveled in an armored car, like Al Capone, and she never had a problem with the bootleggers who backed her clubs. She was, after all, best friends with Dave the Dude. It wasn't only raucousness that surrounded her. "Better a square foot of New York than all the rest of the world in a lump," she said, without the least bit of sentimentality. Tex wasn't a snob. "She seated guest stars next to nobodies and made sure they talked." The dance floor at the El Fey "was the size of a small white envelope." But it didn't matter. Tex helped her customers get through the night. She wasn't part of the Algonquin Round Table—Tex didn't believe in lunch. At dawn she would disappear in her armored car to her Greenwich Village flat, sleep through the day, with dark curtains covering the windows, and rise a little before midnight to have breakfast in bed. "Practically nobody saw her except at the El Fey. I don't think she ever went around," said Ben Finney. She was like a phantom who only existed inside her clubs, as if the El Fey lent her whatever lyricism she had, and *nighttime* was the only time a citizen could breathe, and here, in that hidden spot, some little scratch of a room, in a narrow building with a peephole in the door, with watered-down whiskey and champagne that was a joke, Broadway was on fire. With Tex around, you didn't have to be afraid. You could give up the mask you wore as a banker or a debutante, and find your own anonymity in the anonymity of Texas Guinan, Queen of the Night. . . .

—Damon Runyon publishes "Romance in the Roaring Forties," and Runyonland is born, featuring Mindy's, Missouri Martin, and Dave the Dude.

—For a brief moment William Van Alen's Chrysler will rule as the tallest building in the world, taller than Woolworth and the Eiffel Tower. It's disliked by contemporary architects. Kenneth Franzheim calls Van Alen "the Ziegfeld of his profession." Chrysler does have the daring and the whimsy of show business, like Urban's staircases. It's a descendant of William H. Reynolds' Dreamland (Reynolds was also Chrysler's developer and Van Alen's boss). From Coney Island to Chrysler there seems to be a capitalist arc or arrow let loose in a funhouse, a funhouse that will disappear with the Depression. Chrysler's silver crown could be the hat of a benevolent witch guarding over the metropolis. . . .

1932

—July 22, tired, worn, half a million in debt, with no more Follies to sustain him, Ziggy dies of a heart attack in LA. His safe at the Ziegfeld Theatre is opened and all that is found are eleven rubber bands, two five-dollar bills, "a small bronze-black elephant, his talisman against misfortune" . . . and the bitterness of Broadway.

CHAPTER THREE
THE MILK AND COOKIE MAN

1.

In *Terrible Honesty*, Ann Douglas' marvelous study of "Mongrel Manhattan" in the 1920s, its language, its literature, its jangly popular culture—white and black—we meet Bert Williams, Scott Fitzgerald, Texas Guinan, Bix Beiderbecke, Al Jolson, bandleader Paul Whiteman, blues singer Bessie Smith, Dorothy Parker and her fellow wags at the Algonquin Round Table, but there isn't even a glimpse of Arnold Rothstein, or the least mention of Lindy's, which was much more potent than any round table or Algonquin wit. There's Robert Benchley, but no Legs Diamond, Dutch Schultz, or Owney Madden. Ann Douglas lingers on the "tall, tan, and terrific" chorines of the Cotton Club, but never mentions that Madden was one of its owners. There would have been no "Jazz Age," and very little jazz, without the white gangsters who took black and white jazz musicians under their wing.

And there was little room for jazz at Rector's, which wasn't a gangster hideout.

As George Rector recalls: "We had four orchestras playing in relays and they all played like mechanics repairing a locomotive." But saxophonist Bud Freeman remembers a different and more appropriate tale: "The better hotels and restaurants employed violinists and pianists who played . . . very old fashioned music. We were happy to have a [mobster] place to play the kind of music we loved."

Legs Diamond once tipped Duke Ellington a couple of grand to play "St. Louis Blues," and Legs was a very mean and stingy man. But the greatest devotee of jazz among Prohibition mobsters was "Scarface" Al Capone, a Broadway character, even if his *Broadway* was Chicago's South Side. He idolized Gershwin and could whistle every note of "Rhapsody in Blue." Capone would explore nightclubs and cabarets with his bodyguards behind him, all wearing tuxedos. He liked to drink whiskey out of a teacup. "Scarface got along well with musicians," according to jazzman Jimmy Hines, and would follow each one's career. When he was sent to jail in 1931 for income tax evasion, the jazzmen also disappeared, as his prison term "marked the slide of local jazz into oblivion."

Bootleggers—not Broadway dilettantes and producers—were the real modernists. They redesigned their clubs to accommodate the flappers and young heiresses who were among their biggest clients. Women could sit alone in a gangster bar, listen to music, and not be disturbed by any prowling males. The bootleggers had become their chaperones . . . and their accomplices in finding jazz motifs for their clubs, with hints of Art Deco and the "bizarre, surrealistic zig-zag patterns" of Moorish, Mayan, and Mexican art. It's almost as if the nightclubs *feminized* the gangster owners, or at least provided them with a curious education: suddenly they were connoisseurs, and had an awareness they could never have dreamt of as they moved into café society, whether it was Owney Madden at the Cotton Club, Legs Diamond at the Hotsy Totsy, or Dave the Dude at the Silver Slipper. By becoming an entrepreneur, "You were no longer a highwayman, you were a host."

Diamond was a brutal killer, of course. But he had the rhythm and the strut of a star. And that rhythm was as much of

a language as Jolson's daemonic delivery on stage or the high
kicking at the Cotton Club. And Diamond, in the 1920s, became
a creature of the American imagination, larger than his own miserable roots. Perhaps no one understood that better than Robert
Warshow, a peripatetic student of popular culture who died of a
heart attack in 1955 at the age of thirty-seven and left behind a
pair of prophetic articles, "The Gangster as Tragic Hero" and
"Movie Chronicle: The Westerner," which isolate and scrutinize
America's own maddening dream. Warshow came to the gangster
through his study of gangster films. But he could have been talking about Legs or Madden when he wrote: "The peculiarity of
the gangster is his unceasing, nervous activity. . . . He is without
culture, without manners, without leisure. . . . But he is graceful,
moving like a dancer among the crowded dangers of the city."

It's almost as if he were a dancer in a new kind of Follies,
where Urban's designs become the lights of Broadway, six-foot
headdresses become a black hat, and Ziegfeld's unblemished
showgirls—whiter than white, without an ethnic trace—become
scarred Italian, Irish, or Jewish immigrant men, who moved with
an overwhelming lyrical menace that spoke to a nation's hidden
desires with more clarity and heartbreak than any musical.

"The gangster is the man of the city, with the city's language
and knowledge, with its queer and dishonest skills and its terrible
daring." And like Gatsby or Dave the Dude and Legs Diamond,
he's a creature embroidered with myth, who inhabits "that dangerous and sad city of the imagination . . . which is the modern
world."

The gangster touches us, as the Jazz Age was touched by
Legs Diamond, because "he is what we want to be and what we
are afraid we may become." If the twenties was a time of infec-
tious consumerism and enterprise, of magnificent, almost god-

like, success, then it's no wonder that for a magical moment America worshiped at the gangster's shrine: the speakeasy-night-club, where the gangster dwelled when he wasn't doing mayhem somewhere else.

He was, as Warshow imagines him, a misanthropic Christ: "the story of his career is a nightmare inversion of the values of ambition and opportunity." The gangster is doomed, as Legs was doomed, with his countless look-alikes in gangster films, "because he is under the obligation to succeed, not because the means he employs are unlawful. In the deeper layers of modern consciousness *all* means are unlawful . . . one is *punished* for success."

The gangster dares for us, dances toward his own death, and with his death, "he 'pays' for our fantasies, releasing us momentarily from the concept of success, which he denies by caricaturing it, and from the need to succeed, which he shows to be dangerous."

Readers of the *Daily News* would marvel at Diamond's resurrections, as he would rise from the grave each time he was shot, until he was trapped in an Albany rooming house and had his head blown off while he was asleep. But Diamond's resurrections were delicious, an extraordinary thrill, as he died and died for the *Daily News* and rose again. His very name—Legs Diamond—had the aura of a jubilee or religious carnival. He was much more tantalizing than his boss, Mr. Big, who carried a gun but never used it and conducted most of his business sitting behind a table at Lindy's. Or, as Madden once remarked: "Rothstein wants to rob people sitting down."

Perhaps Owney was slandering the one person he depended on. He couldn't have thrived without Rothstein's bankroll, none of Manhattan's bootleggers could. But A. R. didn't always sit. He had his own peculiar steps, a "pantherish quickness," according to Donald Henderson Clarke, The Brain's first biographer. He loved to scrutinize his own kingdom, march up and down Broadway, sniff the night air, as the Bambino often did. But he wasn't looking for prostitutes. A. R. had other *material* in mind. He was whispering, pointing to the next locale of the floating crap game that he ran. . . .

2.

He remains a mystery man. If we remember him at all, it's through Fitzgerald's fictional portrait of him in *The Great Gatsby*, a gargoyle called Meyer Wolfsheim. Fitzgerald claimed to have met A. R. out on Long Island, where his neighbor, Edward Fuller, was partners with A. R. in a "bucket shop" (a cut-rate brokerage house that often bilked clients and helped make Rothstein *and* Jay Gatsby very rich). But that meeting with A. R. was never documented, and I doubt that it ever took place. There is little, almost none, of A. R. in Wolfsheim. Fitzgerald had a merciless eye for detail; and when he "painted" Irving Thalberg, MGM's boy wonder, into Monroe Stahr in *The Last Tycoon*, one can almost *taste* the resemblance and feel Fitzgerald's sympathy for Stahr (Fitzgerald once belonged to Thalberg's rogues' gallery of writers in Hollywood). Monroe doesn't speak with a broken accent, as Meyer does. Like Gatsby, Stahr reinvents himself. A bandit out of the Bronx who took one night course in stenography, he now runs a Hollywood studio. "He was born sleepless, without a talent for rest or the desire for it." He's fast and furious, like Legs Diamond, and frail, a killer without a gun. The corpses he leaves are all on the cutting room floor. The studio big shots are afraid of him. Only Stahr has the entire warp and weave of the studio inside his head. And he's no Meyer Wolfsheim. He doesn't talk about "business gonnegtions" or "Oggsford men." Meyer is "a denizen of Broadway." He's a gambler "with two fine growths of hair which luxuriated in either nostril." He eats with "ferocious delicacy," and when he talks "his tragic nose" starts to tremble. He's a character right out of vaudeville. Edith Wharton would congratulate Fitzgerald for having created "the perfect Jew." She was the *perfect* anti-Semite, together with F. Scott Fitzgerald. "I remember a fat Jewess, inlaid with diamonds, who sat next to us at the Russian ballet and said as the curtain rose, 'Thad's luffly, dey ought to baint a bicture of it,' " Fitzgerald writes in *The Crack-Up*. His fat Jewess could have been Wolfsheim's wife.

But Wolfsheim is still a man to be reckoned with: he fixed the World Series of 1919, which impresses Nick Carraway. "It never occurred to me that one man could start to play with the faith of fifty million people—with the single-mindedness of a burglar blowing a safe."

It's 1922. We're at a cellar restaurant on the Main Stem. Fitzgerald introduces the scene with two little words, "Roaring noon," which suggest the summer heat, the glaring sun, and the wildness and abandon of Broadway. Gatsby's a bootlegger, after all, and Wolfsheim created him, as Rothstein helped create Legs Diamond. But A. R. didn't have a trembling, tragic nose. . . .

He wasn't a bandit from the Bronx. He was born on the Upper East Side in 1882, where there were very few gangs. His father, Abraham Rothstein, aka Abe the Just, was a millionaire manufacturer from Bessarabia, a philanthropist, a deeply religious man. A. R. had an older brother, Harry, born in 1880. Harry was the adoring son of an adoring dad, a boy scholar who held close to family tradition and Manhattan's tribe of Russian Jews. Young Arnold loved Harry and was morbidly jealous of him. "He was a baby who did not laugh," insists Leo Katcher, author of *The Big Bankroll: The Life and Times of Arnold Rothstein.* Apocrypha springs all around the book. It's a text filled with half a dozen myths, flawed perhaps but with precious pieces of truth. A. R. was a mathematical wizard, like Monroe Stahr, but he couldn't have run a studio. He didn't have much imagination . . . except when it came to Harry. He went around like a sleepwalker with a knife in his fist, mumbling "I hate Harry." And Abe the Just had to put him to bed. "He sought dark places—cellars, closets—in which to play. He liked the dark."

He attended Boys' High, but left after two years, in 1898. He'd already started to gamble, and was soon a fixture at one of the dice games in the prop room of Hammerstein's Victoria Theatre on 42nd Street. Among the other crap shooters were members of Manhattan's toughest gangs, the Hudson Dusters, the Gophers, and the Monk Eastmans, including Monk himself, a bullet-headed gangster whose infamy inspired no less a writer than Jorge Luis Borges: "He was a battered, colossal man. He had a short, bull neck; a barrel chest; long, scrappy arms; a broken nose . . . and legs bowed like a cowboy's or a sailor's." He wore a derby several sizes too small, and soon half the Bowery and the Lower East Side, his particular kingdom, affected the same kind of hat. He was the darling of Tammany Hall, captain of his own ward, who would batter people into submission if they failed to vote the Democratic line. For a little while A. R. ran with the Eastmans. But he wasn't really a hooligan, and he fell under the sway of Big Tim Sullivan, Tammany sachem and boss of the Bowery. He would gamble in Big Tim's poolroom, run errands, collect bets without bothering to scratch little reminders in a book. He could hold a swirl of numbers inside his head. "My smart Jew boy," Big Tim called him.

Wandering around for Tim, he became the Wolf. He was seventeen. To satisfy Abe the Just he took a job as a traveling salesman, with a line of derbies like the one Eastman wore, but while he was hawking hats, Harry died of pneumonia at the age of twenty, and the Wolf couldn't stop blaming himself. "Somehow, I had the feeling that I was responsible for Harry being dead. I remembered all the times that I'd wished he was dead, all the times I had dreamed of killing him."

And he couldn't seem to recover. The scowl he wore, a constant mask, was related to Harry. Harry would appear and reappear in his dreams, and whisper, "I'm not dead. Go into my room and you'll find me there." And he might wake from these nightmares and stumble toward some phantom room.

He stopped selling hats, moved into the Broadway Central Hotel, a boy with chalky cheeks. He had a new mentor, Nicky Arnstein, a suave gambler and confidence man with blue eyes and a baritone voice, who could discuss politics, art, and literature and liked long ocean voyages where he could prey on wealthy widows who didn't mind being swindled by such a bon vivant. He was even more of a mystery than the Wolf. Nick might have been born in Norway, or might not. He seemed to be Jewish, but who could tell? He had so many monikers, it was difficult to keep track of all the names. But Nick befriended the green little gambler who'd dropped out of Boys' High. "He was just a kid," recalled Nicky. "He didn't look like a gambler. . . . But no one could read his eyes. They were always hooded," like the boy who was still mourning Harry.

He became a loan shark and hired Monk Eastman to collect the *vig*. Monk was the best bill collector in town. But he'd bumped and battered too many people in too many gang wars, and the Wigwam (Tammany Hall) abandoned him. Eastman, who'd been untouchable, was sent to Sing Sing. And when he was released, Monk "found himself a king without a kingdom and a general without an army." He peddled dope and went back to work for the Wolf, who now had a small empire on Broadway. Monk became A. R.'s chief enforcer and bodyguard, shoving folks out of the way as the Wolf went from card game to card game at Rector's or Shanley's and the Knickerbocker Hotel, where Caruso lived. He rented two brownstones in the Roaring Forties and turned them into casinos.

In 1907 the Wolf fell in love with a blonde actress, Carolyn Greene. "He had so many interests that time for romance had to be rationed." But he did ration enough time to marry her, and when Abe the Just learned that Carolyn had been raised a Catholic, he sang the song of the dead for that prodigal son who'd survived Harry.

By 1910 Nick Arnstein was already working for him as a part-time steerer who could entice customers to his casinos. But Nicky continued to entice on his own. Fanny Brice—Flo's star, the anti–Follies Girl—fell in love with him. She refused to see the con man in Nick; for her he would remain an elegant dreamer with an aura of gentility. She loved the idea that he'd been the prison librarian at Sing Sing. Such was the power of Nick.

In 1911, A. R. lost his old Tammany protector, Big Tim Sullivan, who became partially paralyzed, perhaps as a result of syphilis. He would scream, make impossible demands, rattle off numbers, cuff at those around him like a great black bear, and he had to pay a band of roughnecks to pose as nurses and watch after him. A. R. survived Big Tim's fall, but Monk was sent back to Sing Sing. The Wolf needed fresh bait for his lair. He pursued Follies Girls and was often seen in the company of Lillian Lorraine. A. R. wasn't looking for a mistress to complement Carolyn.

He hired the hot-tempered Lillian as one of his steerers. She would bring millionaires with her into the Roaring Forties and deposit them with A. R. or Nick.

His fortunes multiplied, he found himself with too many numbers inside his head. From this moment on The Brain began to scribble coded messages in a little black book. He would sit inside Reuben's delicatessen at Broadway and 73rd (it was long before Leo Lindemann) and leave his black book on the front table; neither the customers nor the cashier could decrypt A. R.'s messages. It was the language of a wolf.

"I own Broadway and anybody who doesn't think so winds up in the gutter," A. R. boasts in Jimmy Breslin's book. But it doesn't sound like A. R., who adored silence and wasn't given to braggadocio. As his lawyer, William J. Fallon, said: "Rothstein is a man who ducks in doorways. A mouse, standing in a doorway, waiting for his cheese." A mouse who could quickly become a wolf, and whose cheese might be converted into thousand-dollar bills.

A. R. was known to carry incredible amounts of cash on his person—three hundred thousand dollars in "bricks" of thousand-dollar bills. He might bet that much on a horse, on the color or shape of a cloud, on the batting average of Babe Ruth. Few other gamblers could afford to bet such stakes or to walk around with so much cash. And that's why he always had a chief enforcer and bodyguard. First it was Monk Eastman and then it was Abe Attell, "The Little Hebrew," who had reigned as featherweight champion from the beginning of the century to 1912, when his title was taken away for throwing a fight. He was as much of a gambler as A. R. And he would serve as A. R.'s point man in the Black Sox scandal.

It was common knowledge that the Chicago White Sox were fed up with their owner, Charlie Comiskey, who paid them a pittance. The "Old Roman" wouldn't raise their salaries a nickel or a dime. Eight of the White Sox banded together, including Eddie Cicotte, the team's best pitcher, and a bumpkin who couldn't even scratch his own name, outfielder Shoeless Joe Jackson, the idol of Chicago fans and the greatest natural hitter in the American League. Cicotte was the ringleader of this little tribe, and he agreed to throw the World Series against the Cincinnati Reds for a hundred thousand dollars, in advance.

The Sox were heavy favorites. By simply whispering Rothstein's name, Attell got Cicotte to accept a token sum up front, with a "guarantee" of a hundred grand. To cover himself, A. R. bet on both the Sox and the Reds to win, but he had many side bets on the Sox noted in his little black book. The Brain had distanced himself from the fix and the fixers, had never talked to Cicotte, had never made his intentions known. It was "The Little Hebrew" who was out on a limb, who went to Chicago and Cincinnati with A. R.'s chief bookkeeper, Rachel Brown, and Rachel kept a record of all her dealings with the Sox.

Cincinnati won, of course. But the whole damn Series was "a Greek tragedy that was played as a farce." The fixers "were inept. They were naïve. They were stupid." Some of them, like Shoeless Joe and third baseman Buck Weaver, performed much, much better than the players who hadn't been involved in the fix. It was *those* players who made costly errors and lost crucial games, and not the fixers themselves, who would become the poor boys of baseball—total pariahs. There'd been rumors of a fix ever since the Series, but in September 1920 a grand jury met in Chicago and returned indictments against Shoeless Joe and the seven others, against Attell and Rachel Brown. . . .

The Little Hebrew fled to Canada, and A. R. was free to put the entire blame on him. "Abe Attell did the fixing," he told the State of Illinois. "I don't doubt that Attell used my name to put it over. That's been done by smarter men than Abe."

Kenesaw Mountain Landis, the newly appointed "emperor" of baseball, would ban the fixers for life but none of them ever sat in jail. The records of the grand jury had disappeared. The signed confessions of Shoeless Joe and Cicotte were lost. Joe vanished from baseball with Black Betsy, his celebrated bat. His fans couldn't stop mourning him. Prohibition had already arrived, and Manhattan was the new American outlaw. There was a furor against A. R. and Broadway itself. A gang of Jewish gamblers, led by A. R., had destroyed Shoeless Joe and nearly wrecked baseball, whose stars were "folk heroes. [Any] man who would trifle with the honor of the game was a Benedict Arnold."

But as Joe drifted into obscurity, A. R. was becoming a national icon, more and more notorious, a power broker who could break into anything, even America's number-one sport. Wherever he went on the Main Stem, people stared at the man behind the Big Fix. It seemed that A. R. "had money in everybody's mouth, all the way up to the Presidential cabinet." Thanks to Big Tim Sullivan, he'd gotten closer to Charles F. Murphy, grand sachem of Tammany Hall, the shrewdest political boss New York has ever had. Murphy controlled the police—he made and unmade captains and commissioners—the courts, the mayor's and the governor's office. The most unbridled gangs were beholden to him. The city's prostitutes were practically his own private union. And when white Protestant America breathed down his neck, he would button up the Tenderloin and close the red-light district, until taxicabs became the only brothels in town. . . .

Murphy had his own "office" on the second floor of Delmonico's, where he received visitors like some pope or prince who was surrounded by clumsy, brutal men. Murphy needed someone with finesse who could dance among politicians, bankers, and the police, who could talk and dress "Park Avenue," who was as com-

fortable in a palace as the local precinct. There was only one candidate—Arnold Rothstein, who would serve as Tammany's private banker and bondsman, who could bribe judges and district
attorneys, could control ferocious, feuding criminals, create his
own little school for crime.

3.

Enter Legs Diamond. The Brain needed a new bodyguard.
Attell was gone, and Legs had just gotten out of Leavenworth, where he sat a year and a day for going AWOL from the
army. He and his kid brother Eddie had been vicious little thieves
for Madden's Gopher Gang. That was when Jack Diamond supposedly earned the name "Legs" for stealing packages off delivery
trucks and running right past the police. He'd been a burglar too.
"He'd failed at that as a teen-ager and graduated to the activity
that conformed to his talent, which was not stealth but menace."
He was an Irisher who liked to advertise himself as a Yid, because
that seemed more appropriate and enticing in Rothstein country,
on Broadway. He was "a moving gob of electricity," cruel and effi-
cient and crazy, "Rothstein's crazy nabob." He would collect for
A. R., and soon Rothstein put him in charge of his bootlegging
operations, made him a chief. And Legs Diamond was "the
dauphin of the town for years."

No one seemed to like Legs. For Stanley Walker, who lived
through Prohibition, he was "a frail, tubercular, little rat [who
loved] to burn men's feet with matches." Why did Rothstein pick
such a little sadist as his dauphin? Was it sound business sense,
his desire to cash in on Diamond's reputation for cruelty? Or was
it something much more tribal? Did he see in Jack and Ed Diamond a curious echo of himself and Harry? Jack was the older

brother, Jack took care of Ed, and they were suicidal together, "making enemies like rabbits make rabbits." Was A. R. touched *and* disturbed by their devotion? The Diamond boys had only themselves as friends. Jack was feared because of his "insane gang tactics"—he would hijack his own trucks, kidnap bootleggers who belonged to him—and his "gonnegtions" to A. R. He was like a snake who would spit anywhere, and at anyone . . . except A. R. And he could dance like the Devil. Jack was never still. He was a walking contradiction, cowardly *and* courageous. And he had a sense of style, with his chinchilla coats, his white on white silk scarves, his wide-brimmed white felt hat.

Perhaps A. R. needed a stylish, provocative gangster to front for him and bring a little terror onto the Main Stem. And perhaps he secretly relished in Jack, who couldn't control his thievery. Whenever the cops found a murdered gambler with emptied pockets, they would ask themselves, "Did Legs take him home?" He'd started the first modern gang, with Lucky Luciano and Dutch Schultz as raw recruits. Jack had no attachments (other than Ed), no allegiance to a neighborhood, no political dues to pay. He was a corporation who hired himself out for mayhem and didn't believe in territories or territorial disputes, like the Gophers and the Hudson Dusters, who kept annihilating each other. But Legs himself was a bit old-fashioned . . . and as anarchic as the old neighborhood gangs, and just as unpredictable; that's why his own gangs would constantly fall apart. Every other gangster seemed to want the dauphin dead. But that only added to his allure. He was unstoppable. "Jack had imagined his fame all his life and now it was imagining him."

He would freelance, with A. R.'s blessing. The Brain had gone heavily into drugs. Jack went to Germany and bought heroin for himself and A. R. He'd taken over an entire town in the Catskills called Monticello, and his gang was headquartered in the Monticello Hotel. He grew estranged from A. R., who must have known that Madden or Costello or one of the other corporate gangsters would kill Legs sooner or later. Legs' "lust for blood and torture" was bad for business. But Jack Diamond continued to dodge bullets and dance, like a poisonous spinning top. . . .

4.

Rothstein's marriage began to fail. It was 1927, and he'd been married twenty years. The Wolf lived with Carolyn at 916 Park Avenue, but he'd never once been inside his wife's bedroom. Lindy's was his main lair. "Regular as clockwork, he comes here. Sunday night, Monday night, any night. Everybody knows that . . . this place is like an office to him. . . . Mr. Rothstein you see, but you do not watch," recalled Abe Scher, Lindy's night cashier.

He'd return to Park Avenue after dawn, have a snack of milk and cookies, try to sleep. He was still haunted by Harry, and he would have long bouts of depression. Carolyn told him that she wanted a divorce. She sailed off to Europe without the Wolf. He scribbled a note to her:

Dear Carolyn,
Things are quiet here. Have a good time.

And he ended the letter with "*Love. Arnold.*"

His brevity had little to do with his lack of romance. The Wolf had no language. He lived in a dream of money. A. R. had narrowed himself to nothing. "He was a man who had no inner resources; his own company bored him." That was the curse of Broadway. Jolson suffered from the same disease; so did Eddie

Cantor and Damon Runyon and Walter Winchell. The long electric night kept them alert; without it they were sleepwalkers . . . and Rothstein was merely a milk and cookie man.

He had his own separate table at the delicatessen; nobody else could touch it a little after dark. Leo Lindemann or Abe Scher would bring him his messages. He might whisper a few words into Lindy's phone. The number was CIRCLE 3317; anyone could ring up A. R., who might or might not take the call. After he was done with the telephone, he held court at his table, but it wasn't the same kind of principality as it had been before.

A few years back, Madden might have petitioned him for a loan; his breweries were expanding and he needed more trucks to carry his best beer, "Madden's No. 1." Or it could have been Luciano and Schultz who were short of cash. But by 1927 the beer barons lived like royalty and were as rich as the Wolf. His bankroll didn't seem quite so big. His ablest pupils—Costello, Luciano, Lepke Buchalter—were beginning to outgrow their master and have as long a reach. But they couldn't penetrate Park Avenue and Police Headquarters or the Wigwam and Wall Street without A. R. The grand sachem, Boss Murphy, had died in 1924. And no one was clever enough to replace him or rein in "irregularities." Jimmy Walker, the new Jazz Mayor, had risen under Murphy's star, but with Murphy gone he was like a lost child adrift in some wonderland that would soon eat him alive. . . .

The Brain was a chronic worrier—and a hypochondriac. He carried a bag of figs in his pocket, because Lindemann or some Broadway gangster had told him that figs were good for his health. He worried about his upper teeth, which "had been soft and chalky since childhood." He'd lost every one and had to wear an upper plate, which gave him a wolfish grin that bothered so many gamblers. He couldn't bear the sight of his own body. "He removed the last of his clothes in the dark," so that he wouldn't have to see himself naked. And for the first time he worried about his bankroll.

He'd abandoned his interest in bootlegging—that's why he didn't need so much of Legs—and had gone deeper and deeper into heroin and cocaine. But he had to expend enormous sums of cash to keep his merchandise moving. And the milk and cookie man couldn't charm Carolyn into a reconciliation. He moved out of the Park Avenue flat and returned to Broadway, hopped like a wolf from hotel to hotel. He continued to gamble. "I think I gambled because I loved the excitement. When I gambled nothing else mattered. I could play for hours and not know how much time had passed."

And he had another incentive now. Cards could ease his cash flow. He took up with a new lady, Inez Norton, a flashy blonde and former actress. She lived at the Fairfield, a hotel that belonged to him, that was part of his real estate empire. But he still had to keep scrambling for cash. He could build up equity with each card game, because win or lose, the Wolf would always be ahead. Rothstein was a "slow pay"—whatever the circumstances, he would pull cash out of the pot and offer his marker. If he lost fifty grand, he would write an IOU for a hundred, and the other gamblers had to subsidize A. R., become his banker. And then there was that wolfish look, the Rothstein grin. He was losing his stride on Broadway. He would seem forlorn at Lindy's, agitated, as he nibbled on a Danish.

In one particular poker session, he'd raided the pot and owed a bundle to George "Hump" McManus, a burly bookkeeper-gambler who was over six feet tall and weighed 210 pounds, with one brother who was a priest and another a cop. He'd pulled McManus' own money out of the game and left him a marker. But

McManus couldn't collect. The Wolf spread word that the card game had been crooked and that he wouldn't pay such a weasel.

McManus called CIRCLE 3317, got Leo Lindemann on the line, asked for A. R., told the Wolf to meet him at the Park Central Hotel. It was almost eleven P.M. A. R. had been to the Colony Club with Inez Norton. He wasn't despondent, according to Inez. The Wolf was in a splendid mood. "We spoke of many subjects, but mainly of love." He hoped to marry her soon, she said, but A. R. wasn't free. He still had a missus on Park Avenue. . . .

He arrived at McManus' hotel without a bodyguard or a gun. It was the one instant in his life when he could have used his dauphin, Jack. Would Hump McManus have shot A. R. if Legs had been right behind him? Would he have risked Legs' crazy wrath?

But A. R. went to Hump McManus all alone. Was it a suicidal dreamwalk? Did he have Harry in his head? Or was it the brazen act of a Broadway wolf? How will we ever know?

"I shot him right through the prick," McManus bragged to Damon Runyon. A. R. was found on the back stairs, rushed to the Polyclinic Hospital. He wouldn't reveal McManus' name. Leo Lindemann offered A. R. a pint of his own blood, and he kept vigil as the Wolf lay dying.

Broadway would soon die with him. Lindy's was never the same. Who could have inherited Rothstein's table? And there was no longer a silken line between the cops and the pols, the bankers and the bootleggers. Franklin Roosevelt, who would become governor of New York with the help of a Democratic machine that had cracked skulls for him in Syracuse and other places, distanced himself from the Wigwam when he prepared to run for president. He would sit in judgment on the Jazz Mayor, who'd been accused of rampant corruption.

"No man could hold life so carelessly without falling down a manhole before he is done," said Ben Hecht of Beau James. But *carelessness* had defined Broadway. And the cut of your clothes. The Jazz Mayor spent more on his wardrobe in a few months than he earned in a whole year. He would change outfits three times a day, and he kept a complete wardrobe at City Hall and at his tailor shop in the Ritz-Carlton. He drank Black Velvets with Betty Compton, she of the "caplike hairdo and the Chiclets smile." And with his own administration in tatters, and Roosevelt ready to pounce, Walker resigned on September 1, 1932, and sailed for Europe with the Chiclets Girl. He threatened to run for reelection, but he never did. His own era was already gone. He was an ex–Jazz Mayor without Ziegfeld, without Texas Guinan, without Rothstein's magic table, without much jazz.

5.

And the milk and cookies man? Fitzgerald may have mocked him, may have put extra hairs in his nose, may have taken away his whisper and his soft brown eyes, but it was Runyon who understood his loneliness, his wanderings as a wolf, and the perverse sadness of his death. . . .

In "The Brain Goes Home," Runyon's homage to Rothstein, we meet Armand Rosenthal (The Brain) walking in front of Mindy's. The Brain is forty years old and beginning to "to get a little bunchy about the middle," like A. R. himself. Careful of his health, he buys an apple from a red-headed raggedy doll, gives her a finnif, tells her to keep the change. This Apple Annie blesses him and starts to cry. And Armand meditates on his love life. "I give Doris Clare ten *G's* last night and she does not make half as much fuss. . . . I guess that love costs me as much dough as any guy that ever lives."

The Brain has three different dolls and an ever-loving wife. But "think of the many homes it gives me to go to in case I wish to go home. . . . I guess I have more homes to go to than any other guy on Broadway."

Naturally "he never picks a crow." Doris is an ex–Follies Girl who's very blond, like Inez Norton, while Cynthia Harris' hair is "black as the inside of a wolf." She's a graduate of Mr. Earl Carroll's "Vanities," where The Brain spotted her while she was in the raw. And Bobby Blake, who's from Flatbush, "is a very smart little doll."

While Armand is out walking, Daffy Jack shoves a shiv into his left side. Daffy was hired by Homer Swing, a gambler who owes Armand money and is annoyed when Armand puts the pressure on him. Runyon reenacts A. R.'s "agony" with an ironic twist. A. R. becomes the hunter rather than the hunted, a collector of beauties rather than cocaine—not the man who took money from McManus.

The narrator and Big Nig, a crap shooter, find him stumbling on 52nd Street long after midnight. "I wish to keep this a secret . . . if you take me to a hospital they must report it to the coppers. Take me home."

"Which home?" the narrator asks.

The Brain ponders like a philosopher and says "Park Avenue," which is where his ever-loving wife Charlotte lives.

The narrator and Nig put him into a taxi and ride with him to Park Avenue. But Charlotte is in the middle of a big soiree. "I am entertaining very important people tonight, and I can't have them disturbed by bringing in a hospital patient." Besides, "It is twenty years since he comes home so early."

They can't try Doris, because she's already gone out. Cynthia won't take him, and neither will Bobby Baker, who slams the door on the narrator and Nig. Then the cab driver disappears. They lug Armand around until the raggedy apple doll pops out of a basement, where all the raggedy dolls live. She takes him in, and in typical Runyon fashion, he draws up a will as he's dying and leaves all his money to the redhead and her five kids.

It's Runyonland, where beauties are self-absorbed, and only a raggedy redhead can take Armand in. But "The Brain Goes Home" is a cautionary tale. Runyon doesn't condemn the beauties. They live in a mechanical universe and are doing what gold diggers have to do: protect their goods. And by writing Rothstein's *real* obituary, Runyon scratches at the brittle heart of Broadway, with its band of outsiders, where the rulers—gangsters and gamblers—rush after dolls who dance in the raw, where women are beauties or nothing at all, where A. R. was a citizen of the night whose only furniture was a delicatessen table. He had no "gonnegtion" to another human being apart from Harry's ghost. His existence was as chalky as his own absent upper teeth. He sat astride an endless want, where *home* was nothing but a dance of thousand-dollar bills, and A. R. had nowhere to go, except to meet his fate in McManus' room.

CHAPTER FOUR
MADDEN AND MONK

1.

The first edition of *The Great Gatsby* has a painting on its cover by Francis Cugat, an art designer who once worked in Hollywood. It's a spooky rendering of Daisy Buchanan, the object of Gatsby's desire. Daisy's eyes peer out of a cobalt sky. She's wearing a cloche hat, like a pirate, with three little beads hanging from the edge. We can catch a tiny female nude swimming in the iris of each eye. A green tear like a splotchy exclamation mark has fallen from her right eye. The lady lacks a nose but her mouth is like a red kiss in the cobalt. The lights of Coney Island seem to explode under the masklike face, with the dark somber city in the background. She resembles Nick Carraway's dream of Daisy, "whose disembodied face floated along the dark cornices and blinding signs" of Manhattan, as Charles Scribner III points out in his afterword to the book.

But the quote isn't as innocent or romantic as it seems. Nick Carraway is the least reliable of unreliable narrators. He's riding in a carriage through Central Park with Jordan Baker, the golf champion who is Daisy's best friend and is obliging Nick to act as the "pimp" who will bring Daisy and Gatsby back together again. Nick is furious but he can never show it. He simply repeats a mantra inside his head that could have been the mantra of Broadway: "There are only the pursued, the pursuing, the busy and the tired."

The carriage ride occurs *after* the scene with Gatsby and Meyer Wolfsheim at the cellar restaurant on 42nd Street, *after* Wolfsheim talks about Gatsby being "an Oggsford man," *after* Gatsby tells Nick that Wolfsheim fixed the World Series, *after* Nick compares Wolfsheim to a man toying with the faith of fifty million people like a burglar with a blowtorch.

He's the disingenuous Nick, the naïve Nick, who asks Gatsby if Wolfsheim isn't a dentist by any chance. Nowhere do we learn that Nick's in love with Daisy, his second cousin once removed, and that his own carelessness has conspired to bring about Gatsby's death.

He accuses Jordan of being "incurably dishonest." But it's Jordan who realizes that she and Nick are twins: "I hate careless people. That's why I like you."

If *The Great Gatsby* grows more powerful and poignant with each decade, it isn't necessarily because of our nostalgia for the twenties, or our romance with Jay Gatsby, the most elusive character in all of American literature. The book remains a total mystery, a kind of palpable illusion, like Francis Cugat's portrait of Daisy, who might not be *our* Daisy, but some modern gold digger leaving her imprint on us all. . . .

The originality of the novel lies in its narrator. We can never really pin Nick down. He claims to have a certain moral pedigree that allows him not to make judgments, but he judges all the time—with language, with his sense of style. He's a kind of cannibal who feeds on others, turns them into gargoyles, like Meyer Wolfsheim or Myrtle Wilson, Tom Buchanan's mistress—or masks, like Gatsby or Daisy, his dream creature, who comes to us out of Nick's very own dream language. Nick isn't nameless or faceless, like Runyon's narrator, who lives within a monochrome and can never crawl out of it. Nick has Fitzgerald's own modulations, like a superb musical instrument that can invent and reinvent. He also has an emotional range that's beyond Runyon's, even if it's subversive and masked. Nick's hidden anger and jealousy fuel the narrative, and mirror Scott Fitzgerald's own complex relationship with Zelda, whom he cannibalized as he created Daisy's character and voice. Nick understands what her voice can do to a man: "I think that voice held him [Gatsby] most with its fluctuating, feverish warmth because it couldn't be over-dreamed. . . ."

—*couldn't be over-dreamed*, like the novel itself, which relived Fitzgerald's courtship with Zelda, the wild pain and wild delight, and their almost public marriage, as they were immediately mythologized into the two most gorgeous people in America. Scott couldn't write when Zelda was around or when she was away. "I was in love with a whirlwind and I must spin a net big enough to catch it." But he couldn't find a net big enough to catch his own jealousy.

Zelda was his *wound*, and that wound invades the novel as Scott invests himself, through Nick, in Tom Buchanan, the fallen football hero who has to fight to hold onto Daisy; in Gatsby, the young lieutenant who didn't have the means to marry Daisy, the little debutante—his riotous success as a bootlegger will play upon Scott's own riotous early success as a novelist; and in Daisy herself. "In the last analysis," Scott would write, long after *Gatsby*, "she [Zelda] is a stronger person than I am. I have creative fire but I am a weak individual. She knows this and really looks upon me as a woman."

And it's Fitzgerald's fear of his own femininity, his obsessive need to wear a masculine mask, that distorts and controls *Carraway*, the man who carries himself away, who comes home to the West after Gatsby disappears, plucks out his narrator's eye and all "privileged glimpses into the human heart."

But Nick, the unreliable narrator, is perfectly reliable in his description of New York. In fact, *Gatsby* is the ultimate Broadway novel, even if only one or two scenes happen on Broadway. He doesn't take us into Mindy's or the Silver Slipper—Runyonland didn't exist when Fitzgerald wrote the novel. Nick's Broadway isn't about nostalgia. Published in 1925, the novel focuses on the summer of 1922, when New York had its own film studios and was a much bigger Babylon than Hollywood would ever be. On his ride with Jordan Baker in Central Park, Nick notices that the sun "had gone down behind the tall apartments of the movie stars in the West Fifties. . . ."

It's still the great age of the Follies, when a Ziegfeld Girl could create a furor wherever she went. At one of Gatsby's parties, "there is a burst of chatter"—about a particular girl—"as the erroneous news goes around that she is Gilda Gray's understudy from the 'Follies.' "

And Nick falls in love with Broadway itself as he watches an armada of taxi cabs "bound for the theatre district. . . . Forms leaned together in the taxis as they waited, and voices sang, and there was laughter from unheard jokes, and lighted cigarettes outlined unintelligible gestures inside. Imagining that I, too, was hurrying toward gayety and sharing their intimate excitement, I wished them well," as Scott might have done when he was a very young man coming into Manhattan from a prep school in New Jersey.

He also understands the Broadway that celebrates energy and success, that has little tolerance for defeat—"there was no difference between men, in intelligence or race, so profound as the difference between the sick and the well."

Gatsby *is* Broadway, even if his mansion's on West Egg (Great Neck). Like most Broadway creatures—Texas Guinan, Al

Jolson, Owney Madden, Fanny Brice—he reinvented himself. It was Wolfsheim who sponsored Gatsby, the way A. R. sponsored Legs Diamond and Frank Costello. "I raised him up out of nothing, right out of the gutter." As Matthew J. Bruccoli has noted, Gatsby is a pun on *gat*, a word Runyon's own gangsters might have used for "gun." Gatsby had graduated from the Great War with a fistful of medals, a few months at Oxford, and little else. He had to keep wearing his uniform because he had nothing else to wear. Wolfsheim sensed immediately how this "Oggsford man" would be helpful to him in his own business "gonnegtions." And Gatsby rose out of some phantasm of himself to become Wolfsheim's dauphin and nabob, and much, much more than that. The astonishing, surreal wealth is nothing to him. He's a monomaniac. His only ideal is to recapture Daisy after five years of separation and her marriage to Tom. It's Daisy and Tom who are careless and corrupt, not the bootlegger, who may have killed people or had them killed, but not, we imagine, out of carelessness. Daisy isn't a gold digger, like Myrtle Wilson, she's "the golden girl," the implacable daughter of some implacable king. . . .

If Gatsby continues to intrigue us, it's because he's that creature of the New World—the American gangster, who has no antecedents other than himself, who can buy palaces out on Long Island, like horse-faced Larry Fay; who can hire Broadway dance instructors to teach him to walk, like Al Capone; who can rent an entire restaurant for his beloved, with an orchestra and a herd of French-speaking waiters, like Noodles (Robert De Niro), the sad-eyed Jewish gangster in Sergio Leone's *Once Upon a Time in America*; who can fabricate an entire world to fool a Spanish nobleman, like Dave the Dude; who can ride around in an armored car with the melancholy look of a gangster, not a gun moll, like Texas Guinan; who can dart across the city with all the pluck of a little rooster, like Owney Madden; who can dance with Kiki Roberts while bullets twirl at his feet, like Jack Diamond; who can rise out of nowhere with a lightning leap, like Gatsby himself, with the smile of a schoolboy, so that his very existence seems spectacular and unreal. There was "something gorgeous about him," and that gorgeousness won't go away.

2.

Matthew J. Bruccoli, Fitzgerald's Sherlock Holmes, tells us that Gatsby's pet phrase—"old sport"—was borrowed from Max Gerlach, one of Fitzgerald's neighbors in "West Egg." Gerlach, who may have been a bootlegger, had nothing of Gatsby's aura about him. He might also have been a German baron, or a car dealer who tried to kill himself in 1939 and couldn't complete the job. That doesn't sound like Jay. We can't imagine Max staring forever at that green light near the edge of Daisy's dock, caught up in her glow, irreparable as any remade man.

The gangster himself was reborn, with Broadway, at the start of Prohibition, when the town was fast and furious, and one could declare that "anything goes." Gatsby's contradictions—his innocence and his murderous means—feel as modern to us as our very bones. His mannerisms, such as "old sport," are like a nervous tic. He's more than a relic, a piece of history left over from Fitzgerald's Jazz Age. With all his treasure, he's a lithe man who dances at the very edge of time. . . .

The gangster who most resembles him isn't Legs Diamond or even A. R., who has his own mythic pull, and escaped from the Jewish bourgeoisie of his father to prowl among lowlifes—it's Madden, who's relatively undiscovered. He doesn't even have his own listing in *The Encyclopedia of New York City*, and he's the nearest thing that Manhattan ever had to a crime czar, even if his reign was very short, five or six years. He didn't travel from South Dakota to Broadway, like James Gatz.

Owen Victor Madden was born in Liverpool—same as John Lennon—or Leeds, in 1891 or '92; the date and place seem to vary according to the scant biographical notices that were ever written about him. His parents were dirt-poor Irish immigrants. His papa died and his mama sailed to New York with Owney and his sister in 1902, settled on Tenth Avenue in Hell's Kitchen, Manhattan's wildest neighborhood, a little northwest of the Tenderloin. Owney was ten or eleven, depending on which of his biographers you believe. He joined the Gophers, the gang that ruled Hell's Kitchen and robbed from the railroad and broke heads for Tammany Hall, like the Monk Eastmans. But the Eastmans were strictly downtown. The Gophers' rivals were the Hudson Dusters, whose territories touched upon their own. Cops and criminals would describe him as "that banty rooster out of hell." He was always getting into fights.

According to Herbert Asbury, he was "almost the exact antithesis of Monk Eastman; he was sleek, slim and dapper, with the gentle smile of a cherub and the cunning and cruelty of a devil." He became boss of the Gophers at seventeen, the most feared hoodlum in Hell's Kitchen, where he was called "Owney the Killer." He was good with a lead pipe (wrapped in newspaper), a blackjack, a slingshot, and a gun.

But with all his dapperness, was he that different from Monk? He combed his hair, and Eastman did not. He had fewer scars on his face. He was never a bouncer, or "sheriff" of New Irving Hall, and didn't carry a cudgel—a Monk Eastman shillelagh—with which to crack a hundred heads. Ambulances would shuttle between the New Irving and Bellevue Hospital so often that drivers took to calling the accident ward at Bellevue "Eastman Pavilion." Madden had no hospital wards named after him. Perhaps he had a little more brains and ambition than Monk, "and frequently let it be known that he aspired to be the acknowledged king of all the gangs."

—*king of all the gangs.*

That almost sounds like one of Meyer Wolfsheim's nabobs, but Meyer's nabobs weren't penny-poor, like the old gangs of New York—the Dead Rabbits, the Bowery Boys, the Monk Eastmans, and Madden's Gopher Gang—minions of Tammany Hall who never had a bookkeeper or a bank account. Madden was the Wigwam's pet bulldog, like Monk. And if Madden thrived while Monk was in Sing Sing or Dannemora, abandoned by the Wigwam because his gang warfare had gotten out of control, he—Madden—was destined to have a similar fate. With all his dreams of conquest, Owney the Killer wasn't big enough or smart enough to chase down Tammany Hall, which was like a cartel of bribery and plunder that used the gangs as often as it could and discarded one after the other.

Few gang leaders ever became lieutenants of Tammany Hall. Grand sachems were seldom seen in their company. Madden was as much a pawn as Monk. In fact, he modeled himself after Monk Eastman, even if he didn't wear a derby that was too small for his head. He wouldn't walk through his territories with a "great blue pigeon" perched on his shoulder, but he adored pigeons, tamed them, had his own coops.

Ferocious and lazy, he loved the adulation of gangster life. When suspicious characters approached him, he would smile and say, "I'm Madden. Who are you?" And his would-be attackers would run. He kept a diary for several days to please a local reporter who wanted to learn the "lowdown" on Madden. And in its matter-of-fact way, this little diary reveals more about Madden than any thumbnail sketch of Hell's Kitchen mores.

Thursday—Went to a dance in the afternoon. Went to a dance at night and then to a cabaret. Took some girls home. Went to a restaurant and stayed there until seven o'clock Friday morning.

Friday—Spent the day with Freda Horner. Looked at some fancy pigeons. Met some friends in a saloon early in the evening and stayed with them until five o'clock in the morning.

Saturday—Slept all day. Went to a dance in the Bronx late in the afternoon, and to a dance on Park Avenue at night.

Sunday—Slept until three o'clock. Went to a dance in the afternoon and to another in the same place at night. After that I went to a cabaret and stayed there almost all night.

Madden was girl-crazy; it was Freda Horner and other of his Hell's Kitchen "fiancées" who would bring about his fall. Once, when a clerk named Henshaw began to court one of his fiancées, Owney the Killer tracked him to a trolley car, and "in full view of a dozen passengers, he shot the man to death, pausing long enough to ring the conductor's bell."

Neither the conductor nor the passengers would testify against Madden, and the police couldn't touch him. And it was while he was at a dance hall with his fiancées on November 6, 1912, that eleven gunmen from the Hudson Dusters shot Madden to pieces. The cops let him wallow on the ground and then called an ambulance. "Surgeons dug half a dozen bullets out of the gangster's body," and it took months for him to mend. But Madden plotted from his hospital bed, and all eleven gunmen began to die, one by one.

He never really recovered from his bullet wounds, and he would have a cough for the rest of his life. But he recovered enough to dance with Freda Horner, whom he had wooed away from Patsy Doyle, a minor member of his own gang. When Doyle went to the cops and squealed on Madden, Madden had him killed, after Freda helped lure Doyle into a saloon and set the trap. But the Wigwam had tired of Madden as it had tired of Monk, and Owney the Killer was sent to Sing Sing. It was 1915. The Gophers were already a dying breed. Boss Murphy had to fight off reformers and became as sanctimonious as a church mouse. He dropped the gangs from his payroll and permitted the police to pick away at them. Meanwhile, Madden coughed up blood and tended to Sing Sing's flock of pigeons.

And Monk Eastman? Lost, in and out of jail, he joined the National Guard under an alias and served overseas in 1917. "Bullets in the mass held no terror for him after the gunfights of the East Side," and he killed as many Germans as he could. Wounded several times, he escaped from his nurses and returned to the war half-naked and unarmed. He received no medals, but when he got back to New York, the captain of his company wrote to Governor Alfred E. Smith, stating that Monk was a good soldier, "and toward all his comrades he evinced the greatest kindness and devotion."

Like other ex-convicts, Monk had been shorn of his citizenship, and on May 3, 1919, Al Smith signed an executive order that pardoned Monk and made him a citizen again. The Wig-

wam smiled on its war hero. The cops got him a job. But he disappeared, and on December 26, 1920, he was found outside the
Blue Bird Café near Fourth Avenue with five bullet holes in him.
Manhattan's trenches were too much for Monk. A Prohibition
agent had shot him after a quarrel. It seems Monk had been
bootlegging and selling dope for The Brain. A. R. was never
implicated, of course. He was untouchable behind his table. . . .

3.

In 1923, Madden was paroled from Sing Sing after serving nine
years. Like Monk, he found himself a king without a kingdom.
The ex-Gophers had all gone into bootlegging. "A lesser man,"
according to Stanley Walker, "a man of more limited imagination,
or one who had been broken in prison, would have slipped back
into the underworld as a mere punk, a nobody. Madden had iron
in his gizzard." He discovered a city with a new kind of gang—
competing brotherhoods of bootleggers with their nightclubs and
speakeasies and cabarets. Madden was obliged to reimagine himself. Owney the Killer became a quiet man. He attached himself
to taxi czar Larry Fay, a disciple of his from the Gophers. Fay,
who'd started as a bootlegger with one taxi cab, now had a whole
fleet, financed with a loan from A. R. He put his imprint on each
"El Fay" cab, redesigning the doors and fenders with a silver trim,
supplying a musical horn and a battery of lights—the lavender-
colored cab with gray upholstery that Myrtle Wilson selects for
Tom, Nick, and herself in *Gatsby* could have been an El Fay.

Madden went to work as a "counselor" who kept El Fay's drivers from going out on strike. And Larry Fay ended the feud
between Madden and "Big Frenchy" DeMange, an old rival from
the Hudson Dusters. Soon he and Big Frenchy were inseparable,

and now Madden worked with Larry Fay, not for him. Larry had perpetuated a Broadway style. He could have strolled outside Mindy's with Dave the Dude. He bought nightclubs, invested in Broadway shows, hired Texas Guinan as a hostess, went to Europe to shop for chorus girls and clothes, bought a mansion out in Great Neck, where he was Scott Fitzgerald's neighbor, mingled with the high and the low, threw miraculous parties that served as a model for Gatsby's, with buffet tables that snaked across an entire lawn, but Larry Fay was no organizer or elder statesman. He couldn't have monitored and policed prima donna bootleggers such as Waxey Gordon, Dutch Schultz, and Legs Diamond. Manhattan was a minefield, and he had to seek Madden's protection to stay alive. Suddenly Madden was more than a partner. . . .

"His face was small. In profile its lines were like a falcon's. His forehead was not high, and it receded a little. The nose was a fierce beak. . . . His body bore the scars of many bullets, and the condition of his lungs made him fear that he would die of tuberculosis. . . . His hair was black and sleek. His eyes were blue, a very bright and piercing blue."

And this "frail and almost forgotten man of legend" began to take over the town, not with his "typewriters"—machine guns— like Scarface. And not with his fists, or his gang of bomb throwers from Hell's Kitchen. . . .

Scarface had turned Chicago into his own private bloodbath. There would be six hundred unsolved murders during his rule of the South Side. He even wore a badge. (The suburb of Cicero had elected him sheriff.) He would howl and have temper tantrums. He had General Motors design him a dream car with armor noble enough to break through brick and portholes to house his machine guns. He had seven hundred soldiers. And Scarface bivouacked like an army, riding across Chicago in a "traveling fortress" of nine or ten cars. He might decide to have lunch or dinner in his fortress, with his bodyguards doubling as waiters. When his sister got married, he invited ten thousand guests and delivered a nine-foot wedding cake to the bride and groom. Politicians and judges sat at his feet. He was a graduate of Brooklyn and the East Side waterfront, and had grown up in the Five Points, that ferocious fountainhead of nineteenth-century gangs. But Scarface didn't have the curious chivalry of the Dead Rabbits and the Short Tails, who fought only among themselves. He ran with Johnny Torrio and his James Streeters, terrorizing whole neighborhoods and burning their enemies alive.

He continued his tactics on the South Side after Torrio brought him to Chicago. But he eclipsed his old boss and sat on a throne inside his headquarters at Cicero's Hawthorne Hotel. Capone loved the glamor, like Jack Dempsey and the Bambino did. He was the number-one bootlegger in the world. *Scarface.* He had his own mansion in Miami, where he entertained Winchell and Runyon, giving them exclusive interviews. His profile was as famous as Valentino's. There were thousands of photographs circulating in the press—Capone meditating like Mussolini, Capone congratulating the next Caruso, Capone with his favorite jazz musician, Capone catching a marlin, Capone with a bathing beauty. But there were only *two* pictures of Madden available, both of them mug shots. "All publicity, to Owney, was bad publicity." He had a bulletproof Duesenberg, but it wasn't meant to display his armada. He had no armada. The Duesenberg ferried him from place to place, particularly after he took over the Cotton Club as a showcase not only for "tall, tan, and terrific" chorines but for "Madden's No. 1" beer.

He was into all kinds of rackets. In the old days, a "racket" had been the false tickets sold at some benefit dance. Now the same philosophy had spread to a multitude of businesses, and was in itself a big business. "During his period of ascendancy it would have been possible to pass an evening having one's cab driven by a Madden man, the door of [one's] night club opened by a Madden man, the food and drinks served by a Madden man, and [one's] clothes brushed by a Madden man back in the washroom," all ex-convicts who might not have found work without Madden.

He never abandoned his native ground. Scarface might usurp an entire hotel in Cicero or downtown Chicago, build machine-gun turrets, and line the halls with soldiers who served him champagne. But Madden didn't stray far from Tenth Avenue, his first address in America. His headquarters, from his time with the Gophers through the Roaring Twenties, was the Winona Club on West 47th, near Tenth. It wasn't Mindy's, with its guys and dolls. The Winona didn't generate as many myths. But it's where Madden percolated and played cards; it was his post office, where messages could be left for him. And Madden was in demand—"his largesse, merely to appease the army of harpies who thought he had all the money in the world, was tremendous."

He also had another address, the Harding Hotel, on Broadway, off Times Square, a haven for boxers, vaudevillians, showgirls, and gangsters and gamblers, such as Legs Diamond, Dutch Schultz, and A. R. himself. Mae West's mom, Tillie, managed the hotel, acting as a front for Madden. Tillie and her husband Jack, a boxer and "special policeman"—strong-arm man—had always been involved with the underworld, and Mae grew up in that milieu. Madden would live at the Harding from time to time, and Mae met him there. She found him "so sweet and so vicious," and might have had a love affair with him right in the hotel, but Mae never wrote about it, and Madden wasn't much of a documentarist.

The Harding was often where gangland disputes were settled, with Madden as presiding judge, or "Grand Old Man" of the
rackets. "His word, except among madmen and low competitors
who had designs upon his life or his money, was always, in the
days of his glory, regarded as absolutely good." Capone thrived on
chaos, but Madden insisted "always on outward order." Once
upon a time he'd attacked the whole of Hell's Kitchen. "Wildest
bunch of roosters you ever saw," he said of the Gopher Gang. But
now he was a businessman, backer of nightclubs and Broadway
musicals, the owner of taxi cabs and laundries and a cereal bever-
age business on West 26th Street that produced the best beer on
the continent. "He saw no reason for killing anyone." Legs Diamond's lust for blood and torture was bad business "when there
was no need for anything except a smile and an occasional firm
command on the telephone."

Another man hung out at the Harding, a "taxi dancer" who
worked at Texas Guinan's El Fey Club and was a part-time bootlegger for Madden. George Raft, né Ranft, who'd grown up in
Hell's Kitchen and idolized Madden as a boy. Though young
George had never been a Gopher, Madden befriended him, and
when he resurfaced after Sing Sing, he befriended Raft again.
According to jazz pianist Willie (the Lion) Smith, Raft was
"about the best dancer in New York," and whenever "he showed
up at the Cotton" with or without Madden, women would plead
with the headwaiter "to ask Raft if he would dance with them to
the hot music."

He danced his way to Europe and then to Hollywood, where
the studios tried to puff him into a second Valentino (the first had
died of a perforated ulcer in New York in 1926 and had a *Broadway* funeral, where thousands of women wept in the streets). But
the world didn't seem to want another smoldering sheik, and Raft

was "discovered" in his seventh film, *Scarface* (1932), Howard Hawks' homage to Al Capone, where he plays a melancholy hoodlum with the habit of flipping a coin. That would become his Hollywood signature, flipping a coin. He would parody the same role in Billy Wilder's *Some Like It Hot* (1959). But he seemed to sleepwalk through the '30s and '40s, as Cagney and Bogart became bigger stars, playing gangsters with much more finesse. Still, he was enough of a star to become engaged to bombshell Betty Grable with her million-dollar legs (she dumped him to marry bandleader Harry James), and to maintain a long friendship with Benjamin "Bugsy" Siegel, Lower East Side bootlegger turned Hollywood hood. Raft could have used some of Ben Siegel's manic energy and flair in front of the camera. Instead, he modeled himself after Owney Madden, who at times "was enveloped in bitterness and melancholy."

Like Madden, he was tight-mouthed, and delivered his lines in some strange slow motion that disrupted the constant blinks of the camera's eye. The world's fastest Charleston dancer could barely keep awake on the screen.

Cagney and Bogart were movie-time gangsters, and George Raft was as close as one could get to the real thing (though Cagney had been raised near the Five Points and had developed his gangster strut watching Monk Eastman look-alikes on the Lower East Side). And that haunted image we're left with of George Raft might well have been Madden. Madden was constantly sick. In 1920, while he was still in Sing Sing, he'd had a major operation when his old bullet wounds began to bother him. And in 1930 he was driven back to Sing Sing in his Duesenberg when the same wounds suddenly flared again. He could "entrust himself to no one but Dr. Charles Sweet," the surgeon at Sing Sing.

Capone had already contracted syphilis and was about to fall. But the reformers of white Protestant America had "created out of old New York a gaudy, upside-down metropolis . . . [that] Madden was born to rule." He and Big Frenchy fixed the entire fight game, fabulating a heavyweight champion, Primo Carnera, a gentle giant who wept whenever he had to throw a punch. But it didn't matter. He won all his matches while Madden had money on him. But Madden grew more and more melancholy. On July 6, 1932, he was sent back to Sing Sing on a parole violation regarding one of the laundries he owned. It was a Hamlet-like gesture. He had a battery of lawyers and the resources of Tammany Hall. He and "Charley Lucky" (Luciano) owned the Wigwam now. But a siren must have been whispering in his ear. *Sing Sing*. Perhaps it was his own sad song, or the realization that his racket days in New York were over. He sat in the prison hospital and looked after Sing Sing's pigeons again. He'd been breeding fancy pigeons ever since he was a boy—Nun's Caps, Hollanders, Tipitzers. . . .

4.

It was already the end of an era. Horse-faced Larry Fay had run into bad luck. Bootleggers had lost their clout, even one with a mansion out on Long Island. No one came to his parties, neither the high-born nor the low. And pretty soon the parties stopped. The mansion itself began to rot. Texas Guinan couldn't help him. She was on the road with her Guinan Graduates and in another year she would be dead. Without her, his clubs had closed. He would drift through his mansion in a nightshirt. He opened one last seedy club, the Casa Blanca, and on January 1, 1932, a disgruntled employee who had to take a pay cut shot

Larry after an argument over a few dollars. "None of Fay's Broadway friends attended his funeral." And the bootlegger of Broadway, who'd once owned the Big Street with his Fay's Follies and his silver cabs, had nothing to remember him by. Cagney would play a racketeer who was supposed to be Larry Fay in *The Roaring Twenties* (1939), with Gladys George in a good imitation of Tex, but the film couldn't recapture Fay. Cagney was much too agile and didn't have a horse face. . . .

While Madden sat in Sing Sing, Jimmy Walker resigned as New York's Jazz Mayor. It was September 1, 1932. Madden had helped make the little guy. He was the force and the money behind the Central Park Casino, a nightclub that Joseph Urban had remodeled in 1926, right after Jimmy was swept into office. It had a ballroom of black glass where Jimmy could dance unmolested with chorus girls, and an upstairs retreat that had become a second City Hall. Beau James conducted his business under a ceiling covered in gold leaf. He drank Black Velvets with several tycoons, who provided him with his own railroad car. "Flattery was sweet to him—and so fatal," said his first wife. He accepted bribes with all the insouciance of some Sun King. After all, the Central Park Casino "was Jimmy Walker's Versailles." He would prance about in shoes thin as a toothpick, his fedora cocked over one eye. He'd never read a book in his life. "What little I know, I've learned by ear."

He was a lovable lightweight. Wristwatches had come into fashion during his reign, and he joined a crusade "to put an illuminated wristwatch upon the forearm of the Statue of Liberty."

Like Madden, he distributed a lot of largesse. He would stuff his trouser pockets with bills of various denominations and drop five hundred dollars in tips during a single afternoon in Central Park. And while he danced on black glass, the city crashed around him. Housewives were plucked off the streets and arrested as prostitutes, and might sit in jail for months, trapped by a "cabal of crooked vice-squad policemen, court clerks and magistrates," with a wink from the Wigwam.

It was the biggest disgrace New York had ever endured, a government of troglodytes that was burrowing into the city's bowels, eating the flesh of its own people. And the Jazz Mayor didn't even care to open his eyes. "He loved like a woman; he played like a child; he hoped like a saint," said Joe Laurie Jr., a witness to Walker and his times. . . .

Madden was paroled on July 1, 1933, and for the second time he found himself in a foreign universe. Prohibition had been repealed, and Owney was one more ex-bootlegger. "Madden's No. 1" meant nothing now. He abandoned Primo Carnera, who was knocked senseless by Max Baer, and "retired" to Hot Springs, Arkansas—a health spa famous for its mineral baths. It was also a mob town, with illegal gambling and politicians who were as cunning and corrupt as the Wigwam.

Madden bought into a gambling casino, the Hotel Arkansas, which he turned into a gangster resort. Meyer Lansky visited him, so did Frank Costello and Big Frenchy. It would become a vacation ground for the Brooklyn soldiers of Murder Inc., like Abe Reles. Hoodlums with a price on their heads would grab a train to Hot Springs, hide in a luxurious room, bathe in Madden's waters, gamble away whatever little fortune they had left.

Madden was no longer lean, hard, and catlike. He didn't require any more operations. The waters had soothed his old war wounds. He married the postman's daughter. There isn't a single photograph of him during this period. Lansky's biographer insists that Madden "paraded the gaming rooms [of Hot Springs] like a Rothstein in retirement." But it doesn't sound like Madden. Or perhaps he was secure enough to parade in his own parlor. He was never in the news. He didn't run for any office. He was the secret captain of his domain. Unlike Rothstein, unlike Legs, unlike Larry Fay, he died peacefully in his own bed on April 24, 1965. He'd outlived Prohibition and his own precious beer by almost a third of a century. . . .

5.

Even Herbert Asbury, America's poet laureate of gangsters and the nineteenth-century gang, misunderstood Madden. In *The Gangs of New York*, he claims that after his first "sit" in Sing Sing (1915–1923), Madden "more or less dropped out of sight." Asbury couldn't comprehend a gangster who worked behind the scenes, and he had no inkling of what a twentieth-century gangster might become, a gangster divorced from his gang, like Owney. It's Francis Ford Coppola, *auteur* of *The Godfather* epic, who finally celebrated Madden in an otherwise mediocre film, *The Cotton Club* (1984), which should have been a masterpiece. But Coppola hadn't quite recovered from his breakdown during the shooting of *Apocalypse Now* (1979), when one of his stars (Martin Sheen) suffered a heart attack, when his entire set was destroyed in a tropical storm, and when Marlon Brando arrived in the Philippines like a Buddha without having read a line of the script. Coppola still managed to impose his own madness on the madness of the film, and *Apocalypse Now* is a spooky mirror of America's descent into the hell of Vietnam. One can only imagine the madness he could have found in Jazz Age Harlem and its most notorious spa, the Cotton Club. Coppola's co-scenarist was William Kennedy, who happened to write *Legs* (1975), a novel that charts Jack Diamond's own dance of death.

But Coppola's *Cotton Club* exists in a kind of aesthetic bubble. The "tall, tan, and terrific" chorines can barely breathe. We never experience the authentic stink of the place. The feisty geometry of kicking legs is narrowed down to one or two camera angles. The girls never engulf us. Besides, the Cotton is only a pretext for a pretty-boy cornetist named Dixie Dwyer (Richard Gere), "the first white musician to sit in with the Cotton Club [orchestra]." Gere is a melange of Bix Beiderbecke and George Raft, but without Raft's silence, Raft's sullen charm. There's no hint of sadness in Richard Gere's eyes.

Dixie is hired by Dutch Schultz (James Remar) to mind his little protégée, Vera Cicero (Diane Lane), because Schultz, the snarling killer, is a henpecked husband who's scared to death of Frances, his wife. Unfortunately, Dwyer and *Cicero*—a passing blink at Al Capone—are at the heart of the film, and there's no electricity between them, nothing at all.

"You do move me—in unusual places," Dixie says to Vera in a voice that's as wooden as the lines he has to speak.

The Cotton Club is a film in search of its own rhythm, and it can't seem to find it in the fancy footwork of Sandman Williams (Gregory Hines), or in the loveliness of Angela (Lonette McKee), a Lena Horne look-alike. Both Sandman and Angela are part of the décor, like walking, talking furniture within an empty whirlwind.

But that whirlwind comes alive when the film moves from lovers and Harlem strivers to the white (and black) gangsters surrounding the Cotton Club. Bumpy Johnson (Larry Fishburne) is one of the rare black hoods who could muscle his way inside Madden's club. Fishburne was only fourteen when he first auditioned for the role of "Mr. Clean," the young black broomstick of a grunt from the South Bronx, in *Apocalypse Now*. By the time of

Cotton Club, he wasn't such a broomstick. His body had filled out, and he uses it to bump his enemies aside. Johnson hadn't been invented by Coppola and Kennedy. He was as historical as Jack Diamond and Dutch Schultz. Luciano called him "the toughest nigger to ever live on 125th Street."

Like Madden, he was a bit of a Robin Hood. He couldn't find many rich people to rob, but in the territories he'd carved out for himself he did protect the poor from the mayhem of Dutch Schultz and other white racketeers. And the cops knew better than to hustle Bumpy Johnson's runners. He would take revenge by attacking an entire precinct; the cops would have to barricade themselves and beg Bumpy to go away.

Coppola's Harlem is still Hollywood, or Bumpy would have swallowed the film. He's only given a little piece to play. But Fishburne's natural swagger removes him from the stilted romance of Dixie and Diane Lane. Gere does his own cornet solos in the film, but that doesn't make him Bix Beiderbecke, who was so involved in his music he'd forget to bathe or comb his hair. Bix was "hauntingly borderless without his music"—dead at twenty-eight, a sort of alcoholic suicide—and Dixie Dwyer has too many borders, too much *self* to die of anything. Black jazz lions like King Oliver supposedly wept when they heard Bix play. Bix could howl at the moon with his horn. And Gere is just Dixie playing Dixie. He ought to rip our heads off whenever he blows. But he can't. He's part of the film's negative space, a nothingness that eats up the screen.

But then there's Bob Hoskins and Fred Gwynne as Madden and Big Frenchy DeMange. They steal the film as often as they can. We have more "romance" between them, more tenderness, than in the big love scene between Dixie and Vera, spangled light on their faces like a load of chain mail that serves as a substitute for genuine emotion. Hoskins is short and chunky, and very *untubercular*. But he's pure Hell's Kitchen. He looks like a rooster. He captures Madden's slight brogue, his sadness, and the rage he has to bottle up in order to survive as gangland's chief negotiator.

The best image in the entire film is of Madden and Big Frenchy pissing side by side in a pair of urinals at the Cotton Club. It's much more intimate and detailed than shots of Harlem's dancing sons and daughters. Gwynne plays Frenchy as a subdued giant in a dinner jacket, and for a moment we can't help remembering him as Herman, the mournful monster, in a hit television series—*The Munsters*—that would tag him for life. He doesn't try to escape the Munsters in his delivery of DeMange. He's Herman come back to haunt us in a mobster's coat. Hoskins and Gwynne make the perfect odd couple—Tiny and Tall.

And the crux of their performance is triggered by a real event, the kidnapping of Big Frenchy by Vincent "Mad Dog" Coll. Coll was a baby-faced killer who loved to kidnap people and collect ransom. His biggest prize was meant to have been Madden himself. But he never had the chance. Madden was much too suspicious. Kidnappers and killers would often pose as policemen to grab their prey. "No strange cop is ever going to arrest me," Madden promised himself. And so Coll decided to hit at Madden through Big Frenchy, grabbing DeMange outside one of his nightclubs and hiding him at a house in White Plains. Madden paid the ransom. The figure is often quoted as twenty thousand dollars, but Madden might have paid less. In the film he pays a lot more.

Dixie's kid brother, "Mad Dog" Dwyer (Nicholas Cage) steals Frenchy away from Madden. And when Frenchy's returned to the Cotton Club, Madden, his eyes red and raw, says, "I'm worried sick about you."

There's a slight contretemps between them, like a broken soft-shoe dance. Big Frenchy sulks. He'd heard that Madden only agreed to pay five hundred dollars for him. The king of the Cotton Club has to correct Big Frenchy. It was fifty thousand, not five hundred. And the mournful monster almost smiles. His true value has been proclaimed. He's content. . . .

And in one short glimpse Madden has been revealed. He will remain Bob Hoskins in my mind's eye, that short, turbulent mick, not simply because of the hypnotic power of film and Hoskins' charm on the screen, but because outside of Hoskins we have no picture of Madden, who preferred not to be seen at all.

Kennedy and Coppola do make one thing pretty clear. Madden orchestrated his own return to Sing Sing; he was going on permanent vacation from the New York rackets. We meet him with Frenchy at Grand Central. He mentions "a nice horse farm in Arkansas," as marshals lead him toward the train. . . .

And perhaps Madden wasn't wrong to cling tight to his anonymity. In 1930 he moved into a penthouse in London Terrace, a block-long series of buildings with Romanesque markings that was the largest housing complex ever built for Manhattan's middle class. It was on West 23rd, between Ninth and Tenth, the lower limit of Hell's Kitchen. The doormen were dressed like London bobbies, in hard hats. Had they been put there to watch over the mick? Children and adults kept demanding his autograph. He was London Terrace's most notorious tenant.

From his penthouse he could survey his old kingdom and catch the sun glinting on the silver tip of the Empire State Building, completed just as Madden was moving in. Was the silver needle Madden's own green light? Wasn't he as fictional as the Great Gatsby, with some unknown Daisy Buchanan to quicken his heart? And weren't the lights of Broadway that burnt through the mist like the mirage of Daisy with her green tear on *Gatsby*'s first cover? Her ruby lips a kiss from which no one could really recover? And didn't Owney the Killer share some of Gatsby's peculiar chivalry—an almost fatal flaw?

He must have been like a caged animal inside that penthouse of his. And that mirage with the green tear, the sweet menace of Broadway, must have lost its hold over him. He abandoned London Terrace, abandoned the Cotton Club, abandoned Broadway. People began comparing him to Scarface. Everyone wants to meet the New York Capone, somebody said in "Talk of the Town." It was like poison in Owney's ear. "I'm not Scarface," he hissed in his Hell's Kitchen accent before running to that horse farm in Arkansas.

CHAPTER FIVE
"She's a Chandelier"

1.

Five Points was a volatile, chaotic cradle of crime long before Hell's Kitchen. Charles Dickens visited it during his voyage to America in 1842. "Let us . . . plunge into the Five Points," he remarked in *American Notes*. "From every corner, as you glance about you in these dark streets, some figure crawls half-awakened, as if the judgment hour were near at hand, and every obscure grave were giving up the dead. Where dogs would howl to lie men and women slink off to sleep, forcing the dislodged rats to move away in quest of better lodgings . . . all that is loathsome, drooping and decayed is here."

Five Points opened onto a small park called Paradise Square, one of the few places where the poor could meet and clutch at whatever small pleasures they might find. Paradise Square "became the Coney Island of the period." But *this* Coney Island bred hovels like the Old Brewery, where children were born "who lived into their teens without seeing the sun." That's all one needs to explain the gangs of Five Points, which sprang from the common culture, yet existed outside of it, an order unto themselves.

They had their own mythical chiefs, like Mose, who was at least eight feet tall, Herbert Asbury reminds us, and could swim the Hudson River in two strokes. "But when he wanted to cross the East River to Brooklyn he scorned to swim the half mile or so; he simply jumped."

Not every gang had a giant who could jump across a river, but they did have their own fire brigades. Nine or ten gangs would compete to put out a single fire, battling one another while the fire raged. Local politicians learned to redirect their rowdiness. The gangs were paid a pittance for each skull Tammany begged them to break. Most of the Five Pointers were Irish—either immigrants or the sons of immigrants. Half the population in the 1850s was foreign born, and the Irish were the poorest of the poor.

Later the landscape of the gangs would enlarge to include Italians and Jews, who fell into the same black hole of poverty. As Luc Sante has noted in *Low Life*, the gangs of New York "demonstrated their mingled respect and derision for the world outside their turf through parody: parody of order, parody of law, parody of commerce, parody of progress."

It was an endless vaudeville act played out in the brutal theatre of the streets. If the gangs of New York are like no other gangs on earth, it's because New York was an impossible labyrinth, where wealth and poverty existed side by side (and still do), where commerce was like a conflagration, and where law and order were the right of the very rich. . . .

New York didn't have a single public high school until the end of the nineteenth century, which means the poor left school at twelve or thirteen, if they had any schooling at all, and apprenticed themselves to whatever tradesman they could find. That was the fate of most boys. Girls either became servants, seamstresses, or slaved at home until they were old enough to marry . . . or sought adventure out on the street as some kind of showgirl or prostitute (often the same thing). Over fifty thousand "street dancers" roamed Manhattan in the 1850s, about 16 percent of the population! And the Irish prostitutes of Five Points were like ancestral sisters to the Jewish prostitutes of Allen Street who flourished after 1890. What connected them was a mindless, suffocating squalor, a system that said education was only the birthright of the upper classes, and did not belong to immigrants arriving like little shock waves to the American shores.

Between 1880 and 1905 about a million and a half Jews from Siberia and Eastern Europe settled in New York. By 1910 Jews composed a quarter of the population. The other three quarters began to look upon them as an Asiatic horde that would soon smother the entire town and wipe out its traditions. Even an expatriate like Henry James worried over "the Hebrew conquest of New York," with East Side cafés that served as "torture-rooms of the living idiom."

But the "living idiom" was changing all the time, and the Jewish "torture-rooms" would lead right to the language of Broadway. In fact, there might not have been a modern Broadway without the "Asiatic horde" of comedians, gossip columnists, songwriters, and singers that grew out of the ghetto, whether it was on the Lower East Side, Harlem (a Jewish ghetto before it was a black one), Newark, or Washington, DC. Sophie Tucker, Irving Berlin, Walter Winchell, Al Jolson, Fanny Brice, and the Marx Brothers were educated in one "torture-room" or another, and none of them, except Fanny Brice, ever saw the inside of a high school. Jolson joined a circus at ten. Tucker was a vaudevillian by the time she was twelve. Berlin was a singing waiter in a cellar saloon (with a bordello upstairs) at fifteen. And Brice was a tall, gawky street urchin who ran with a tough gang of girls.

Each had an incredible ability to mimic and mime. They were all *magpies*, even if Harpo Marx was a silent one and Berlin did most of his chattering with songs. And they were bitterly poor—Winchell's family had to hop from address to address, eluding landlords. The nihilism of vaudeville would have been natural to them, part of their own interior landscape. They could have been eluding landlords all their lives, no matter how wealthy they would become. Their wealth was almost *illegal*—ill-gotten gains.

If Berlin was more conventional, that was only a mask. He would *feel* poor until the day he died. He might donate millions from "God Bless America" to the Boy Scouts and still be afraid to spend a dime. He would become a hermit who lived and cooked in one room of his mansion on Beekman Place. He'd remained a bedouin, Izzy Baline, who started his career as a songwriter by busking for pennies on the street, the way Fanny Brice would busk . . . and steal pennies from other kids, since she was so damn tall. Groucho Marx "retired" to a suite in the Sherry-Netherland, where he camped out like a bedouin, a wise *and* senile child-man. Jolson, the greatest bedouin of them all, would wander from hotel to hotel, unable to bear the affliction of a permanent address. . . .

They hollered, howled, fought, and poked fun, like those parodists from the Five Points, the nineteenth-century gang. In truth, they all had a gangster streak, even Berlin. Their maddening drive for success must have seemed dangerous to them. Their art was a little outside the law. However hard they might scream yes, yes to American culture, there was also an *undersong*, an unconscious will, "expressing that part of the American psyche which rejects the qualities and the tenants of modern life, which rejects 'Americanism' itself."

They'd grown up in a culture that mocked their own kind. If New York had become a nation of immigrants by 1900, then

vaudeville and popular music would imitate their babel of different dialects and tongues. And Jewish comics and singers would
develop into the fiercest imitators of them all, as if their mockery
were hiding a certain hysteria, an obsession to succeed at any cost,
an eagerness to play the clown and the fool, because it was an
excellent cover for one's aggression. "They did 'Dutch' [German]
dialect routines, Irish imitations, Yiddish parodies, blackface,
slapstick, sentimental ballads, standard hoofing, and a little ragtime."

Blackface would become a Jewish "specialty," with Jolson
turning it into the touchstone of his repertoire. He'd seldom
appear on stage without blacking up. For years and years he did
variations on a single stock character, Gus, a sly black slave, who
might resurface as Bombo, Christopher Columbus' navigator, or
a gondolier, or Inbad, the foil of Sinbad the Sailor—colossal hits
with audiences everywhere. Once, in San Francisco, while Jolson
was traveling with *Bombo*, the audience wouldn't let him off the
stage, and he was like an enchanted prisoner who "sang and sang
and sang."

Jolson loved to tell audiences at the Winter Garden how he
first decided to put burnt cork on his face. "I had a Negro dresser
who told me, 'You'd be much, much funnier, boss, if you blacked
your face like mine. People always laugh at a black man.'"

And they did laugh at Jolson playing a black man with a lovable white soul.

It's hard to reimagine the perverse racism of the period.
Blacks weren't welcome on Broadway unless they were comedians
in blackface, like Bert Williams, or tan chorus girls in an all-black
show who could titillate and serve as "forbidden fruit,"
temptresses with a tricky whiteness stolen from some black silver.

Jolson's apologists will swear that he "deepened" Bombo with Jewish humor, that he transformed blackface "into something emotionally richer and more humane. Black became a mask for Jewish expressiveness, with one woe speaking through the voice of another." But Jolson was a bigot and a son of a bitch. And Bombo humanized no one but Jolson himself, who was a miserable human being without his black mask. . . .

What united Berlin, Jolson, Brice, and Winchell was not their humaneness, but the savagery of success. They were like stunted children who had to become adults at the age of ten. None of them had the power to reflect—"the very pace at which they lived, the compulsiveness with which they worked, made reflection unlikely," says Irving Howe. Or impossible. And robbed of reflection, they could fall into silence, like Irving Berlin, or couldn't stop howling, like Fanny Brice, as she rediscovered her own gangster girlhood on radio, where she was "Baby Snooks" from 1937 right up to her death, a brat who could eat her mother's coat and delight millions of listeners with her irrevocable lack of remorse. . . .

2.

He conquered songwriting like a Kublai Khan, presided over his empire for fifty years—America's foremost balladeer—until he was dethroned by Elvis Presley and the new empire of rock 'n' roll. Israel Baline, born in Siberia in 1888, the son of an itinerant cantor. Fleeing a pogrom in 1893, the Balines arrived in New York harbor, passed through the "cattle station" at Ellis Island, settled on the Lower East Side, moved from Monroe to Cherry Street, near the Five Points. The cantor, who worked in a kosher meat factory, suffered from chronic bronchitis, and died in

1901. "Izzy" ran away from home, lived from hand to mouth, singing, stealing, steering customers to the bordellos of Allen Street, and made his way uptown to Tin Pan Alley, where he plugged songs for music publishers by the time he was fourteen.

Like Broadway, Tin Pan Alley was both an idea and a physical place with its own mythology. It began in the 1880s "as a cluster of sheet music publishing houses" that sprang up on the Bowery. These publishers were like gypsies who followed the upward thrust of theatres and lobster palaces and cabarets, and by the early 1900s many of them had relocated to West 28th Street, between Broadway and Sixth, where songwriter Monroe Rosenfeld heard the constant crash of pianos that sounded "like a cacophony of clashing tin pans," and he dubbed this gypsyland "Tin Pan Alley."

And soon Izzy Baline, the minstrel of Cherry Street, was a nascent balladeer and vassal of publishers that would "post" him, put him to work plugging songs at various vaudeville houses, planting him in the audience as a "singing stooge" who would suddenly break into song and urge everyone in the house to sing along with him.

He continued this musical feast as a waiter at Nigger Mike's Pelham Café in Chinatown, where he sang in dialect, mimicking kikes, micks, dagos, and coons, and began writing songs for Nigger Mike (a swarthy Russian Jew). Izzy worked from eight at night until six in the morning, and it was here at the Pelham that he began his lifelong habit of intense activity during the night and total hibernation during the day.

Berlin was a "faker," a self-taught pianist who could only strike the black keys, but he still managed to compose on the piano with a special lever "that enabled him to learn how his tunes sounded in any other key." Thus a star was born, Irving

Berlin, who would have his own publishing house on Tin Pan Alley and his own theatre, the Music Box, on Broadway.

Like everyone else, he was writing rags, "coon songs" with a slightly syncopated, ragged beat that borrowed shamelessly from the great black syncopators like Scott Joplin to manufacture "white rag," bouncy tunes that either mocked blacks or rendered them invisible. And in 1911 he was catapulted out of relative obscurity with "Alexander's Ragtime Band," which brought international acclaim to him and Tin Pan Alley. Berlin's output was so expansive, so absolute, with variation upon variation, like a diabolic player piano, that his competitors accused him of keeping little Scott Joplins in the closet. But they'd underestimated Berlin's bounty, the restlessness, the electric pull, that turned him into a nighthawk, like Winchell and Jolson, and wouldn't allow him to sit still.

Ann Douglas calls him "unstoppable," the man who could parrot whatever he heard. She compares him to Bix Beiderbecke. "Bix was not doing with black jazz what Berlin was doing with ragtime. He played brilliant apprentice, not robber, to black music. He was not coopting Negro jazz by adapting it to white tastes but pushing it to new frontiers of expressiveness."

Douglas is absolutely accurate *and* a bit unfair to Berlin. He was a ghoul, a grave robber of black rags, like most other white musicians of his era. But he was simply a much greater robber, and in his best robberies, he did provide something new, like Bix. "Alexander's Ragtime Band" is a demonic song, much, much darker and more complex than any other white rag. Berlin is related to Alexander—he's Alexander's white twin, a ragged gangster man who's inviting all his listeners to some strange, marvelous destruction; he's asking everybody to go to war.

Hollywood would seize "Alexander" and shoehorn it into a thirties musical, starring Tyrone Power and Alice Faye, that's both a laughable pastiche and a poignant commentary on the song and the ambiguous magic of Irving Berlin. The film's "Alexander" is an aristocratic white musician, Roger Grant (Tyrone Power), with classical training who lives on San Francisco's Nob Hill but breaks away to start a ragtime band. He has a code name like a common criminal—"Alexander." And his band, full of white musicians, has an invisible black aura. Charlie Dwyer (Don Ameche), his pianist and best friend, is a white man with "nigger lips." The band's reluctant torch singer, Stella Kirby (Alice Faye), is in love with "Alexander," who's a conceited hot-head and does everything he can to put her down. Broadway beckons, but it wants Stella Kirby and not a ragtime band.

"Alexander" spurns her, she jumps the band, becomes a sensational songbird on Broadway. We arrive at 1917—"Alexander," aka Alex, ends up a soldier without his band. Free of ragtime, Charlie Dwyer is a successful composer (à la Berlin) married to Stella Kirby.

The war ends and we find Alex almost a derelict—or an unemployed gangster—living in a little room. But Prohibition unites him with Bill, the saloonkeeper who gave Alex his first job in San Francisco and now owns a Manhattan speakeasy. Alex is back in business. He has a new songbird, Jerry Allen, played by Ethel Merman, the girl with the terrific tonsils who would star as Annie Oakley in Berlin's biggest hit on Broadway, *Annie Get Your Gun* (1946). She loves Alex, but no one can carry the torch like Alice Faye.

Stella breaks up with Charlie Dwyer and goes to hear Alex. As she knocks on the speakeasy's door, an eye peers at us through the peephole. It belongs to John Carradine, the club's bouncer, who jolts us for a second and brings a sinister tone to the fluff of a Hollywood fairy tale.

But the romantic strings start all over again. Stella can't have her "leader man," who's engaged to Ethel Merman. Of course her life is a mess without him. Alex goes to London with Ethel and Charlie Dwyer. Away from San Francisco and New York, Alex is appreciated for the first time. Londoners adore America's "ragged meter man."

With his new foreign credentials, Broadway beckons *him*, and "Alexander's Ragtime Band" is invited to perform at Carnegie Hall. The prodigal son has redeemed himself, gone from classicism to becoming a classic, by way of ragtime. But Stella is still alone. The night of the concert, she gets into a taxicab, tells the driver to take her *anywhere*. She wants to drift. But this is no ordinary cab and no ordinary driver. He belongs to ex-bootlegger Bill. We've seen this chauffeur before . . . at Bill's club. It's John Carradine, and he plays a gangster man with a quiet verve that's chilling to watch. He isn't George Raft, the borderline gangster who mimicked gangsters all his life, or Cagney, the hoofer who went to Stuyvesant (Manhattan's classiest high school), or Bogart, the mama's boy who was expelled from Andover. Carradine was a Shakespearean actor who bummed his way across the South sketching people in office buildings. But in his limousine he takes us outside the fakery of 20th Century-Fox and lets us glimpse at what the Roaring Twenties might have been about. He's murderous and gentle. We can feel his menace and his desire to protect Stella Kirby, just as the bootleggers would protect unescorted ladies who entered their clubs. He incarnates a little of Legs and a lot of Owney Madden—the quiet man with violence under the skin. He listens with Stella Kirby to "Alexander" on the radio, then drives to Carnegie Hall—soon as she's out of the limo, we're back in the land of 20th Century-Fox, where "Alexander" is always white and gets to marry his blindingly blonde girl, Alice Faye, while Don Ameche and Ethel Merman, his "black" accomplices, have to wait somewhere in the wings. . . .

3.

She was a tomboy with a great big nose and a very wide mouth, a little lady Robin Hood, stealing from stores so she could buy things for neighborhood brats. She would become the biggest and most beloved star of the Follies, even though Florenz Ziegfeld could never "glorify" such a gawky girl. But she would play on her very lack of romance to distinguish herself from Ziggy's beautiful chorines, poke fun at the Ziegfeld Girl's "requisite whiteness" and Anglo-Saxon charm. She was a "great farceur," says Gilbert Seldes in *The 7 Lively Arts*, a book about the birth of popular culture. She was "one of the few people who 'make fun,'" who could parody Pavlova, Salome, or Ziegfeld himself, and could shed her antics and her Yiddish accent in an instant to sing "My Man," in homage to her current husband, Nicky Arnstein, who was either going into or coming out of jail. She was the most adored comedienne of the twentieth century, or at least its first half. Kings would call upon her in London; movie stars sat at her feet; she could talk like a socialite or curse like a cab driver. Fanny Brice.

She was born Fania Borach on the Lower East Side in 1891. Her mother was a saloonkeeper, and that's where Fanny discovered how to curse, in the slightly illegal atmosphere of a saloon, with its variety of local hoodlums and alcoholics. But Fanny seemed to develop amnesia about her own childhood, that is, the

ten years the Borachs spent in Newark, away from the heart of
Manhattan—ten years she didn't mention to a single soul. She
was a bit of a juvenile delinquent, but she had the loudest voice
wherever she lived and she loved to entertain. She was onstage at
fifteen, performing in vaudeville and burlesque. She could never
kick her feet correctly in a chorus line, and she had to turn dancing into a comic routine.

Ziggy would discover her at eighteen and a half, after watching her as "Sadie Salome" (in a song by Irving Berlin), the Yiddish temptress who danced behind a veil. She swore that she did-
n't know any Yiddish but had learned it for her act. Yet she'd been
around Yiddish ruffians in her mama's saloon. It's difficult to
determine what to believe from a "mytholept" like Fanny Brice,
who nourished her own personal legend.

In 1912 she met another mytholept, Nicky Arnstein, the love
of her life. Nicky kept fabulating names and pasts for himself. He
could talk like a college professor and art historian but had barely
gone to school. He was notorious for conning rich women, and
he conned Fanny Brice, the funny girl who'd become famous at
the Follies. "One Saturday afternoon, I was introduced to a man
who stood then and forever after for everything that had been left
out of my life: manners, good breeding, education and an extraordinary gift for dreaming."

Fanny was both shrewd and dumb in her assessment of Nick.
His manners hid the mean streak of a gambler and a gangster who
was like a relentless preening bird of prey. "Nicky is a long man.
He is long-faced, long-nosed, long-chinned, long-waisted and
long-armed. His hands are long and delicate, as are his fingers. He
can palm a card—or a full deck of cards—in those beautifully kept
long hands." But he did dream his way into an aristocratic world
of heiresses and high rollers with a softness for some "long man"
who could talk about Rembrandt and the pointillism of Pissarro,

and Nick brought Fanny Borach, the saloonkeeper's daughter, along on the ride.

Fanny married Nick in 1918, after he did a stretch in Sing Sing. He'd started out as Arnold Rothstein's mentor, but as A. R. rose in the underworld with his knack for manipulating money and hiring enforcers like Monk Eastman and Legs Diamond, Nick continued to scheme and get caught: he sat in the best jails of Europe—Paris, London, Monte Carlo.

He could dream with Fanny, but he didn't have much of an imagination for crime. He ended up as Rothstein's silent partner, who steered his aristocratic friends to the Wolf's card games. He got involved in a caper where five million dollars' worth of Liberty Bonds were robbed from bank messengers over a period of four years. The district attorney's men were looking for a "mastermind"—probably A. R.—but one of the supposed robbers fingered Nicky Arnstein, the fall guy, and Nick was grabbed up by the police. By now Fanny Brice knew her man. "Mastermind! Nicky couldn't mastermind an electric bulb into a socket."

The mastermind acted out his own burlesque; he ran away to some mob town in Ohio and then surrendered himself, but he couldn't even do that correctly. He got caught in a parade with Fanny and had to let the cops find him. He was sent off to Leavenworth after a sensational trial, and Fanny, the farceur, went around in black. She stood in front of a bare black curtain at the Palace and sang "My Man" to a mesmerized, weeping audience.

Nick was released from Leavenworth in 1927 but he never lived with Fanny and their two children again. She would get her long nose fixed and run to Hollywood, but Hollywood had no room for her brand of farce. It was only on the radio that she could score, as Baby Snooks. It was as if she'd gone full circle, from the wild child with the loudest voice in Newark to the raucous make-believe child with the loudest voice on radio. . . .

But 20th Century-Fox didn't forget the old, reliable legend of Fanny Brice and her ne'er-do-well gambler husband, Nicky Arnstein. *Alexander's Ragtime Band* had been an enormous hit, and the studio was looking to reunite its star couple, Alice Faye and Tyrone Power—"Alexander" and his blindingly blond girl. Fox reached into its bag of tricks and came up with *Rose of Washington Square* (1939), a retelling of Fanny Brice's torch song romance without the ethnic trimmings. "Second Avenue Rose" moves to Washington Square. Alice Faye never rolls her eyes or screams in a Yiddish accent. She's a songbird rather than a farceur.

Bart Clinton (Tyrone Power) is the con artist and gambler she happens to fall for . . . and marry. Bart is even a bigger louse than Nick. But there was no film noir in 1939, and Fox tossed in Al Jolson as Rose's fairy godmother and former partner. Jolson plays himself under the guise of Ted Cotter, a minstrel singer known as "Mr. Blackface." He pops up throughout the film in burnt cork, looking like a pathetic, aging apparition. Singing "Mammy," he's much better served when we view him from the rear and can't see his awful, painted mug. Ted supplies the bail when Bart is arrested in a phony bond scheme. Frightened of "the big stone cottage up the river," Bart jumps bail. Rose sacrifices her career for him. Ted Cotter calls her "the only girl on Broadway who would rather listen to her heart than her own voice," just like Fanny Brice. Tyrone Power repents and goes to jail, after hearing Alice Faye sing "My Man." But it's not Fanny Brice we remember. It's the ghost of *Alexander's Ragtime Band.* Tyrone Power seems lost without his baton. The film desperately needs a "ragged meter man."

Meanwhile Fanny was like a submarine submerged in Baby Snooks. She moved to Hollywood, took up interior decorating, and was about to write her autobiography when she died of a brain hemorrhage in 1951. We can only dream of the book she might have written. *The Loudest Voice* by Fanny Brice. Would it have been the memoirs of a mytholept, without the "lost" girlhood in Newark and the Jewish face that haunted her in Hollywood, but with the blue-eyed mediocrity of Nick? She was only a comic Cassandra who could intuit everyone else's fate with Sadie Salome's veil, poke fun of all pretence, but couldn't really practice the art of introspection. She was much more comfortable as the ferocious brat she'd always been: Baby Snooks.

But she would have her own dark redeemer in a girl from Brooklyn with a bigger nose and a louder voice than hers. Barbra, who would finally bring the Second Hand Rose to Hollywood. Barbra, the snake charmer with feline features who was an exotic, *almost* beautiful Fanny Brice. Barbra Streisand was Fanny even before *Funny Girl* (1968). The role of Yetta Tessye Marmelstein in the Broadway musical *I Can Get It For You Wholesale* (1962) was pure Fanny Brice. Then there was *Funny Girl*, the musical, and *Funny Girl*, the film, with Walter Pidgeon as Flo and Omar Sharif as Nicky Arnstein without Nick's Norwegian blue eyes—it was almost as if the film had captured Brice's own mytholepsy, where the duckling becomes a magnificent swan, where the brooding Mephistophelian Omar Sharif is more like Arnold Rothstein than the bumbling Nick, and a Second Hand Rose is much, much more vibrant than any Rose of Washington Square.

4.

He was the biggest gangster of them all, who once held more power than most presidents . . . and also abused it. In his heyday half the adult population of America either read his column or listened to him on the radio. "Good evening, Mr. and Mrs. America and all the ships at sea."

His great pal was J. Edgar Hoover of the FBI, who shared his private table at the Stork Club. Both of them dressed like gangsters and demolished more people than an army ever could. Both of them hated the rich and liked to talk baseball. Both of them were snarling paranoiacs who loved Broadway. Because of his association with "Edgar," he could bully whomever he wanted and win any feud. His enemies *and* his friends were frightened to death of him. His column was like a sacred font. He could destroy you with a few words or build your career. "The way to become famous fast," he often said, "is to throw a brick at someone who is famous."

Playwright Clifford Odets wondered "how a human being could have so little sense of other human beings." And comedian Jack Paar claimed that this king of gossip, this Broadway gangster and gallant, had "a hole in his soul."

His family name, Weinshel, meant "sour cherries" in Yiddish. And that's what he was, the sourest of sour cherries. His father had been an itinerant cantor, like Berlin's, but couldn't make a living in America. Walter Winchell was born in 1897 on the Lower East Side and grew up in East Harlem. He had "large blue eyes, a thin, almost feminine mouth." But unlike his dad, he was never "a real lady killer." He was too busy dodging landlords.

His friend Ernie Cuneo said that Walter's childhood "had left him with four inches of scar tissue around his heart, and with a heart full of fear." Walter would explain his *modus operandi*: "I didn't want to be cold. I didn't want to be hungry, homeless or anonymous."

—*hungry, homeless or anonymous.*

Like Jolson and Berlin, he had a pathological need *not* to be poor, *not* to be unknown. Everything he did was defined by hunger and want. He couldn't bother about public school. He ran away from home at ten to join a vaudeville troupe of child performers. He was once part of a quartet with comedian George Burns, né Nathan Birnbaum. He'd become a little song-and-dance man. The singing and dancing would hold him in good stead. "Vaudeville made Walter an entertainer for life . . . he not only absorbed its diversity, its energy, its nihilism," but like a real trouper, he would juggle with the world and make journalism into a deeper, richer vaudeville.

That was his lasting contribution to the Big Street, not so much the "slanguage" he would develop with Sime Silverman about "the hardened artery" of Broadway, but the sheer force of his persona, his panoramic presence. He was everywhere and nowhere at the same time, like a mischievous bantamweight hoofer with two toes in every single door. He was the original "Nighthawk of the Roaring Forties" and the original *newsboy*, "immature in everything but nerve." Walter was a piece of "human electricity," five-foot-seven (like Jolson and Berlin). He'd developed his own Broadway strut. "He walked fast, airily, like the dancer he once was."

No one could keep up with Walter Winchell. He was gone before you could say hello. He would make his rounds—Lindy's, Reuben's, the "21" Club, and the El Fey, where he might linger a bit because of Texas Guinan. "We learned Broadway from her," he would confess. "She taught us the way of the Street."

It was at Tex's place that he would also meet Madden. He was considered Madden's protégé, and he didn't have to worry about getting kidnapped or roughed up by racketeers. During the thirties he would start carrying a snub-nosed .38 after two American Nazis attacked him. But it never happened again. Lucky Luciano had promised to "even things up" for Walter. Madden might have done it, but Madden was in Hot Springs. . . .

Walter had already become the mythic man of Broadway, a gangster who didn't need a gun to kill (though he had one now). Whenever Scarface came to town, he'd beg Walter to teach him how to rumba and how to talk. He "polished" Capone the way he "polished" Costello. He was more celebrated than any of the celebrities who sought him out. He didn't pretend to be a pioneer. He wasn't the first columnist to write about Broadway. *Variety* had had a Broadway beat long before Winchell. But no other "newsboy" from outside the entertainment weeklies had ever declared the Street as "his exclusive domain." Walter's column, "Your Broadway and Mine," had its debut in the *Evening Graphic* on September 20, 1924. And American journalism would never be quite the same. Walter uncoiled a live snake that had been largely unexplored—the slitherings of Broadway. And he himself would become a citizen of this new country-within-a-country that had emerged after the Great War: a lawless, unbridled mecca where everybody could meet—hoodlums, heiresses, jazz singers, funny girls, dentists from Des Moines (so long as they had a little money)—and eventually did meet at Texas Guinan's El Fey Club.

Tex practiced a raucous, rude democracy. She welcomed whoever she could fit into her speak. "I call every man I don't know Fred and they love it." The powerful cocktail she produced had come from this mingling and shaking together of the celebrated and the utterly unknown. "She wheedled bald, dignified millionaires into playing leap-frog on the dance floor." A great big peroxide blonde with much too much makeup, "her gown glistening with sequins, [Tex] used a clapper and a police whistle to prod her guests into greater din," her own brassy voice rising above the orchestra of other voices.

She built a crazy cathedral out of loneliness and isolation and a primordial fear of the dark that "attracted a set of largely root-

less, dissatisfied people, people without families or commit-
ments," like Madden and Jolson and Rothstein and Tex herself,
or Runyon and Winchell, who were more rootless with a family
than without.

This imagined and very real country-within-a-country was a
land of nighthawks, where people like Winchell loved to wander,
where nothing could hold you for very long, not even Tex, where
all you could ever discover came in short shifts, like the kinetic
language of Walter's columns, each entry an isolated island; and
his own coinages—a new mistress was a "keptive," a recently
divorced couple was "Reno-vated"—made you feel a little less
alone by marking other people's foibles, malaprops, and essential
isolation. . . .

Walter was "a moveable feast, flitting from one nightspot to
another," and then the dervish came to a full stop. It might not
have happened if Tex had still been around. But Prohibition
agents and the city's own cops had banished her from the Big
Street, and Walter Winchell needed his own *Reno-vation*. He
began to favor a small-time speak, the Stork Club, on West 58th,
owned by Sherman Billingsley, with the backing of Frank
Costello.

Billingsley was a nebbish from Enid, Oklahoma, where his
dad had been the chief of police. He'd come to the Big Bad Town
during Prohibition, studied Texas Guinan like a little guru, and
got involved in the business of speakeasies. Unlike Tex, Sherman
Billingsley was a snob. If "Miss Guinan blended the Social Register, Broadway stars and showgirls, top-drawer racketeers and a
few intellectuals into a novel, heady mixture" that would become
"Café Society," there was never any sense of exclusion. But Sherman Billingsley meant to exclude. "I decided that my clientele
would be strictly carriage trade or nothing."

He didn't like Jews (Walter would be the exception, since the nebbish needed him), didn't like most Catholics, didn't like dentists from Des Moines. He didn't want the *unfamous* and the *unloved* at the Stork. And by endorsing Sherm, by dubbing the Stork Club "New York's New Yorkiest place," Walter helped kill the Broadway of Texas Guinan and the profound mingling that she inspired.

The Stork's Café Society would *harden* Winchell's "hardened artery," turn Broadway into a series of boring, dead masks. Walter would become one himself as he sat every night at table 50 in the Cub Room. Even Sherm would admit that the Stork only "arrived" after Winchell arrived in 1930. Soon Walter had his own barber shop on the club's second floor. He was even more of a fixture than Rothstein had ever been at Lindy's, the little man's delicatessen.

Sherm was no longer a little man. He severed his ties with Costello, and without his mob "gonnegtions," he was promptly kidnapped by "Mad Dog" Coll, tucked away in a Bronx garage, and tortured until he could come up with twenty-five grand. It only made him more of a snob. He moved the Stork closer to Fifth Avenue, at 51 $\frac{1}{2}$ East 51st, and finally to an old furniture shop at 3 East 53rd, where his club would become the first speak to introduce champagne cocktails and to have a canopy over the door.

The thirties would bring a new hero, not the boisterous, rambunctious Babe Ruth, but the Yankees' brooding celebrity center fielder, Joe DiMaggio, with his impeccable manners and aristocratic mien. He was a perfect candidate for the Stork Club. He loved starlets and let others pick up the tab, pay for the pleasure of his company. Walter never wrote an unkind word about this intensely private, complicated man who had such a difficult time dealing with adulation. There was a common bond between the inarticulate DiMaggio and the magpie in the Cub Room, one of them "a man without a private life at all, who was always onstage," and the other a gifted athlete who could only find his language and a little bit of grace out on the playing field. . . .

Winchell had drifted a world away from Tex's world. Tex had been about curiosity and constant movement. She had to keep ahead of Prohibition agents who were right on her tail with their padlocks. But the hoofer no longer had to dance. He sat behind a table now, while seekers hovered around him, begging for an audience. Walter was totally absorbed in his own vendettas—fighting with Jolson this season, Franklin Roosevelt the next. He'd become a stationary target, full of bile. Sherm would suck up to Walter with a champagne cocktail. In his hands, Texas Guinan's magnificent lonely hearts club had become a vitriolic court. . . .

That court was revisited in Alexander Mackendrick's *Sweet Smell of Success* (1957), starring Burt Lancaster as J. J. Hunsecker, the magpie's taller, handsomer double, with his own column, "The Eyes of Broadway." His kid sister, Suzy, is hanging out with a young jazz musician, Dallas, whom he prepares to break. His instrument of destruction is a slippery press agent, Sidney Falco (Tony Curtis). Falco is constantly on the move, whirling around Hunsecker, whom we only meet at fixed locations, like his table at "21"—the "21" Club was Sherman Billingsley's greatest rival during and after Prohibition.

"Be warned, son," J. J. says to Dallas, "I'll have to blitz you," and he means it.

"He's told presidents where to go and what to do," Falco says of J. J., his terrible tin god. And like the little pair of eyeglasses that serve as the logo for J. J.'s column, we peep at Hunsecker and his narrowly focused, frightening power. He can squash whoever he wants. But in his penthouse, above Broadway, he's a hollowed-out man, removed and *Reno-vated* from humankind, an insect, like Walter must have been, with or without his column. . . .

5.

Everybody called him *Mr. Broadway*. "Watch me—I'm a wow!" he would announce in *Variety*. He was a shameless self-promoter who liked to think of himself as the World's Greatest Entertainer, and he probably was, for a decade or two, but of all the denizens of Broadway, including Meyer Wolfsheim, he's the one who seems remote, as if his jangling energy were frozen into the burnt cork on his face.

His persona has faded more than Fanny's, more than Winchell's, more than Berlin's. Yet Jolson *was* the Jazz Age, its ultimate white jazz singer. As Zelda said to Scott's little band of expatriates in the South of France, "Don't you think that Al Jolson is just like Christ?"

She was much more clairvoyant than Scott Fitzgerald. Zelda could *read* Jolson and his era, his ability to cannibalize himself, to give his own guts to an audience, to become a kind of human sacrifice. Gilbert Seldes sensed this in *The 7 Lively Arts*, when he wrote that Jolson (and Fanny Brice) were possessed of a daemon that could otherwise only be found "in religious mania, in good jazz bands, in a rare outbreak of mob violence," but not on the American stage. Jolson "never saves up for the next scene, or the next week, or the next show. His generosity is extravagant. . . . And on the great nights when everything is right, Jolson is driven by a power beyond himself."

Arnold Rothstein, 1928. He lived in a dream of money. A. R. had narrowed himself to nothing. "He was a man who had no inner resources; his own company bored him." That was the curse of Broadway. Jolson suffered from the same disease; so did Damon Runyon and Walter Winchell. The long electric night kept them alert; without it they were sleepwalkers. CORBIS

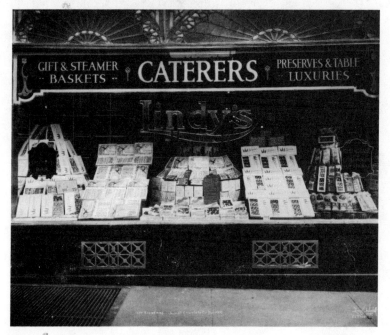

Lindy's opened in 1921, and it would become Rothstein's lair until the day he died. It didn't have mirrors wall to wall, or a griffin and four full orchestras. It was a dump, but Arnold, who didn't drink anything stronger than a tall glass of milk, preferred boiled potatoes and borscht to lobster Newburg. CORBIS

We revere Fitzgerald and hardly read Runyon at all. We dismiss him and his cartoon characters as cannon fodder for musicals. Yet we ought to look again. There's an hysteria underlying Runyon's monochromes, a desperate desire to block out the sunlight, to limit Broadway to four o'clock in the morning at Mindy's. And if we look, we might find a whole dominion, a hunger that marked Broadway. CORBIS

Babe Ruth. The Babe had grown up at a bad boy's school in Baltimore, St. Mary's, which would become his dormitory for life. He didn't leave until he was twenty, and perhaps he didn't leave at all. His jibes, his pranks, his cruel taunts were like the antics of an orphan let loose in the world, and somehow in his psyche he had to return there every night. CHICAGO HISTORICAL SOCIETY

Fanny Brice, circa 1925. She would become the biggest and most beloved star of the Follies, even though Florenz Ziegfeld could never "glorify" such a gawky girl. But she would play on her very lack of romance to distinguish herself from Ziggy's beautiful chorines, poke fun at the Ziegfeld Girl's "requisite whiteness" and Anglo-Saxon charm. CORBIS

Louise Brooks, circa 1925. Unlike Jolson, who was cruel and egotistical and couldn't see beyond his nose, Brooksie had the power and the curse of reflection. She was a failure in the land of success, a gold digger who didn't know how to dig. CORBIS

The Follies caught on like a house on fire, and soon Ziegfeld was as famous as the Follies itself. Life was dangerous and swift for Ziggy's girls—most of them wouldn't survive their twenties on and off the stage. There were other divas around, other choruses, other revues, "but the most modern and daring of all female occupations was that of the Follies Girl."
DUKE UNIVERSITY

W. C. Fields would claim that Bert Williams was "the funniest man I ever saw and the saddest man I ever knew." Even if he'd lived longer and had gone out to Hollywood, like Fields, he couldn't have had much of a career as a black comedian in blackface, the one role that white (and black) audiences were eager to have him play. His signature song was "Nobody."
DUKE UNIVERSITY

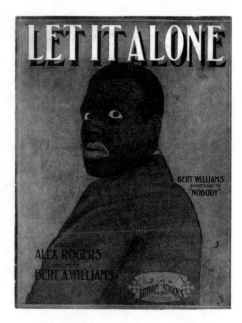

At least now, in the twenty-first century, we have to talk of *two* Fitzgeralds, Zelda and Scott, not as the definitive Jazz Age couple, with his songs and her heartbreak, and not because she was "beautiful, female, mad; and he was handsome and a drunk and died a failure," but because she had her own real claim as a writer and as a combatant in a world that gave women, beautiful or not, so little room to breathe. CORBIS

Marion Davies and William Randolph Hearst, 1942. It was Broadway's best tale— romance between the owlish millionaire and the chorus girl with a crooked face. It would outlast Orson Welles and the brilliant satire of *Citizen Kane*. It was simple, almost outside language itself. Once upon a time, in 1915, his little whale's eyes had fallen on Marion Davies as she danced, and would never, never let go. CORBIS

Owney Madden (left) leaving Sing Sing. "A lesser man, a man of more limited imagination, or one who had been broken in prison, would have slipped back into the underworld as a mere punk, a nobody. Madden had iron in his gizzard." CORBIS

Ruby Keeler. "Ruby wasn't much of a tap dancer. She was flatfooted. . . . But she had appeal. She was only fourteen when she started dancing in clubs—an innocent amid a world of sophisticates, corrupt politicians, show people, and gangsters. It was to the gangsters that the teen-aged girl appealed most." CORBIS

Jack Johnson. That "golden smile" disturbed a nation used to obedient, barely visible blacks. It wasn't simply the gold teeth in Johnson's mouth, it was the constant, provocative grin, like that of a wolf, a wolf with yellow eyes. CHICAGO HISTORICAL SOCIETY

Bessie Smith. She was a female Jack Johnson, six feet tall and two hundred pounds. And she loved to fight, knocking down men and women at will. She had the loudest, strongest voice and the richest register in an age when every voice had to be strong or you couldn't survive as a singer. She was also a renegade who sang about "me and my razor and my gun." LIBRARY OF CONGRESS

If Louise Brooks was Manhattan's secret bride, then George Gershwin was its bachelor prince. Broadway seemed to prosper whenever he was near. He might show up at some rehearsal or in the middle of a party, ask for an ice cream soda or a Scotch highball—his two favorite drinks—and hold an audience captive for a couple of hours. LIBRARY OF CONGRESS

Al Jolson visiting Jack Dempsey's training camp, August 11, 1920, when Jolson was the most popular entertainer on the planet, as he mugged and sang in blackface. He considered himself a tough guy. He would battle with everybody—men, women, stage managers, other performers, wives . . . and Jack Dempsey, heavyweight champ. CORBIS

There were other witnesses. "When Jolson enters [the Winter Garden]," wrote Robert Benchley of the Algonquin Round Table, "it is as if an electric current has been run along the wires under the seats where the hats are stuck. The house comes to tumultuous attention . . . such a giving-off of vitality, personality, charm and whatever all those words are, results from a Jolson performance."

Or, as screenwriter Samson Raphaelson remarked: "Every person has an aura about him, a kind of electricity he generates. Someday, there will be a way of measuring it. No one, though, had it like Jolson. That's what made him so great—so unique."

But we only have the word of those who witnessed him, who had fallen under his sway—like Gilbert Seldes, or Raphaelson, or Robert Benchley and Zelda Fitzgerald. We ourselves cannot "visit" Jolson, and he seems truncated, almost puny, on the screen—a man robbed of his persona. His detractors and idolaters have both declared that Jolson's particular talents did not translate to any medium other than live theatre. Ann Douglas belittles him by saying that even Irving Berlin "outgrew Jolson's all-powerful but limited gifts." Perhaps it is our own limitation—and the stigma we attach to blackface—that doesn't permit Jolson to reveal himself to us.

He considered himself a tough guy. He would battle with everybody—men, women, stage managers, other performers, wives. He loved to box, and he would often race down a boulevard, whether Broadway or Rodeo Drive, ducking imaginary blows. Sometimes the blows were real. Like Winchell and Berlin, he ran away from home, bummed around in circuses and carnivals, was beaten up, and was found living like a rat in a Baltimore bar when he was eleven or twelve—it's hard to fix Jolson's age, since like many Russian immigrants from the Jewish Pale, he had no birth certificate. He chose May 26, 1886, but he might have been born in 1884 or '85, in April or June, July or August. . . .

From that bar in Baltimore he was sent to St. Mary's, Babe Ruth's alma mater. And when both of them were big stars, Al and the Babe would brag how they'd met at the bad boys' school and had run the school ragged. It's an apocryphal tale. Ruth was only a toddler when Jolson spent a couple of months at St. Mary's. But they enjoyed clinging to that lie.

Jolson entered vaudeville in 1904, joined several minstrel troupes, and reinvented himself the moment he put on his black-face mask. Jolson became "Jolie." That's what the minstrels called him and that would be his signature and mythic, almost magical, nickname for life. None of the other minstrels could compete with him. "In those days you must remember there were no microphones," recalls his manager, Art Klein. "But this man had the most resonant voice of any human being I ever knew."

He took over the runway at the Winter Garden, turned it into his private country, from which he could practically plunge into the audience or retreat. "He teased, cajoled, and thrilled [an audience] in the manner of a great violinist or lover." He was a maniac on opening nights, and his little retinue of followers had to pluck a prostitute off the street to perform fellatio on him. It was the only thing that could soothe the satyr. Columnist Sidney Skolsky became one of his pimps. " 'She's a chandelier,' " he'd whisper to Jolson, "meaning she was good at sex in the wildest positions, including hanging from a chandelier."

—*She's a chandelier.*

That best describes the bullying vulgarity of the man: exploitation more than appetite. The mindless milling around— Jolie as a perpetual motion machine—the panorama of showgirls and prostitutes, the two wives he would slap and dump, slap and dump, then beg to return, because he couldn't bear to be alone, dump them all over again, in the same cruel cycle. He could attach himself to nothing and no one but an audience, which was constantly fickle and changed all the time, and had to be wooed every single night.

And then there was Ruby Keeler, the little gold digger who loved to play dumb.

Al first saw her at Tex's 300 Club in 1926. She was a member of Guinan's Graduates, but she watched her toes when she danced and she sang with a lisp. Jolie didn't care.

"Who's that cute little dark one?" he asked.

That's Johnny's girl, he was told, and the jazz singer was intrigued. Johnny "Irish" Costello was a baby-faced bootlegger and beer baron with part interest in the 300 Club. He was also Owney Madden's lieutenant, and a prime salesman of "Madden's No. 1"—no nightclub owner ever refused the beer that Johnny Irish offered to let him buy. He was the sleekest dresser in town, with his headquarters in a haberdashery shop on Broadway. Irish was helping Ruby with her career. He got her a gig as a headliner in a floor show at the Silver Slipper, a club that Madden owned with Rothstein and Frenchy DeMange. Ruby wasn't much of a tap dancer. "She was flatfooted . . . stationary to the point of almost moribund. But she had appeal. She was only fourteen when she started dancing in clubs—an innocent amid a world of sophisticates, corrupt politicians, show people, and gangsters. It was to the gangsters that the teen-aged girl appealed most." And tough guys like Al Jolson.

She was born Ethel Hilda "Ruby" Keeler in Dartmouth, Nova Scotia, on August 25, 1904, the eldest of six. The family moved to Manhattan when Ethel was three. Her dad delivered ice, and the Keelers barely survived. Ethel was discovered by one of her teachers at St. Catherine of Sienna grammar school and started to take lessons at Jack Blue's School of Rhythm and Tap before she was ten.

She was in the chorus of a Broadway musical at thirteen and went to work for Tex at the El Fey Club when she was fourteen and a half. She wasn't a particular prodigy.

Most of Guinan's Graduates were between thirteen and sixteen, and chorus lines were flooded with fourteen-year-olds. But she was clearly Tex's favorite. Tex adored her and watched out for little Ruby. "It was frightening out there on that little floor," Ruby would later admit. "But she [Tex] just stood out there and kept everything going on around us."

It's Budd Schulberg who articulated the appeal Ruby must have held for Al Jolson and Johnny Irish and countless other tough guys. "Where Ruby had it over the rest of the line was she was beautiful in an unusually quiet way . . . even in the scantiest, she carried herself with an air of aloof respectability which had the actual effect of an intense aphrodisiac."

But Jolson forgot that aphrodisiac for a little while. He didn't chase after Johnny Irish's girl. But Al happened to be out on the Coast in the summer of 1928; Fanny Brice was arriving from New York and he'd come to greet her . . . when Ruby Keeler stepped off the train. And he didn't stop pursuing her after that. He sent roses to her backstage at Grauman's Egyptian Theatre, he sent a lynx coat, a silver comb. She ran back to Johnny Irish in New York.

But wherever Ruby went on the road, Jolson was there. His relentless, manic energy overcame her. He proposed to Ruby Keeler in DC. "Jolson is here in Washington," she told her manager, who was also one of Johnny Irish's partners in a speak. "I've fallen in love with him. Will you break the news to Johnny?"

Johnny Irish didn't scream.

"Larry Fay found him standing outside Dinty Moore's restaurant in tears."

But he was still looking out for Ruby Keeler. Johnny summoned Al to the haberdashery shop, with Jolson "like a prospective bridegroom calling on his father-in-law." Irish had heard about Jolson the wife-beater. Al promised never to harm Ruby and offered to bring his own dowry to the wedding—one million dollars for his future bride.

Legs Diamond learned of this dowry, decided that the jazz singer was "a soft touch," called Jolson and demanded fifty thousand dollars.

Irish had already given his word that the jazz singer wouldn't be harmed, but he didn't have the muscle to go after Legs. It was Owney Madden who made Legs back off. Jack Diamond apologized to Jolson, said it was all a joke.

Al and Ruby Keeler were married in Port Chester, New York, on September 21, 1928. She was nineteen, and the jazz singer was forty-three, give or take a couple of years. They sailed for Europe aboard the *Olympia,* neither of their names on the passenger list, but people still mobbed them at the boat. Jolie had brought several of his pals along. He was a man "who could feel awfully lonely on a honeymoon."

His child bride was no longer a child. She'd matured under the tutelage of Tex. "She was a stubborn, somewhat sassy young woman who had been around and who knew all there was to know about speakeasies, Broadway night life, and gangsters."

But neither Johnny Irish nor Tex had prepared her for the whirlwind that was Al Jolson. *The Jazz Singer* had made him the most visible entertainer on the planet, and he couldn't stop entertaining. He cannibalized Ruby's career. She was now billed as

Ruby Keeler Jolson, and agreed to star in *Show Girl*, a Ziegfeld musical about Dixie Dugan of the "Zigfold Follies." During the out-of-town tryouts at Boston's Colonial Theatre, Ruby was about to go into her tap-dancing routine when Jolie jumped out into the aisle from his seat in the second row and sang "Liza" in the voice that never needed a microphone. *Show Girl* was an enormous hit while it had Al Jolson. . . .

Forty years later Ruby was asked why Jolson had jumped into the aisle. "I was just as surprised as anyone. I guess he just liked to sing. But I don't *know* why he did it. I'm not very bright, you know," said the disingenuous gold digger.

Ruby and Al moved out to Hollywood in 1929, and Ruby would become a sweetheart of the Depression, the backstage girl who scrambles to the top on the sheer force of her own goodwill. She was the same flat-footed dancer with a lisp, but audiences loved her for it. Jolson had become "Mr. Keeler." He was losing his popularity and his looks. He couldn't seem to face "the prospect of having a wife with a career more dazzling than his own." He would fall into jealous rages, knowing that other men had the privilege of kissing her in a film. They were fighting all the time, though he never dared hit her. She left him in 1939. "Al was a possessive man, which was difficult for me. . . . If I was gone for ten minutes—just shopping, mind you—I had to explain."

He "bought" a black prize fighter, Henry Armstrong, together with George Raft. He gambled, went on golfing expeditions. He even had some sort of a revival when Larry Parks played him in *The Jolson Story* (1946). But he still seemed like an orphan of an earlier era, when live sound at the Winter Garden had much more resonance than radio or silent film. Jolson ruled at the very beginning of the "age of mechanical reproduction" that Walter Benjamin writes about, when the artist still had his "aura." And that aura disintegrated, disappeared, with Mr. Broadway.

"Even the most perfect reproduction of a work of art is lacking in one element: its presence in time and space, its unique existence at the place where it happens to be." Like Jolson at the Winter Garden. And when Jolson lost the "ritual" of singing at a particular time, in a particular place, for a particular audience, there was really little room left for Broadway.

The movie star didn't have any less of a measure than Al Jolson, with his (or her) ghostlike transformation on the screen, but the movie star, as Benjamin imagines him, responds to the "shriveling" of his aura with the fake spell of personality that the studio builds around the star, turning him into a commodity.

Benjamin may have been a bit reductive about the movies. Jolson was also a commodity, in place to sell tickets for his producers, Lee and J. J. Schubert. But he was his own animal onstage, without a microphone, without a mechanical edge, with a daemon that could never quite fit onto a screen. Tex had some of Jolie's daemon. "She has neither beauty nor youth, voice nor figure," as one critic noted. "She is the human wisecrack with magnetism in it. She seems to think in flashes of electric light."

And her Guinan Graduates—Ruby tapping with two flat feet—had some of the ritual that Benjamin talked about. A certain warmth and vigor, the magic of being in a little cave (the nightclub), a gold digger with some dream of an infinite future inside her head. That dream was Broadway itself.

CHAPTER SIX

THE MAN WITH THE GOLDEN GRIN

1.

No critic captured the spirit of modernism and the new lively arts better than Gilbert Seldes. He insisted that a popular culture had arisen in America that was full of turbulence and fun—whether it was the antics of Charlie Chaplin or the antics of Krazy Kat. Seldes was one of the first to investigate the *seriousness* of the comic strip, in particular the genius of George Herriman's *Krazy Kat*, "the most amusing and fantastic and satisfactory work of art produced in America to-day," meaning the twenties.

The Kat is ambiguous in every sense but one—he's in love with Ignatz Mouse, whose main ambition is to brain the Kat with a brick. Krazy sees this missile as a mark of affection. Both kat and mouse are obviously immigrants, but Ignatz is *acclimated*, and Krazy is not. He talks with the chopped-up poetry of some divine ghetto that would have caused Henry James to shiver in his underpants.

—Things is all out of perpotion, Ignatz.
—In what way, fool?
—In the way of 'ocean' for a instinct.
—Well? asks Ignatz, bored with Krazy's metaphysics.
—The ocean is inikwilly distribitted. . . . Take 'Denva, Kollorado' and 'Tulsa, Okrahoma' they aint got no ocean

a tall—while Sem Francisco, Kellafornia, and Bostin, Messachoosit, has got more ocean than they can possibly use. . . .

And while he talks, the scene keeps shifting, oceans become mountain peaks, trees that look like triple-decker sandwiches shrink into mushrooms. "The strange, unnerving, distorted trees, the language inhuman, un-animal, the events so logical, so wild, are all magic carpets and faery foam—all charged with unreality. Through them wanders Krazy, the most tender and the most foolish of creatures, a gentle monster of our new mythology."

And Seldes, who's so perceptive about Krazy Kat, so willing to investigate new forms of art, to champion the daemonic in Al Jolson and Fanny Brice, can't seem to wrestle with his own demons when blacks intrude upon this art.

In 1921 an all-black musical revue from Harlem burst upon Broadway, with songs by Noble Sissle and Eubie Blake. The show was called *Shuffle Along* and would never have gotten to Broadway if it hadn't been backed by Arnold Rothstein. A. R. hardly ever went to musicals, but when asked why he sank money into *Shuffle Along*, he said: "I like to hear them people talk."

Or perhaps he was fond of the black gamblers and confidence men featured in the revue. . . .

Seldes writes about *Shuffle Along* and its population of "cheats and scoundrels" with a praise that also shuffles along. The show lives "without art, but with tremendous vitality." Its "appearance of unpremeditated violence" distinguishes it from "the calculated and beautiful effects" of the Follies. *Shuffle Along* has Florence Mills, with "her superb, shameless swing . . . and her baffling, seductive voice" (a minor talent, he suggests, compared to Follies star Gilda Gray). But the wild cry of Florence Mills and the other singers and dancers "is a little too piercing at times, the postures and the pattings and the leapings all a little beyond the necessary measure. It remains simple; but simplicity, even if it isn't usually vulgar, can be a bit rough."

In other words, Seldes himself is superior to the show. And he reveals his own hidden treatise, which is a hundred times less eloquent than the tangled wisdom of Krazy Kat.

"I say the negro is not our salvation because with all my feeling for what he instinctively offers, for his desirable indifference to our set of conventions about emotional decency, I am on the side of civilization. To anyone who inherits several thousand centuries of civilization, none of the things the negro offers can matter unless they are apprehended by the mind as well as by the body and the spirit."

I wish I could say that Seldes had scribbled this on some private moon, but he didn't, and Seldes isn't alone. Hemingway and Fitzgerald had the same cold indifference to the "negro," as if all blacks were just plain pests.

And H. L. Mencken, that great interpreter of *living* language, who attacked middle-class America and its Rotarian culture, was even more threatened by black music and black art than was Gilbert Seldes.

"Can it be that the Republic, emerging painfully from the Age of Rotary, comes into a Coon Age? . . . No dance invented by white men has been danced at any genuinely high-toned shindig in America since the far-off days of the Wilson Administration; the débutantes and their mothers now revolve their hips to coon steps and to coon steps only."

—like the coon steps of *Shuffle Along*.

Broadway should have been more adroit than Mencken, more welcoming to Sissle and Blake. But it was scared to death of *Shuffle Along*. And this would be its undoing. *Shuffle Along* was a kind of anti-Follies, a parody of the Ziegfeld Girl's "requisite whiteness." And the Follies struck back. In 1922 Gilda Gray introduced her shocking shimmy shake—stolen from Florence Mills and half a dozen red hot mamas—and sang "It's Getting Dark on Old Broadway."

The message was unmistakable. "Ev'ry café now has a dancing coon." *And* if it wasn't stopped, the Great White Way would go dark—dark would lead to darkness in a double sense. Broadway would turn black and then disappear, and whites would flee to some more exclusive space, build another Broadway.

The black population of New York increased by 66 percent in the decade following 1910; the influx of Italians and Jews had already led to the "mongrelization" of Manhattan (and America), and Ziggy, who'd been bold in 1909 and 1910, bringing the first black comedian to white Broadway (Bert Williams) and the first Jewish comedienne (Fanny Brice), had now become the defender of the faith. He would guard the Ziegfeld Girl's purity until his own death. The Follies registered "not simply the exclusion of color but also the protection of whiteness." He forbid a suntan on any of his girls, lest her whiteness fall into doubt. And in 1925 he found a perfect logo for the Follies: "Florenz Ziegfeld Glorifying the American Girl, an American Review in America for Americans."

He couldn't have realized how ossified he'd become, how old-fashioned, vis-à-vis the Follies. His funny girl wouldn't appear as often in a Follies show after 1920, and neither would Bert Williams, his very best clown, who was constantly fighting with Flo . . . and died in 1922. And without Fanny and Bert, he lost that sense of the daemonic, that ability to mock his own girls, who were always silent onstage, statuesque (and silly) in six-foot headdresses.

2.

Another Follies star, W. C. Fields, would claim that Bert Williams was "the funniest man I ever saw and the saddest man I ever knew." Even if he'd lived longer and had gone out to Hollywood, like W. C. Fields, he couldn't have had much of a career as a black comedian in blackface, the one role that white (and black) audiences were eager to have him play. His signature song was "Nobody." Throughout his life, whether he was Rufus Redcap or the catastrophe-riddled "Jonah Man," he played "the slovenly, lazy, dull-witted and slow-footed half" of any comedy team. His movements and his will were meant to be "excruciatingly slow."

But Williams wasn't slow. And he never slouched or shuffled when he wasn't onstage. He was tall, handsome, athletic, and very light-skinned. He was born in the West Indies in 1874, Egbert Austin Williams. His family moved to California when Bert was still a child. He toured lumber camps with a minstrel show by the time he was eighteen. He was an autodidact who carried Voltaire, Schopenhauer, and Mark Twain around with him in his trunk. He would read wherever he went, an introspective man who seldom laughed.

It was in San Francisco that he met his "other half," George Walker, a dark-skinned dandy from Kansas who was a year older than Bert. Walker was short, feisty, and a ravenous ladies' man who couldn't bear to read a book. He had a consuming interest in clothes, would run after chorus girls in his silk cravat.

George and Bert had great ambitions—to break the stereo-
type of black performers as shuffling darkies and dim-witted
coons. But the work they wanted was impossible to find. They
ended up as a pair of fake Africans in animal skins at an exhibition of a Dahomean village in Golden Gate Park, because the real
Dahomeans hadn't arrived in time.

In 1895 the team of Williams and Walker went east to find
their fortune. But while crossing Colorado, they were nearly
lynched in Cripple Creek by an angry white mob that could have
come right out of Mark Twain. Deciding that "a couple of coons"
shouldn't be caught wearing such fine clothes, the mob obliged
them to undress and march around in burlap. . . .

The team flopped in Chicago, flopped in New York, until
they put on burnt cork and advertised themselves as "Two Real
Coons." They were simply capitalizing on the success of "white"
blackface. Walker played some kind of "Alexander," a grandilo-
quent black dandy, and Bert was the "Jonah Man," a dreary clown
in mismatched clothes. And suddenly their act had become a lesson in black and white, as black performers like themselves "imitated, with variations, the white performers playing, and distort-
ing blacks."

"American entertainment," as Ann Douglas suggests, "had
always been integrated, if only by theft and parody." White enter-
tainers, such as Sophie Tucker, Mae West, Fanny Brice, and Al
Jolson, "absorbed African-American art and performance style,
sometimes consciously, sometimes not." The standard rule on
Broadway was that "you started black and ethnic and got whiter
and more Wasp, as, and if, success came your way." Tucker and
Brice discarded blackface, but Al Jolson didn't; burnt cork had
become such a part of his persona that it was impossible to separate Jolie from his mask.

And Bert? He was like Jolson's demonic double, his blackface twin whose "Jonah Man" had much more pathos than Gus, the perennial black slave at the Winter Garden. But pathos or not, Jonah was just as "artificial" as Gus. The dialect Bert used—or "lies" as he liked to call it—was a stage convention, frozen and false, whether spoken by whites or blacks, and represented "an exaggerated take on the 'incorrectness' of black speech." And unlike the white performer, Bert was stuck with this baggage all his life. He would employ it more brilliantly than any other blackface comedian, but the dialect still destroyed him.

Mae West's biographer, Jill Watts, believes that Bert was "signifying" when he used Negro dialect, that it was a secret coded message to other blacks (and a few whites), that he was acting out the tyranny that had been imposed on him, that his performance was full of play and contradictions; he was poking fun at whites and blacks in blackface, including himself—*his* blackface was a critique of whites and a form of rebellion, cloaked in language games. As literary critic and social historian Henry Louis Gates Jr. reveals in *The Signifying Monkey*: "Free of the white person's gaze, black people created their own vernacular structures and relished in the double play that these forms bore to white forms."

Signifying would become "the slave's trope, the trope of tropes," turning him into a trickster with "the trickster's ability to talk with great innuendo, to carp, cajole, needle, to lie." The African jungle served as the mythic dreamland *and* subtext of the American slave. And in this dreamland the Monkey outwits the Lion with the one weapon he has at hand—subterfuge, or trickster talk. "The Monkey is not only a master of technique, he is technique, or style."

More than any other black comedian at the end of the nineteenth century, Bert had the purest sense of style. But he wasn't an absolute trickster, like the Monkey. He lived among too many Lions, and sought to be accepted in the Lion's lair: Broadway. Finally he was accepted, but he would quit the Follies again and again over the humiliation he had to endure whenever he traveled across the country with Ziegfeld's show—separate toilets, separate hotels, separate lives. During his tenure with the Follies he declared in *American Magazine* that he wouldn't trade his skin with any white man. But he still found it "inconvenient" to be black in America.

—inconvenient to be black in America.

Bert might have been signifying here—doubling back upon his own irony—but it wasn't much of a Monkey's game. There was a little too much sorrow. He inhabited some no-man's-land where white and black Americans could bump along and never really meet. He couldn't feel comfortable in a black mask, like Al Jolson. His dialect stories and songs—"I'd Rather Have Nothin' All of the Time, Than Somethin' for a Little While"—cut too close to the bone. That was the source of his humor, as much as any signifying. *He* was the victim of his word play, not his white audience. "Mr. Nobody," with his "thumpin' bumpin' brain," who was "full of nothin' and pain."

3.

In 1896 the "Two Real Coons" would bring the cakewalk to Manhattan. Audiences loved them in drag as they sang "Two Coffee Colored Ladies Dressed in Yellow" and did the cakewalk—"an ebullient strut" that had started during slavery. Williams and Walker "resurrected a practice originally used by slaves to mock their masters' dance rituals."

Soon all of Manhattan was high-stepping along the Rialto, that part of Broadway between Madison Square and the carriage shops of 42nd Street. But this resurrected cakewalk had arrived together with "ragging," or ragtime, the black musician's means of grabbing the white man's waltz and "teasing" it into a broken, or stuttered time. Having come from piano ticklers in the whorehouses of New Orleans, ragtime was now being played by other ticklers in the honky-tonks of Black Bohemia, right near the Rialto. Years before *Shuffle Along*, Broadway had begun to paint itself black. . . .

In 1898 "the celebrated cakewalkers" posed for a cigarette ad with a tall, light-skinned beauty, Ada Overton, who joined the Williams and Walker company and would marry Walker, in spite of his philandering. Lottie Thompson, "a pretty and demure-looking Chicago showgirl," also joined the company and soon had the mournful Bert under complete control, calling herself "Mrs. Lottie Williams" without bothering to divorce her husband, Sam.

There were cakewalking contests in half the capitals of Europe, thanks to Williams and Walker . . . and Ada Overton, who could kick even higher than the "Two Real Coons." White society had adopted the cakewalk, and the annual world championships held at Madison Square Garden were "mixed," with black couples cakewalking alongside white couples and winning "grand pianos, gold and silver watches, gold-headed canes." But apart from the cakewalk, there wasn't much mixing between blacks and whites.

During the night of August 15, 1900, a race riot began on Manhattan's streets, after a belligerent black man killed a belligerent white cop in Black Bohemia. It was open warfare, as a white mob pulled blacks off trains and trolleys, while the police either watched or went after blacks who were "hurling bricks and bottles" at them and the mob. The "Two Real Coons" were performing at a vaudeville house that evening. Williams returned to his flat after the show, but Walker strolled downtown with a friend and walked right into the riot. His friend was nearly beaten to death, but Walker crawled into a cellar, where he hid until the bottles stopped flying.

That was the curious arc of Williams and Walker, the first blacks to break into white vaudeville and to test that terrifying barrier of race, as the vaudevillians' own union—the White Rats—tried to remove them from the bill . . . or have them perform without any billing, so that the "Two Real Coons" would remain a pair of invisible Black Rats. But the White Rats didn't succeed. Williams and Walker got their billing.

It was during this period that Williams encountered a little girl living in Brooklyn—Mae West. Mae's parents knew Williams and had taken her to watch him in blackface. One night Mae's mom brought Bert home. He didn't shuffle or sing melancholy songs or wear slovenly clothes. He looked like a British lord, but Mae started to whimper when Bert stood outside her door. "Do you know why I didn't recognize him? He was too light. He was a black man but he was too light. . . ."

And there's the rub. Little Mae had a profounder truth than most cultural historians. However hard Bert had been signaling to other blacks, or distancing himself from his white audience, the mask had become the man. His stage persona reflected his own deep sadness and ambiguity. If "blacks had to study whites in order to survive," had to wear a mask that would diffuse white hatred and violence, then Bert had to clown to keep alive. He'd perfected an art that would invade white culture—the lovable, harmless, sexually neutral and silly black clown who would become a staple and a standard cliché in American films, whether a black butler with bulging eyeballs or a black maid, like Butterfly McQueen, who worked for Scarlett O'Hara (Vivien Leigh) *and* Mildred Pierce (Joan Crawford)—prattling the same childish nonsense—and had to quit acting in 1947 to protest the stupidity of her roles and become a waitress to support herself. Butterfly's clowning had rendered her without a real tongue, just like Bert. . . .

In 1903 Williams and Walker brought the first all-black musical to Broadway, *In Dahomey*, and sailed to England with the show, giving a command performance for the Prince of Wales. They were adored in London, but still couldn't stay in a "white" hotel. They lived in a parallel universe. Forbidden to join the Lambs and the Friars, they would introduce the Frogs, a social and benevolent club for black performers. Meanwhile Bert sang, "Sometime I jumps into the river just to try to throw myself away."

The more successful Williams and Walker were with their all-black musicals, the more brutal was their exile from whites. They performed in theatres where they couldn't even have entered as paying customers, except to be hustled upstairs to a seat in the balcony. In 1909 Walker began to stutter on stage and couldn't remember his lines. He was suffering from syphilis. Ada would dress up as George and take over some of his routines. Soon Walker was too ill to perform, and Ada herself left the Williams and Walker company.

In 1910 Ziegfeld would hire Bert. He was billed as "The Blackbird with Songs" and would never appear onstage at the same time as the Follies Girls. He was filler material, like Fanny Brice, who would "feed" the audience with comic lines and give the girls an extra few minutes to change into their elaborate costumes. Most of the white members in the cast rebelled and swore they wouldn't perform with Bert. But Ziggy was much more of a rebel in 1910. The entire cast could be replaced, he said, except for his "Blackbird with Songs." And the white vaudevillians got back into line. . . .

Next to Fanny, Bert was Flo's biggest star. He did Othello in drag "and a burlesque of Russian ballet star Nijinsky." He did wild, hilarious sketches where he would act out every hand in a poker game, or play the switchboard operator of a posh Manhattan apartment house who involves himself with all of its inhabitants. He was Flo's phantom Blackbird, whether he played the sidekick of Eddie Cantor or Leon Errol, dressed like a redcap in baggy pants or like a bum in blackface, the saddest, slowest man on earth. And if there was a lull in the show, a quiet spot, the Blackbird would sing his signature song. "I'm nobody. . . ."

He quit the Follies after 1919, longing to shed his burnt cork and become a "serious" actor, but he failed. He would have bouts of depression. He went back into vaudeville. But he was a very sick man, suffering from heart disease. On February 27, 1922, in Detroit, while touring with *Under the Bamboo Tree*, Bert collapsed. He'd caught a cold in Chicago that developed into pneumonia. He returned to New York, where he died on March 4, an American master not quite forty-eight years old.

4.

America had another master born in Galveston four years after Bert—Jack Johnson, the finest boxer of his era and the first black heavyweight champion, the son of an ex-slave. He didn't have much interest in school and left after the fifth grade. He took part in battle royals, where rich white men would hire young blacks to get into a boxing ring blindfolded and bound together, and have them swing at one another while a white audience cheered and bet on their favorite "boy" . . . until the last battler remained standing in the ring and picked up the pennies that were thrown in his face. The last battler was often Jack Johnson, who was six feet two by the time he was fifteen. Jack had little desire to punish the other young blacks. He would bob and weave and pull a fist right out of the air. His boxing skills were extraordinary. As one friend recalls: "Jack was so fast he could block a punch and hit you with the same fist."

He became a stevedore on the Galveston docks and a prize-fighter in various professional clubs. Black boxers lived in the same parallel universe as Williams and Walker. No white heavyweight champion would ever condescend to meet with them in a ring—they were considered unscientific, stupid, and slow. Yet there had been great black heavyweight champions among the slaves, like Tom Molineaux of Virginia, who could have danced around most white champions and demolished them. These "boxing slaves" were the first black sportsmen, given fancy clothes and a little money by their masters, who made a fortune betting on them in the ring and nurturing them like racehorses. Molineaux, the finest of all "plantation champions," was himself the son of a boxing slave. He was set free after beating every available black man and in 1809 he went to England, where he was known as "The Moor" and became a celebrated boxer allowed to box British champions, white or black. The few portraits of him that survive reveal a strikingly contemporary face that looks out at us from the nineteenth century with a kind of sad-eyed poignance, a poignance that's utterly missing in portraits of John L. Sullivan, the Boston Strong Boy, who took on every white challenger in the field. There's a smugness, a self-satisfaction, a belief in his own infallibility that mark him as a souvenir, a creature from another time, another place—with no awareness that the world will begin to forget him even while his portrait is being taken. . . .

Jack Johnson was a "plantation champion" without the plantation. He couldn't have challenged the current world champion, James J. Jeffries, who retired undefeated in 1905 and went back to his alfalfa farm in California, without having fought a single black boxer, like Joe Jeanette or Sam Langford . . . and Jack Johnson. But Jack pursued the successor that "Mr. Jeff" himself had picked, Tommy Burns, who was never really legitimized as heavyweight champion. He caught up with Burns in Sydney, Australia, and beat him in fourteen rounds on December 21, 1908, winning a very ambiguous world championship. The LA papers called him "a long, lean, bullet headed, flat-chested 'coon.'" Jack was thirty years old. He'd been chasing a championship for almost ten years.

"The fight, if fight it must be called, was like that between a pygmy and a colossus," wrote Jack London in the *New York Herald.* Johnson "made a noise with his fist like a lullaby, tucking Burns into a crib." But as accurate and poetic as he was about the fight, London still brooded over the very idea of a black champion. "Jim Jeffries must emerge from his alfalfa farm and remove the golden smile from Jack Johnson's face. Jeff, it's up to you!"

That "golden smile" disturbed a nation used to obedient, barely visible blacks. It wasn't simply the gold teeth in Johnson's mouth, it was the constant, provocative grin, like that of a wolf, a wolf with yellow eyes. . . .

Jim Jeffries decided to heed Jack London's call. "A giant-killer who was himself a giant," Mr. Jeff came out of retirement. He abandoned his alfalfa farm and his bar in Los Angeles and went into training. He weighed three hundred pounds. He let his sparring partners punch away at him and refused to punch them back. "I'm afraid of killing them." But Jack beat the giant-killer in fifteen rounds on July 14, 1911, in Reno, Nevada. He taunted Jeffries. "Come on now, Mr. Jeff. Let me see what you got." And he tucked him into the same crib with Tommy Burns.

"I could never have whipped Jack Johnson at my best," said Jim Jeffries. "I couldn't have hit him. No. I couldn't have reached him in a thousand years. "

But most of Johnson's trouble started right after the match. He'd married "a handsome blonde divorcée" named Etta Terry Duryea, whom he met in Coney Island. She'd accompanied him to his training camp, and he would juggle her with several mistresses, including Belle Schreiber, a policeman's daughter from Milwaukee who was one of the "divas" at the Everleigh Club in Chicago, "the most elaborate and expensive brothel in the world."

Tommy Burns meant nothing. But Jim Jeffries was a national icon. And Jack's victory in Reno created a long, long bout of hysteria. The country couldn't forgive Jack Johnson—the dancing coon—for humiliating Jeff. And his appetite for white women only deepened the hysteria. There was civil war. Whites went after blacks on trolleys all over the land and blacks tangled with sailors in several sailors' towns, like Norfolk, Virginia. Wayne W. Wheeler, superintendent of the Anti-Saloon League, who didn't have any love for Jack Johnson, sent his band of private detectives into the "dry" town of Newark, Ohio, four days after the fight and started a race riot. Wheeler couldn't win. Blacks in the worst ghettos had found a king:

> The white man pulls the trigger
> But it makes no difference what the white man say
> The world champion's still a nigger.

Jack Johnson drank champagne out of a straw. He opened a saloon on the South Side of Chicago, the Café de Champion, where he and Etta lived in an apartment on the second floor. Champions such as Jeffries and John L. Sullivan had their own saloons where they could celebrate their past and present glory and serve beer to grateful customers, but the Café de Champion was unlike any other saloon. It had silver cuspidors, it had Jack's golden championship bet, and "a few real Rembrandts," according to Jack, who loved to mythologize himself. But the Café de Champion didn't need any Rembrandts. It had Jack Johnson of the golden grin, who played the bass fiddle, sang ragtime in baritone, told stories like he'd done on his hugely successful vaudeville tours—he was one of the highest paid troupers in the world—performed magic tricks, and cavorted with prostitutes on his payroll.

Meanwhile his wife sat like a prisoner above the saloon, reluctant to roam Chicago's black neighborhoods. She'd gone on a tour of Europe's music halls with Jack, who sped across London in a scarlet racing car and delighted audiences with a bit of singing, dancing, and shadowboxing. "I was a bigger attraction than the king." But he was still turned away from the best hotels. He had prostitutes and chorus girls to amuse him, and left his wife with little or nothing at all. "Etta's face in repose had an expression of sadness." That sadness worsened in Chicago. She fell into a profound melancholia. "I am a white woman and tired of being a social outcast. . . . All my misery comes through marrying a black man. Even the negroes don't respect me. They hate me." She shot herself in the head, killed herself with one of Jack's guns.

Jack wasn't much of a mourner. He picked up with an eighteen-year-old prostitute, Lucille Cameron, who'd come from

Minneapolis to work at Jack's saloon. Her mother, a certain Mrs. Cameron-Falconet, complained to federal authorities that Jack had kidnapped her daughter. "Jack Johnson has hypnotic powers, and he has exercised them over my little girl." She demanded that the United States arrest Jack in violation of the White Slavery Act. Federal prosecutors seized Lucille, locked her in a room, but she wouldn't testify against Jack. The government found a more malleable witness in Belle Schreiber, who might have felt chagrined that Jack had dropped her. Belle would claim that she was driven out of the Everleigh Club and other world-class brothels: "They didn't want me because I was Jack Johnson's white sweetheart."

The entire country was against Jack. One Georgia congressman noted that "in Chicago, white girls are made the slaves of an African brute." A federal grand jury moved to indict Jack for bestiality. Federal judge Kenesaw Mountain Landis, who would be brought in to clean up baseball after the Black Sox scandal, issued a warrant for Jack's arrest—a detail of detectives broke into the Café de Champion, kicked over the cuspidors, and handcuffed Jack Johnson, who "wept when he saw the shackles." He spent a week in jail, where he brooded over not having his valet.

On December 4, 1912, he married Lucille Cameron. But the United States didn't need Lucille now that it had Belle Schreiber. In 1913 federal prosecutors pounced on Jack and charged him with "debauchery . . . and crimes against nature." He went on trial in May, was found guilty, fined one thousand dollars, and sentenced to a year and a day in federal prison. Jack jumped bail, and the world champion was suddenly "the world's most notorious fugitive. . . ."

But he kept his golden grin. "My real crime—my real crime—was beating Jim Jeffries." Who would have bothered Jack if he'd played the good little nigger and lost to Mr. Jeff? But Jack wasn't the losing kind. He traveled across Europe as a troubadour who boxed, sang, and performed in circuses. Promoters took advantage of Jack now that he was on the run and paid him a pittance. He was always broke. He wrestled for private parties, ran to South America, and became a strongman-clown who could break chains with his chest. . . .

And while Jack struggled, America was looking for a Great White Hope to beat a black fugitive. It seemed to have found one in Jess Willard, "the Pottawatomie Giant." Willard was six foot six and weighed 250 pounds. No one had ever gotten near enough to the Pottawatomie Giant to ever knock him down. Such was the ballyhoo that surrounded him. He was an awkward numskull who should never have danced in the same ring with Jack Johnson, but Jack was close to thirty-seven when he agreed to fight Jess at the Oriental Park Racetrack outside Havana on April 15, 1915. He tired after eight rounds. A wooden arena had been built inside the racetrack, and it was like an infernal box sitting in the sun. Jack began to bake in that wooden box. His legs began to buckle in the tenth round. By the twentieth he was hardly moving at all, but the Pottawatomie Giant wasn't any lighter on his feet. They looked like a pair of walruses wobbling in a wooden box that was about to burn up.

The defensive demon who could "catch punches in his gloves [like] a shortstop spearing a hot grounder" neglected to catch a punch in the twenty-sixth round, and Jess Willard knocked him out—but it was Jack's own exhaustion that defeated him rather than the force of Willard's blow. The world continued in slow motion, as "Jack Johnson, like a man on the beach who had forgotten his dark glasses, languidly lifted his right arm and positioned it over his eyes to shield them from the bright, hot sun."

The giant's grandeur began to grow. But four years later, in 1919, an obscure light heavyweight from Manassa, Colorado, William Harrison Dempsey, better known as "Jack," knocked Willard down seven times in the first round, and became the "Manassa Mauler," who would tower over the 1920s as Broadway's own child (with Babe Ruth). Gene Tunney would beat him twice, but it couldn't diminish *white* Jack. He'd always be remembered as the man who beat the man who beat Jack Johnson, while the Pottawatomie Giant is a footnote in Jack Dempsey's colossal career. . . .

And black Jack? He would insist that he took a dive. "You know I laid down for Willard so that I could come home to see my mother." That was ungracious of Jack and part of his mythomania. He didn't surrender himself to federal officers in San Diego until 1920, five years after the fight. He would remain a vagabond during those five years. Yet a certain homage was paid to him during the war—Frenchmen called the Germans' heaviest-hitting artillery "le Jack Johnson."

He served ten months inside "The Walls," the federal penitentiary at Leavenworth, where he was worshipped by the prisoners, black and white. He even had his own butcher and a supply of liquor and cigars. He was released on July 9, 1921 and given a five-dollar bill.

He wanted to fight Jack Dempsey, but Dempsey obeyed the unconscious will of a white America that needed to bury all traces of a black champion with a wolf's yellow eyes. He moved to Harlem, where he would live for the rest of his life. But it's during the Jazz Age that his particulars seem a bit blurred. He was in and out of vaudeville, may have had his own jazz band, in which he played the "bull fiddle," opened a speakeasy called the Club Deluxe . . . and lost it to Owney Madden, who turned the

Deluxe into the Cotton Club and had no need of a black bull fiddler. Jack might even have been a bootlegger with Bumpy Johnson, but it was no big deal—half of Harlem was bootlegging for Bumpy. By the end of the decade Jack emerged with a new career: raconteur and exhibitionist at carnivals and circuses. And it was as a small-timer that Jack Johnson finally appeared "on Broadway," at one or more of the amusement arcades that began to replace restaurants and theatres during the Depression.

The lure was a sign that said "Jack Johnson Trains Here." But he didn't train at all. He had a tiny gym in the corner of a basement, where he would stand stripped to the waist like a carnival freak and slap at a punching bag in time to jazz piped in from a phonograph. In 1936 he again appeared stripped to the waist in a walk-on at the Hippodrome as an Ethiopian general in *Aida*. It was his first and last operatic role. That same year he moved his little act to Hubert's Flea Circus and Museum. Hidden among sword swallowers and bearded ladies, he no longer bothered to box—he lectured, danced, played the harmonica. . . .

There was a new black heavyweight champion, Joe Louis, and according to Jervis Anderson, Jack seemed envious and bitter about him. Joe Louis had become a hero of black *and* white America. He didn't go near white women or have Jack's demonic grin. Joe wasn't a vaudevillian. He was deadly earnest in the ring, didn't chatter with his opponents, simply knocked them out. Both his managers were ex-bootleggers, but Joe himself was *clean*. . . .

Jack would spend his winters at Hubert's and his summers at Coney Island or on tour at carnivals and sideshows throughout the country. On June 10, 1946, as he crossed into North Carolina in his Lincoln Zephyr, he crashed into a power pole, was knocked from the car, and died at a hospital in Raleigh. He'd come from a

Texas carnival and was on his way to New York to watch Joe
Louis defend his championship against Billy Conn. . . .

5.

Jack Johnson was the very first hero of the twentieth century,
someone with fierce pride, who would not live by other men's
definitions and desires to humiliate him. He dared to be heavyweight champion in spite of the taboos attached to his color. He
was strong and eager enough to take on the whole white race, not
with anger, but with cunning and craft. Jack was the trickster that
Henry Louis Gates Jr. and Jill Watts talked about. He won with
his wits and with the trickster's absolute sense of form—he was
the signifying monkey god inside *and* outside the ring, "a hieroglyphic in black and gold."

Only once did his anger show. It was during an exhibition
match with Stanley Ketchel, the white middleweight champion
whom Ernest Hemingway considered the best fighter pound for
pound on the planet. Actually, the fight was fixed. It was one of
the first matches ever filmed by motion picture cameras and an
early knockout would have made the match much less valuable to
the film's producers. And so Jack danced with Stanley Ketchel on
October 16, 1909. He was his usual signifying self, weaving
around and wearing an American flag as his belt. But Ketchel
decided to take advantage of the cameras and seize the heavyweight championship. In the twelfth round, he landed a power-
house right behind Jack's left ear. "Jack fell to the floor, then
leaped up as though he had touched a hot stove and struck
Ketchel so savage a blow that it tore off his front teeth at the
gums and stretched him senseless."

But the trickster didn't like to keep such lightning in his bag of tricks. He had no wish to hurt a man but to wear him down, like a tar baby would, a tar baby made of wind. His heir wasn't Joe Louis, who fought to kill, but Muhammad Ali. Ali was a talker in the ring. His credo—"Float like a butterfly, sting like a bee"—also described Jack. His "rope-a-dope" could only have been performed by the ultimate trickster. Before his "rumble in the jungle" with George Foreman in Zaire (October 30, 1974), almost no one gave Ali the slightest chance to win. Foreman was a lethal giant and Ali was a jibbering ex-champ. But according to Dave Anderson of the *New York Times*: "Ali leaned back on the ropes absorbing punches, letting Foreman wear himself out pummeling Ali's arms and ribs. By the eighth round, Foreman was exhausted," and the talker put him to sleep. "The *ropes* were his allies, and his opponent was the *dope*." Jack had a kind of "rope-a-dope" against Jim Jeffries in 1911. Instead of leaning against the ropes, he stood in the middle of the ring, performed his own pantomime and dodged Jeffries' punches like a matador. Jeff the giant-killer wore himself out punching a target that was never there. . . .

We don't celebrate Johnson nearly enough. There might not have been a modern Broadway or a Jazz Age if Johnson hadn't come along and shoved himself against a white world and developed his own secret language and showmanship. He'd turned boxing into stunning vaudeville, and even after he quit boxing he played the bull fiddle and told tall stories—how he'd raced a kangaroo in Australia until it dropped dead—to black and white audiences with that glorious golden grin.

He himself had become a Broadway character during the last twenty years of his life, with a speakeasy, some jazz, and his own sort of "variety" at Hubert's. Both he and Bert Williams were emblematic of a quest to locate a genuine black Broadway; they were both *jazzmen* with peculiar riffs. Jack's melodies often came with his dancing in the ring and with his fists, and Bert's with his cakewalk and his parodies and his pantomime. They were also emblematic of a heartbreaking shout by black men and women with a longing to be listened to. Sometimes it was peaceful, sometimes not, and sometimes that same heartbreaking shout produced the most exquisite, painful, and oddly joyous art. . . .

—Call it 1909. Sophie Tucker, the original red hot mama (in blackface) appears in the Follies. Nora Bayes, Ziggy's pampered star, is jealous of Sophie's popularity and insists that her stage time be cut in half. Sophie leaves the Follies and never comes back. The "World-Renowned Coon Shouter" can get her own bookings. Big, fat, and ugly, she's much more comfortable on stage as a coon—audiences can laugh at her harlequinade, not at Sophie herself. But it's a complicated business, and sometimes audiences can't separate the harlequin from the harlequinade: "After one of her stomping performances in blackface, Sophie Tucker would peel off a glove and wave to the crowd 'to show I was a white girl.' A surprised gasp would rise from the audience, then a howl of laughter, as if in tribute to all that impersonation could dredge up," says Irving Howe in support of Sophie's art. Perhaps Sophie's coon shouting served her own "daemon," allowed her to open up, but it was also part of a conspiracy between the shouter and her white audience that they could both participate in the "daemonic"—a kind of sexual awakening and abandonment—so long as Sophie continued the *dream* of being black. And by peeling off the glove she broke the magic curtain, roused spectators from their pleasurable slumber and forced them to confront the slippery fact that black could become white in the blink of an eye, and that there were no safe boundaries between the two; their "howl of laughter" was only a nervous tic, the reaction of being caught within a lie. How could they enjoy themselves if every damn coon that stomped on a stage decided not to stay black?

—It's 1910. Fanny Brice arrives at the Follies. Two black composers, Will Marion Cook and Joe Jordan, write "Lovey Joe," a song about a black badass "lover man" that Fanny wants to use as her opening number. Abe Erlanger, one of the Follies' producers, watches Fanny rehearse, calls "Lovey Joe" a coon song and doesn't care for the nigger voice that Fanny adopts while singing it. He fires her before she can appear at the Follies, but Flo, that hawklike spotter of talent, hires her back on condition that she doesn't sing "Lovey Joe" on opening night. But she defies the Great Ziegfeld, puts on a dress that's much too small, and sings "Lovey Joe" in blackface, knocking her knees together and wiggling like a cat in heat. The audience goes wild and doesn't want to let go of Fanny Brice. She sings the song again, with her belly bursting out of the tight dress as if she's gotten pregnant in the middle of the Follies. She stops the show, takes encore after encore, but Joe Jordan has to listen from the lobby, since blacks aren't allowed inside the auditorium. . . .

—The 1919 Follies opens on June 23, with a score essentially by Irving Berlin. It stars Marilyn Miller, Eddie Cantor, Bert Williams, and The Fairbanks Twins. Fans will consider 1919 a vintage year, the finest of all the Follies. It has a minstrel motif, with the Ziegfeld Girls appearing as "Pickaninnies" in high-yellow paint. Berlin writes "A Pretty Girl Is Like a Melody" for Flo, who is blissful because he now has a theme song that will immortalize the Follies. In the finale, Eddie and Bert, both in blackface, sing "I Want to See a Minstrel Show," while the "Follies

Pickaninnies" strut in the background. Bert is no longer the coon in the corner: he appears onstage with the "Pickaninnies," dances and sings alongside white girls painted black. Bert has become sick of minstrel shows and the Follies' essential lie: America isn't white and never really was. He won't dance with Flo's fake chocolate babies ever again. He quits the Follies for the last time. . . .

—It's 1922. Florence Mills, the Little Black Mosquito, is appearing at Harlem's Plantation Club. As Stanley Walker notes in *The Night Club Era*: "She was a favorite of the crowd that began going to the hot spots of Harlem right after the war, after the discovery that Negro rhythm, Negro songs, even though they could be astoundingly vulgar, were high art because of their naturalness." Walker wrote this in 1932, and one doesn't know whether to forgive him for *his* own vulgarity, or to scold him for the condescension of an entire white culture toward blacks, a condescension that could also kill. . . .

Flo invites Florence to join the Follies. The Little Black Mosquito with her darting, electric sting will be a perfect foil for the "tall, leggy, and light haired" Follies Girl and the architectonics of her walk. But Florence doesn't want to be another Bert Williams, a black harlequin in a blinding white field. She says no to Ziegfeld and stars in an all-black revue, *Dixie to Broadway*. . . .

—It's 1923, and Bessie Smith, the biggest, baddest red hot mama begins her recording career with "Down Hearted Blues." She's a female Jack Johnson, six feet tall and two hundred pounds. And she loves to fight, knocking down men and women at will. She has the loudest, strongest voice and the richest register in an age when every voice had to be strong or you couldn't survive as a singer. Bessie's also a renegade who sings about "me and my razor and my gun." She doesn't have much use for whites or mulattos who pass for white. She herself is "a deep killer brown." She has an appetite for women as well as men and is constantly chasing after chorus girls in her shows and battling with their fiancés. Her fistfights often land her in jail. Mae West will copy her growl, her strut, her shimmy shake, but it will only be a performance for Mae, a kind of skillful parody. Smith will appear on Broadway in 1929, but like a true outlaw, she prefers honky-tonks and tent shows and black honky-tonk men. . . .

—It's February 24, 1924. Paul Whiteman, the self-professed "King of Jazz," gives a concert called "An Experiment in Modern Music" at the Aeolian Hall on West 43rd. It features the world premiere of Gershwin's "Rhapsody in Blue" and Whiteman's own jazz arrangements. With this one concert, Paul Whiteman will become the biggest graverobber in history. Worse. He will steal a living, breathing style from black musicians. And it isn't out of ignorance. It's out of a murderous self-promotion. He's been to the best Harlem clubs. But he still babbles in his program notes about "the tremendous strides which have been made in popular music from the day of discordant Jazz, which sprang into existence about ten years ago from nowhere in particular."

—*from nowhere in particular.*

Jazz came from the South, long before Whiteman. It came from the work songs of slaves, from spirituals and blues, from funeral marches, from ragtime, from Creole songs, from the "jass" bands inside a honky-tonk car that was "sometimes hooked onto the train that carried [black] itinerant workers from job to job." Early jazz was "folk music without words." And in New Orleans, white and black honky-tonk pianists were encouraged to "Jass it up"—give their music some sexual heat. In the simplest terms, "jazz always meant a loosened beat and Negro origins." But it didn't mean Whiteman, who was never, never a honky-tonk man.

—That same year, 1924, a brilliant young black cornetist from New Orleans comes to town (he will soon switch to the trumpet). He perfects the art of signifying on his horn: he'll take a pop tune and "rib" it, tear it apart and reinterpret it with a satirical sound. No one can "rib" like Louis Armstrong, who monkeys with the white man's music and plays it better than any white man.

—It's 1929. Louis Armstrong reigns over Harlem, but he will electrify Broadway when he appears in *Hot Chocolate*, will drive audiences berserk with his rendering of Fats Waller's "Ain't Misbehavin'" and "What Did I Do to Be So (Black and Blue)?" And for one little moment white Broadway is also black and blue. . . .

CHAPTER SEVEN
THE WILD COMANCHE

1.

If Broadway produced sacred monsters such as Al Jolson, Flo Ziegfeld, Arnold Rothstein, Fanny Brice, and Texas Guinan, who seem like gargoyles rather than creatures of subtle and solid flesh, cartoon characters that waltzed out of Mindy's or one of Tex's nightclubs—flattened rather than complex, like Runyon's talking tornadoes—it also produced Louise Brooks, who called herself "the secret bride of New York." Unlike Jolson, who was cruel and egotistical and couldn't see beyond his nose, Brooksie had the power and the curse of reflection. She was a failure in the land of success, a gold digger who didn't know how to dig. She had a beauty that Jolson and Baby Snooks never had. She was the one Follies Girl who'd ever studied modern dance. She would become in middle age a remarkable writer who captured the dead bones of Hollywood and Broadway, but even without her explorations Louise was a Broadway epic. "As emblematic figure of the twenties, epitomizing the flapper, jazz babies, and dancing daughters of the boom years, Brooks has few equals, living or dead," according to Kenneth Tynan. I would say she has none. . . .

She was from Kansas, like Dorothy in *The Wizard of Oz*, but Dorothy never danced in the Follies, and Dorothy never dreamed of Louise's war cry: "I like to drink and fuck." Mary Louise Brooks was born on November 4, 1906, in the heart of the Bible belt. She was a professional dancer by the time she was ten, performing at fairs and women's clubs across Kansas. In July 1922, she got off the train from Wichita "and fell in love with New York forever." She'd been accepted as a student at Denishawn, the most exciting and innovative dance company in America. Louise was fifteen and she lived in a rented room on Riverside Drive. She didn't really get along with Ruth St. Denis, the company's cofounder. She was far too willful a girl. She went to the Follies with her chaperone, Alice Mills. She adored Fanny Brice's comic portrait of Pavlova, but in the final act, "standing motionless in front of a black velvet curtain, with black velvet sheathing her exquisite figure, [Brice] broke the audience's heart with her singing of 'My Man' "—her husband was still in Leavenworth.

But Louise wasn't impressed with Ziggy's Girls, who "wore smiles as fixed as their towering feather headdresses. I decided right then that onstage I would never smile unless I felt like it."

Martha Graham, the doyenne of modern dance, who began her career at Denishawn, remembered Louise as a fifteen-year-old novice beyond the norm "because she was so extraordinarily beautiful and because of a deep inner power that stood her all her life."

She was asked to join the company after her first season at school and she danced with Denishawn for two years, but rumors began to abound that little Louise was sleeping with all the stage-hands . . . or flirting with them, and her relations with Ruth St. Denis quickly deteriorated. Mary Louise was having too good a time disobeying Miss Ruth's edicts of "no boyfriends, no drinking, and certainly no sex," and in the spring of 1924, St. Denis drummed her out of Denishawn.

Louise was seventeen, and she'd lost her one chance of becoming a serious dancer. She would recapture some of the same discipline when she started writing articles about film that were wondrous to read. But in that gap of thirty years between Denishawn and her monklike existence as a writer for esoteric quarterlies who lived on gin and jam, Louise had the strangest of odysseys—she was the prodigal daughter who could never really find the right dance step. . . .

She went from being a dropout at Denishawn to becoming the youngest chorus girl in George White's Scandals during the summer of 1924. Louise was still seventeen. The Scandals was a racier, skimpier version of the Follies. According to Edmund Wilson, "The Follies is such fantasy, such harlequinade as the busy well-to-do New Yorker has been able to make of his life. Expensive, punctual, stiff, it moves with the speed of an express train." George White couldn't compete with that express train, and he had to capitalize on the near nudity of his girls. Damon Runyon's guys and dolls seem to prefer the less aristocratic Georgie White, who at least lets his girls wear "a few light bandages" rather than "walk around raw" like the chorines in Earl Caroll's Vanities.

But it didn't matter how little or how much Louise wore at the Scandals; she was seen and discovered by the upper crust of Broadway and its crowd of bankers, brokers, newspaper barons, bachelor tycoons, politicians, impresarios, columnists, and playwrights who followed every revue with religious fervor and hunted each new lovely like Louise, the current "black-bobbed teenage rage."

She was a novelty in the lap of millionaires. Or as Louise herself would remark—"as a pussycat, I sat under many a king's chair." She'd been initiated into the club of chorus girls protected by rich and powerful men with their own predictable price. "In New York in 1924 there was a hand-picked group of beautiful girls who were invited to parties given for great men in finance and government. . . . At these parties we were not required, like common whores, to go to bed with any man who asked us, but if we did the profits were great. Money, jewels, mink coats, a film job—name it."

That was the dance of Broadway during the twenties—a kind of glorious gold digging, where the chorus girl suddenly had the power to hunt the hunter she desired. It was still a world where gentlemen preferred blondes, but Louise, according to Anita Loos, was a "black-haired blonde" with a "blonde personality." Follies graduates like Barbara Stanwyck, Paulette Goddard, and Marion Davies, who would go on to miraculous careers, with one or several "kings" beside them, still had to sleep their way to stardom. Money wasn't the main pursuit of the wizards and kings who financed films and Broadway musicals—money was only the means to get beautiful women into the king's bed.

And Louise became "Brooksie" in 1924, when she began to wear "light bandages" at the Scandals and run around to nightclubs with a variety of bankers and brokers. "Ours was a heartless racket." After acquiring an ermine coat from some millionaire, "I let him take me just once to a tea dance at the Biltmore Hotel."

Heartless or not, she didn't have the instincts of a real predator. "I just wasn't equipped to spoil millionaires in a practical, farsighted way." But Louise was irresistible, "a girl in a Prince Valiant bob, with electrifying eyes." And she had a particular advantage, since New York's most eligible bachelors, "finding debutantes a threat, turned to pretty girls in the theatre, whose mothers weren't husband-hunting." Manhattan in 1924 was the hottest place on the planet. Hollywood hadn't really taken hold of the public's imagination, and many film stars commuted from their apartment-palaces on the cliffs of Central Park West to Hearst's Cosmopolitan Studio in East Harlem and Paramount's Astoria Studios across the East River and Hell Gate. A banker like Otto Kahn, patron saint of starving actors, writers, and artists, and chairman of the Metropolitan Opera, was on the board of Paramount—with his Prussian manners and waxed mustache, he ran after chorus girls, actresses, and opera stars, attended every single opening night at the Follies, and was considered Broadway's own banker. Louise was one of his pussycats. When she was alone in London in January 1925, dancing the Charleston at a West End café and unable to pay her rent, it was Otto Kahn who had one of his emissaries ship her back to New York. . . .

Louise had quit Georgie White because the Scandals bored her to death, but now Flo Ziegfeld "smiled his charming, silver-fox smile" and Louise ended up in the 1925 Follies as a Glorified Girl in a white feather headdress and "a four-yard train."

"I'm not a chorus girl, I'm a dancer," she told the Great Ziegfeld, but he still had her swivel down one of Joseph Urban's staircases in her white tower and tail. She felt ridiculous but began to enjoy "the regular nightly excitement of the audience" with its "parade of celebrities"—the mark of Broadway in the 1920s, when there was a magical, almost hypnotic interchange between the performer and the crowd, a palpable, silent energy that passed from one to the other, a *language* that could be found nowhere else. . . .

Louise noticed film star Gloria Swanson in the audience. Swanson had arrived with one of Louise's own "protectors," Walter Wanger, a producer at Paramount. Swanson was Paramount's biggest star, an authentic siren of the silver screen. The giant bathtubs she lounged in for Cecil B. DeMille were copied by millionaires who wanted to impress their mistresses and please their wives. She could create instant fashion with the dresses she wore, the cigarettes she smoked, the paint she used on her eyes. At the Follies, in the first row, she "looked so stunning in a black suit with her legs crossed and her arms folded and her head thrown back, watching the show like a little general reviewing her troops." And she told Walter Wanger that Louise in her white paint and peacock feathers "looked like a corpse."

2.

L ouise had her private coterie in the dressing room she shared with Dorothy Knapp, "the most glorified of Ziegfeld's glorified girls," her own little cultural circle, led by Walter Wanger and Herman Mankiewicz, or *Mank*, drama critic and "Central Park West Voltaire," who would give Louise a book to read every week—*Anna Karenina* or *War and Peace*—and then interrogate her in the dressing room like some cultural commissar. He also started the Louise Brooks Literary Society . . . at Louise's expense. He was poking fun of her and her Kansas accent while attempting to get into her pants *and* watch the gorgeous Dorothy Knapp do a little striptease in front of a mirror. It was exactly the kind of condescension that Louise would have to endure from lovers, friends, and film directors, their inability to believe that a beautiful girl like Louise could possibly have a brain. It's no miracle that she would have bouts of melancholia and finally have to withdraw into an apartment–prison cell in upstate New York, with her books and her jars of jam. . . .

She did have a marvelous interlude with Charlie Chaplin, when she was eighteen and Charlie was thirty-six. And Chaplin, whose origins were even narrower than Louise's—he was a performer in London music halls before he was five—never made fun of her narrow education. "In 1925, he was the most famous person who'd ever lived." He'd just finished *The Gold Rush* and had come to New York for the film's premiere . . . while Louise was wearing peacock feathers at the Follies. She met him at a Walter Wanger cocktail party, and that summer Chaplin had only one woman on his mind—Louise. She moved into the Ambassador Hotel with him.

Louise would swear that she was never in love with Chaplin, that he was only part of her league of "interesting" men, but the two months she spent with him became one of the defining moments in her life, though she couldn't quite ever admit it to herself. Charlie wasn't *Manhattan* or *Broadway*, with its bravura and insatiable need for recognition. He was perversely simple and complex, an autodidact like Louise who'd built his own empire in Hollywood out of a single comic character, a nameless tramp who all by himself seemed to represent the power and seduction of motion pictures. Manhattan may have had Al Jolson, with his electricity that rippled from row to row of the Winter Garden, but Jolson's "daemon" was a little coarse next to Chaplin's tramp, who danced with a lightness and a delicacy that were like the outline and the architecture of our very own thoughts and desires. Chaplin's "daemon" was much closer to Louise's, a childlike, amoral perfection. But at eighteen Louise was a little too old for him. Charlie had a penchant for child brides, like Mildred Harris, whom he married in 1918 when she was sixteen . . . and divorced when she was eighteen. He was currently married to Lolita MacMurray, aka Lita Grey, another sixteen-year-old bride. Lita and her family sat like locusts in his Beverly Hills mansion, prepared to devour him while he went to parties with Louise.

But Louise was already a philosopher-poet lying in wait as she observed Chaplin inside their love nest at the Ambassador. "Do you know," she recalled to Kenneth Tynan, "I can't once remember him *still*? He was always standing up as he sat down, and going out as he came in." His gift for caricature was as profound as his creation of the tramp. He could do imitations of *anybody*. "Isadora Duncan danced in a storm of toilet paper. John Barrymore picked his nose and brooded on Hamlet's soliloquy. A *Follies* girl swished across the room; and I began to cry while Charlie denied absolutely that he was imitating me."

His parting with Louise was like the separate migration of two solitary souls. Chaplin didn't leave her "a bangle from Cartier" that she could "flash" as a souvenir, but a big fat check signed "Charlie," which Louise never bothered to acknowledge— as if a pair of "daemons" had begun to distance themselves. But he'd been an excellent teacher. "I learned to act by watching Martha Graham dance and I learned to dance by watching Charlie Chaplin act."

Nineteen twenty-five was a fateful year for Louise—the Follies, a summer romance, and a five-year contract with Paramount Pictures. Flo Ziegfeld was furious, not at Louise herself, but at the film studios that were stealing his stars. He could do very little about the Hollywood headhunters. Paramount would raid the Follies periodically, and the rest of Broadway. And Louise didn't have to shuffle very fast or very far, or give up her feathery trail. Because of Paramount's presence in Astoria, Louise could "dance in the *Follies* by night and shoot movies by day."

Film work didn't interfere with her pleasures. She would still dine at the Colony or "21," and go to the El Fey, where customers would beg her to do the Charleston on Texas Guinan's tiny dance floor.

In 1926, *Photoplay*, the aristocrat of movie magazines, interviewed Louise: "She is so very Manhattan. Very young. Exquisitely hard-boiled. Her black eyes and sleek black hair are as brilliant as Chinese lacquer. Her skin is as white as a camelia. Her legs are lyric."

But that lyricism didn't last. Paramount began closing down its Astoria studios and shifting its personnel and its stars to a brand-new mammoth studio on Marathon Street in Hollywood. And that was the beginning of the end for Louise. "Making films in New York was okay because I learned so much and discovered Tolstoy and *Anna Karenina*. Nobody could understand why I hated that dreadful, destructive place [Hollywood] which seemed a marvelous paradise to everyone else."

Her exile from Manhattan left Louise in a bitter mood about everything, even sex. "Love is a publicity stunt, and making love, after the first curious rapture, is only another petulant way to pass the time waiting for the studio to call."

Hollywood had become "like a terrible dream I have—I am lost in the corridors of a big hotel and I can't find my room. People pass me as if they cannot see or hear me. So first I ran away from Hollywood and I have been running away ever since."

She would run to Berlin and make *Pandora's Box* (1928) for G. W. Pabst. Louise plays Lulu, an ambiguous femme fatale who's finally murdered by Jack the Ripper. A silent film at the very beginning of sound, *Pandora's Box* was "quickly lost in the void." Louise would make two more films in Europe before returning to Hollywood as some kind of ghost. She should have been the star of a hundred Hollywood musicals that picked the bones of the Follies and relived the same old Broadway romance, but Hollywood preferred Ruby Keeler. Ruby threatened no one. She wasn't a femme fatale with knifelike moves and electrical eyes; she could barely keep awake on screen—like George Raft. . . .

Of course Ruby triumphs with her big fat feet. She's Mrs. Al Jolson. But her real charm comes from having once been Johnny Irish's girl—the seventeen-year-old sweetheart of a bootlegger. And one almost wishes a similar fate for Brooksie. Had she ever danced with Owney Madden at the El Fey, become Owney's girl, rather than the pet of Central Park philosophers, bankers, and film producers, she might not have taken such a nosedive. Madden might have kept her close to Broadway. . . .

Poor Louise couldn't even manage her own private casting couch. She slept with *everybody* except the men who might have helped her in Hollywood. She wouldn't go near one of her own directors, Malcolm St. Clair, who'd been trying "to get in my bed on and off for fifteen years. And considering the hundreds of much less attractive men who succeeded in the hay, I can't understand it. The only thing that comes to mind is that the rims of his round blue eyes were bright pink."

3.

Louise "tried" marriage with director Eddie Sutherland, but it didn't work. "He loved parties. I loved solitude." The secret bride of New York couldn't keep house in Laurel Canyon or Beverly Hills. She was unfaithful during her entire three-year marriage, and so was Eddie Sutherland. She moved out of Laurel Canyon on April 18, 1928, and moved into a suite at the Beverly Wilshire, after having appeared in Howard Hawks' *A Girl in Every Port*, the film that convinced Pabst that Louise would have to be his Lulu. And from her suite at the Bev Wilshire, she could look right into the lap of a local movie palace, where *A Girl in Every Port* was playing. "Staring down at my name in lights on the marquee of the Wilshire Theatre was like reading an advertisement of my isolation."

How different it was when she had a one-page article on Marlene Dietrich published in Paris, with her name on the cover.

"From dancing and acting and getting my name in lights and having my pictures seen by millions I got no feeling whatever. This little ad reaching few—I find overwhelming."

For Louise "acting" had nothing at all to do with one's career: it was closer to the rhythm of writing or the dancing she had done at Denishawn, which was more about intense privacy rather than public display. Film acting, said Louise, "does not consist of descriptive movement of face and body but in the movement of thought and soul transmitted in a kind of intense isolation."

And this is what French and American film critics would notice when they rediscovered Lulu *and* Louise in the 1950s— the absolute purity of line that devoured the space around her and wiped everyone but Louise off the screen. It was like the deep, engulfing dream of an exquisite dance step.

When she was ill with arthritis and osteoporosis, barely able to get out of bed in her cozy Rochester dungeon, she would declare: "In my dreams I am never crippled, I dance. . . ."

Pabst, who was crazy about Louise, grew bitter when she couldn't love him back. "Your life is exactly like Lulu's . . . and you will end the same way."

He'd created *Lulu*, but he didn't understand Louise.

"When I was young, I was unhappy most of the time. The pursuits of my friends: fame, money, power, did not make me happy. . . . Only when I moved to Rochester in 1956 did I find some happiness," with her pillows and her jam, and the sentences that clacked inside her head. . . .

How disturbing it would have been for *Mank* if he'd ever realized that the little idiot of his private book-reading classes could write with a ruthless poetry and wit about Chaplin and Garbo or Marion Davies and W. C. Fields (her friend from the Follies) that was well beyond the music Mank could gather with his own words. But Mank died before Louise ever published her poisonous love notes about *his* Manhattan and *his* Hollywood. . . .

In January 1927, just after she arrived in Hollywood, she met the two idols of the Jazz Age, Zelda and Scott: "They were sitting close together on a sofa, like a comedy team, and the first thing that struck me was how *small* they were. I had come to see the genius writer, but what dominated the room was the blazing intelligence of Zelda's profile. It shocked me. It was the profile of a witch."

But that witch was actually Lulu's soul sister. She was the one other creature—man, woman, or child—who blazed across the 1920s with a courage and a ferocious vitality akin to that of Louise. Zelda was the all-American girl married to the all-American writer, Francis Scott Key Fitzgerald, former scrub of the Princeton football team whose great-granduncle wrote "The Star-Spangled Banner." No other novelist had ever had such a meteoric success. "All in three days I got married and the presses were pounding out *This Side of Paradise* [his first novel] like they pound out extras in the movies." He was as handsome and famous as a movie star, with a glamorous red-headed wife who was "living the American dream, and became mad within it." How could it have been otherwise? She was much too modern for her own time, the casualty of a culture that insisted a wife bear children and blend in, that she remain her husband's extra rib, a simple appendage to his needs and desires. Zelda inspired Scott's writing and had to pay the price. She was Daisy Buchanan, the Southern belle with the sound of money in her voice, married to the brutal football hero that Scott could never be, and caught between Nick Carraway, the cunning Midwesterner with all the weapons of language at his disposal, and Jay Gatsby, the Platonic gangster who has no language other than a dozen clichés, but whose success is even more fabulous than Scott Fitzgerald's. And if the novel continues to haunt us, it's because Fitzgerald's psyche is burnt so deeply into the prose and is split between Gatsby and Nick, neither of whom can ever really conquer Daisy. Fitzgerald's men belong to a masochistic tribe. According to one of his Princeton classmates, Alexander McKaig, "Fitz [is] absorbed in Z's personality—she is the stronger of the two." "Fitz" was certain that Zelda secretly despised him as a weak and womanish man. His writing—and Nick Carraway's—was his one revenge.

She was born on July 24, 1900—Zelda Sayre of Montgomery, Alabama, "named after a gypsy queen in a novel." Right from the start she seemed to have mythological proportions. Her mother nursed the little gypsy queen until she was four. Both her parents called her "Baby" her whole life. She began to take ballet lessons at the age of nine. She had the "bluest eyes in Montgomery" and so many beaus that there was no more time for ballet. She was "a wild Comanche," like Alabama Beggs, the heroine of her autobiographical novel, *Save Me the Waltz*. She guzzled liquor "cut with Coke" and "did what she pleased when she pleased."

The war had come to Montgomery, which was flooded with soldiers and aviators from Camp Sheridan and Camp Taylor, right nearby. And Zelda would have a date with a different young officer every night of the week. She collected their insignias in a glove box. "Soon the little box was filled with gold and silver bars, castles and flags and curled serpents." And in July of 1918 she met a particular first lieutenant from the Sixty-seventh Infantry at Camp Sheridan. He wasn't very tall—five foot seven, like Jolson and Winchell—but he wore yellow boots with spurs and his eyes were "a clear ice green that changed color with his moods";

the two of them were instantly attracted to one another. "They even looked alike."

Scott wasn't like her other dates. He was so serious. He talked about the famous writer he would become and how he would keep her as a princess locked away in a tower. He wired her from New York after his discharge from the infantry:

I AM IN THE LAND OF AMBITION AND SUCCESS . . .

And while Scott pontificated, she went out with other young lieutenants, which drove him insane. But in the end Zelda "would accept being his creature, his fictional girl," and that was both the source of her joy and the beginning of her fall. She wanted to be the princess in Scott's tower and couldn't bear to live in it. She was much less conventional than Scott, who wanted a lovely, charming wife to play with and sit beside him while he wrote. She was utterly fearless, and Scott was not. But it didn't seem to matter at first. . . .

New York had opened up like a gigantic oyster for Scott and his bride. "We were the most powerful nation. Who could tell us any longer what was fashionable and what was fun? . . . [S]omething had to be done with all the nervous energy stored up and unexpended during the War." The mecca of this new, energized atmosphere had become Manhattan. "New York had all the iridescence of the beginning of the world." And on Broadway one could find a strange new intimacy: "[A]t the Midnight Frolic you danced elbow to elbow with Marion Davies. . . . We felt like small children in a great bright unexplored barn."

They weren't the only children in that barn. "[T]here were a lot of lost and lonely people," who would congregate at Lindy's after it opened in 1921, or at Texas Guinan's (after 1923), or at

Flo's Midnight Frolic and at one of the film studios in or around Manhattan if they were "picture people," since "the world of motion pictures had little sense of itself and no center."

But Scott and Zelda were at the center of everything, with an aura all their own.

"They looked as though they had stepped out of the sun; their youth is striking. *Everyone* wanted to meet him," noted Dorothy Parker. Or as Gilbert Seldes said upon first meeting the Fitzgeralds: "Suddenly, as though in a dream, this apparition, this double apparition, approached me. The two most beautiful people in the world were floating toward me, smiling. It was as if they were angelic visitors. I thought to myself, 'If there is anything I can do to keep them as beautiful as they are, I will do it.'"

But there was trouble in paradise, very early on. Scott couldn't seem to concentrate on his work while Zelda was near or far. As Alexander McKaig discovered: "If she's there Fitz can't work—she bothers him—and if she's not there he can't work—worried what she might do." Other people also began to notice "the curiously savage intensity of her look." With all the brouhaha around them, she was growing more desperate day by day. Zelda had nothing to do other than be the flapper who jumped into fountains and went through revolving doors with Scott.

"There began to be a touch of the vaudeville team about their performances in public, and their privacy was almost nonexistent."

After being prodded by Scott in an interview for the *Baltimore Sun*, Zelda described what she would do if she ever had to go to work: "I've studied ballet. I'd try to get a place in the Follies. Or the movies. If I wasn't successful, I'd try to write."

They had a daughter who was named after Scott—Frances Scott Fitzgerald, or "Scottie," who was almost like Zelda's little sister. They moved to Europe, where life was meant to be cheaper and calmer for the Fitzgeralds. Zelda flirted with a French aviator in the South of France. She tried to kill herself. She threatened to leave Scott. But Scott had the "oasis" of his writing. He finished *The Great Gatsby* in a storm of jealousy over Zelda's flier. And one can feel that turmoil in Tom Buchanan's sudden eloquence as he fights to hold onto Daisy (his wife) . . . and wins.

But Scott couldn't seem to see Zelda deteriorate in front of his eyes. Zelda and Scottie were "like two children playing together." At the age of twenty-seven, Zelda decided to pick up ballet again. She would become "a Pavlova, nothing less." Scott felt that her obsession with the dance drove her mad, but the obsessiveness was there long before her ballet lessons. Zelda struggled to make up for the years she'd lost. "I worked constantly. . . . I lived in a quiet, ghostly, hypersensitized world of my own. Scott drank."

She was already quite mad, but Zelda didn't have an "official" breakdown until 1930, when she entered a clinic outside Paris, desperate in her need to dance and no longer able to do so; after that, "she was in and out of mental hospitals, in and out of lucidity, in and out of crushing misery. At times, her beautiful body became covered with painful eczema." But she was no longer beautiful. She began to lose her looks. Yet it was at this point that Zelda, the gypsy queen turned flapper, the ballet dancer turned madwoman, became remarkable. She may have still been married to Scott, but she was no longer his wife. And Scott began to panic. Zelda was writing her own novel, which she completed on March 9, 1932, while she was at a Baltimore psychiatric clinic. Scott scrutinized it, edited it, helped her get it published, but he railed against Zelda and her writing. Her novel was too close to the territory he'd marked out for himself—her life and his—and he believed that Zelda, crazy or not, was cannibalizing his own guts. "He couldn't stand by and 'see her build that dubitable career of hers with morsels of living matter chipped from out of my mind, my belly, my nervous system and my loins.'"

He grew hysterical. "I want you to stop writing fiction." And vindictive. "You are a third rate writer and a third rate ballet dancer." With all his cruelty, he was still very much in love with Zelda, beholden to her and the phantoms that may have been inside her head. "I cherish her most extravagant hallucinations." Scott himself was collapsing. "Liquor on my mouth is sweet to her," said the hopeless alcoholic. In some subterranean manner her breakdown was also his—they looked so much alike that their relationship almost seemed incestuous, and perhaps he had to sunder himself from his "twin" in order to survive, both as a writer and a man. But he went too far, not in his love affair with British-born movie columnist Sheilah Graham, but in his need to dismantle Zelda—wipe her out. "I can't live in the ghost town which Zelda has become," he said like someone in a Broadway melodrama. And worse, he wrote to Scottie upon her graduation from a Connecticut boarding school that "[t]he mistake I made was in marrying her. . . . She didn't have the strength for the big stage."

—*the big stage.*

Scott himself was half mad, eaten up with guilt and a pity he'd had to displace. If Zelda was a kind of haunted house, at least it was her house. And he couldn't acknowledge his own competition with her as a writer. He was stung by the portrait of himself in *Save Me the Waltz.* Zelda had transposed him into a celebrated painter, David Knight, who sounded just like . . . F. Scott Fitzgerald. "You're so thin," he says to Alabama, who's given up her entire being to ballet. "There's no use killing yourself. I hope that you realize that the biggest difference in the world is between the amateur and the professional in the arts."

Fitzgerald, the high priest of professional art, would be forgotten the day he died—his books were barely in print—and would have to be resurrected by writers like Edmund Wilson who were devoted to him and his craft. "His talent was as natural as the pattern that was made by the dust on a butterfly's wings," Hemingway would write of him in *A Moveable Feast*. And whatever Scott or Ernest thought, Zelda, all on her own, had some of the same pattern, some of the same dust. . . .

4.

Mary Gordon calls *Save Me the Waltz* a "jazz *Bildungsroman*, with the potent jerky mistiness of early film," as Alabama Beggs struggles to find a self for her somewhere. The novel proceeds in a series of impressions, and does explode into song like a jazz riff. "Charlie Chaplin wore a yellow polo coat. People were tired of the proletariat—everyone was famous . . . there wasn't much interest in private lives."

But these impressions begin to cohere once Alabama writes about her fragile existence as a ballet dancer, "her toes picking the floor like the beaks of so many feeding hens." Dancing for Zelda had the same intense isolation that defined the art of acting for Louise Brooks—"a feeling for the flights of the human soul divorced from the person." Zelda had to get out of her body through her body. Rather than *make* her mad, dancing had preserved her sanity and her psyche, and had prepared her for the "clothes" she would have to wear as a novelist—the rough but translucent second skin of creation.

Earlier, while Scott was still in vogue, she'd written several stories and articles that were swallowed up by his persona, because magazine editors wanted his by-line, not hers, and the worst of Scott's sins was that he would allow this to happen. But he did keep a record in his own ledgers of what was his and what was hers, and we're left with much more than we could ever have dreamed. "Fitz" might have been her mentor, but like Louise, Zelda had her own fierce gift of language. As a writer, she lived underground, a total *amateur* in the pull of her imagination. . . .

In "The Original Follies Girl," we're introduced to Gay, who once had the best figure in New York, "otherwise she'd never have made all that money for just standing on the stage lending an air of importance to two yards of green tulle." And one can fathom Zelda dreaming her own fate as a Follies Girl in the flush of popularity, who "lived mostly alone" in a silver apartment with mulberry carpets, "and to soften the harsh loneliness she soon began to live in a great many places at once."

In "A Millionaire's Girl," published under Scott's name, she writes about the twilight after the war that "hung above New York like indigo wash."

In "Eulogy on the Flapper," which was her own battle cry, she declares that she "flirted because it was fun to flirt." And she tells us: "I believe in the flapper as an artist in her particular field, the art of being—being young, being lovely, being an object."

—*being an object*.

Zelda was shrewd enough to realize that all good flappers had to "capitalize their natural resources and get their money's worth," as hard-boiled businesslike girls with something to sell—their own loveliness and spectacular flair for fun.

In "Paint and Powder," published by Scott in *The Smart Set* but written by Zelda, she talks about the vitality and necessity of painted cheeks. "And so if our women gave up decorating themselves we would have more time to turn sad eyes on the black telegraph wires . . . the barren desolateness of city streets at dusk, and realize too late that almost the only beauty in this busy, careless land, whose every acre is littered with the waste of day before yesterday, is the gorgeous, radiant beauty of the girls."

In one sentence Zelda Fitzgerald captures the entire credo of Broadway and the myth of Ziegfeld and his Follies—that almost religious need for "radiant beauty" without complication or ulterior design. Flo's Girls were meant to be gorgeous, not complicated, machines, who might go on to marry a millionaire or end up like Gay, forgotten, all alone, while younger girls triumphed with their "wide clear eyes and free boyish laughs."

"Looking Back Eight Years," written by Zelda but published by Scott in *College Humor* (June 1928), allows us to peek at the misgivings of a whole generation. "Success was the goal for this generation and to a startling extent they have attained it, and now we venture to say that, if intimately approached, nine in ten would confess that success is only a decoration they wished to wear: what they really wanted is something deeper and richer than that."

Zelda touches upon the fatal flaw of the twenties and the new Broadway culture that it inspired. It was an age of glitter and six-foot headdresses, of chorus girls who pranced with marvelous precision, of gangsters as rich as Kublai Khan, where the only substance was excitement itself. Or as one particular poet remarked: "The philosophy of our time was written by bootleggers," who like everybody else would move in and out of fashion. And among all the glitter were two dancing daughters—Zelda and Louise—who helped create much of the fury, but lived within their own isolated, independent rhythm. They were casualties of a culture that worshipped teenage goddesses, but wouldn't allow them to grow into anything but appendages and pussycats. And the great secret of the twentieth century is that women, who had been closeted at home and forbidden "to make history" by the males around them, were much more interesting and *historic* than these very males. . . .

Zelda died alone in a mysterious fire at Highland Hospital in Asheville, North Carolina, that started around midnight on March 10, 1948, and shot up a dumbwaiter shaft. She was trapped on the top floor, and she could only be identified by a "charred slipper" that might have been (in my own mind) one of her old dancing shoes. Unlike Scott's, her resurrection was very, very late in coming. It took the devotion of Nancy Milford to bring Zelda out from under the shadow of Scott twenty-two years after her death. And it took another twenty-one years for Zelda's collected writings to be published, when most of us weren't aware that Zelda had anything to collect. And what a gorgeous glimpse she's given us of a dancing daughter in the twenties who was practicing her own craft all the while she "crawled into the friendly caves" of Scott's ear. At least now, in the twenty-first century, we have to talk of *two* Fitzgeralds, Zelda and Scott, not as the definitive Jazz Age couple, with his songs and her heartbreak, and not because she was "beautiful, female, mad; and he was handsome and a drunk and died a failure," but because she has her own real claim as a writer and as a combatant in a world that gave women, beautiful or not, so little room to breathe.

CHAPTER EIGHT
ROSEBUD AND MR. BRICE

1.

History has its own strange currency where anything can be bartered and where personalities can rise and fall and rise again within a decor that shifts with the needs and the music of each particular moment. Take William Randolph Hearst. He was the first and perhaps the greatest of all modern moguls, with an empire of newspapers, magazines, paper mills, and motion pictures, his own "kingdom-by-the-sea" at San Simeon, a mistress who was an ex–Follies Girl, Marion Davies, "the No. 1 whore of the world's biggest son of a bitch," according to a piece of doggerel that is often credited to Dorothy Parker.

His empire began to implode in the thick of the Depression and Marion had to bail him out with her own jewelry. Film critic Pauline Kael once saw them dancing at a posh hotel in San Francisco, circa 1938: "It's like stumbling onto Caligula, as Hearst looked like a Roman emperor mixing with the commoners on a night out. He was a huge man—six feet four or five—and he was old and heavy, and he moved slowly about the dance floor with *her*. . . . When he danced with Marion Davies, he was indifferent to everything else. They looked isolated and entranced together; this slow, huge dinosaur clung to the frowzy-looking aging blonde in what seemed to be a ritual performance."

But they weren't allowed to melt into oblivion. In 1941, Orson Welles, a swaggering young director who'd played The

Shadow, Lamont Cranston, on the radio, and had mounted a voodoo *Macbeth* in the middle of Harlem, completed *Citizen Kane*, a film that parodied the life and times of Will Hearst and Marion Davies in a brutal *and* clinical fashion. Kane's childhood sled, "Rosebud," around which the film's narrative quest unfolds, happened to be Hearst's pet name for Marion's private parts. Marion claimed that she and "Pops" (as she called Hearst) never saw *Citizen Kane*. But one can appreciate his furor at Welles and his desire to destroy the film. He succeeded, but only by half. The film had limited distribution and wasn't advertised or reviewed in any of Hearst's papers, but critics adored it and recognized its worth—it was the first Hollywood film that wasn't made in support of the system and its rules. It was larger, greater, freer and much more baroque than Hollywood and its moguls, who would have killed *Kane* if they could. The film disappeared for ten years, but the damage was already done. Charles Foster Kane was a blowhard and a bird of prey, and Susan Alexander, his mistress and soon his second wife, was an alcoholic opera singer without a touch of talent. It didn't seem to matter that Welles as Kane and Dorothy Comingore as Susan Alexander had a largeness, a brilliance, and a tragic dimension on the screen. Will and his mistress had been laid bare to Hollywood and half the world, and "Rosebud" was the film's great, secret joke.

Slowly, but irrevocably, Hearst the newspaper tycoon was transformed into Citizen Kane, with his kingdom shunted from California to the Florida Everglades, and now called Xanadu—the pleasure dome of Kublai Khan, according to Coleridge—and Marion, the last and longest love of his life, who stuttered and had a comic streak, became a most uncomical *kvetch*. As *Kane* resurfaced in the 1950s, like a fabulous submarine, and was soon on everyone's "ten best" list, Hearst's persona disappeared, swallowed up by Welles' fictional character and by Welles himself, another gigantic man with a gigantic appetite, particularly for film goddesses like Rita Hayworth.

Will died without much éclat in 1951, and slept quietly for twenty years, until Pauline Kael published "Raising Kane" in the *New Yorker*; her aim was to rescue Brooksie's old friend, Herman Mankiewicz, from oblivion. Mank had shared an Academy Award with Welles for co-writing *Kane*, but had been overlooked in the monstrous notoriety of the film, and "Raising Kane" is a long homage to Mank and to screenwriters of the twenties and thirties who delivered some of Broadway's sound and fury to Hollywood, after Broadway itself declined and tumbled into a landscape of burlesque houses, penny arcades, and the musical extravaganzas of Billy Rose, which had Follies Girls without the Follies, without Flo's deliciousness and grand design. He'd even married Fanny, but that didn't make him another Flo.

Pauline Kael shoved at Welles with a vengeance, like a great barrister preparing to redress the crimes of current history. For Kael, Orson Welles' behavior toward Mank in regard to *Kane* was criminal. He'd tried to seize sole credit for the screenplay. And by cinching the character of Kane irrevocably to Hearst, Kael hoped to discredit Welles once and for all. If *Kane* was a portrait of Hearst, parodied or not, then how could Welles have discovered that portrait? It was Mank who knew Marion and Will, not Welles; Mank who'd been a guest at the "ranch" (San Simeon); Mank who'd seen Marion hide her gin bottles and grow obsessed with her jigsaw puzzles; Mank who'd uncovered the story of "rosebud," not Orson Welles. And it was Mank who really betrayed Will and Marion's trust, not Welles, who could never have found the material for *Citizen Kane*. He was a brilliant usurper, nothing more.

Of course Kael had been wrong about Welles' participation in the script. He'd built his own megalomania into the character of

Kane; much of the dialogue was his, but Kael's devotion to Mank
blinded her to Welles. Mank was the *writer*, and Welles was the
upstart who hadn't been old enough to be in Hollywood when
movies went from silence to sound. But Mank, and other expatriates from the Algonquin Round Table, had been there, and
"they could bring to the screen the impudence that had given
Broadway its flavor in the twenties . . . and liberate movies into a
new kind of contemporaneity."

And it's curious. No matter how close Hearst comes to Kane
and Welles *and* Mankiewicz, once Kael cuts Welles out of the
narrative, she also liberates Will, frees him from the mythology
of Orson Welles, and we can examine the peculiar, perversely
touching romance of Will and Marion without the gargoyles of
Kane and Susan Alexander looming behind them and sucking
up all the space. Kael may not be totally accurate in the details
of how they met, but the primal force of their first encounter is
accurate enough: Kael has Hearst spot Marion at the 1916 Follies, which he attends "every night for eight weeks," buying two
tickets—one for himself and the other for his hat—just to "gaze
upon her." And gaze upon her he did, for thirty-five years. He
would start a film company, make her a star, without giving up
that gaze: "leading men were afraid to kiss her; Hearst was
always watching." She was a funny girl, a terrific mime, but he
wouldn't allow anyone to glimpse at her sexuality or her humor.
His wife, Millicent, who was sixteen when he discovered her in
a chorus, wouldn't give him a divorce, so he built Cosmopolitan
Pictures and San Simeon for a queen he couldn't marry; he had
detectives follow her everywhere; she had to hide from Will and
his detectives when she had a short romance with Charlie Chaplin. While Will ruled, she ruled over Hollywood as its reigning
queen *and* courtesan. Will "took a beautiful, warm-hearted girl

and made her the best-known kept woman in America and the butt of an infinity of dirty jokes, and he did it out of love and the blindness of love."

2.

He was born in the Wild West in 1863, the son of a rich miner and future senator from California barely able to read a book. His mother Phoebe spoiled him, and he would become her accomplice and companion, going on a world tour with her when he was ten years old. He remained an "arrested" child all his life, full of mischief and a distrust for adults *and* their civilization. Winston Churchill would say of Will after a visit to San Simeon: "I got to like him—a grave simple child—with no doubt a nasty temper—playing with the most costly toys."

He went to Harvard and hated it. Philosopher George Santayana, who was a member of his class, recalled: "He was little esteemed in the college." This was almost a compliment, coming from a man who believed in faith and reason and retired to a convent, while Will believed in chorus girls and the *unreasonableness* of Krazy Kat. In his freshman year he inherited a mistress from another fellow. She was a waitress in Cambridge—Tessie Powers—and he was devoted to her for ten years. He brought her back with him to San Francisco after he was expelled from Harvard, lived with her in Sausalito, took her on a tour of Europe in 1892, and might never have parted with Tess if Phoebe hadn't given her money to leave on her own or be whisked away by the police without a cent. Will "was furious at his mother. He was missing Tessie." But he was already a tycoon, even though Phoebe controlled the purse strings. His dad had bought the *Evening Examiner* in 1880 for "the Boy" while he was still at Harvard—

and Will would always be "the Boy," with his high-pitched voice and feeble handshake.

The Boy was looking to spread his wings. In 1895 he bought the New York *Morning Journal* and moved to Manhattan. He began to steal reporters from Joseph Pulitzer's *World*. Phoebe paid all the bills. He was already "a master at constructing news from nothing." He could invent a war if he had to or a spectacular case of domestic violence. High society had to share the front page with New York's common folk, who preferred the "funnies" to world affairs. And Will's Sunday edition was like a constant carnival flushed with color comics that followed the adventures of the Katzenjammers and the Yellow Kid, and later—as Will continued to steal—Little Nemo, Mutt and Jeff, Popeye, Blondie . . . and Krazy Kat. The Kat was one of Will's particular favorites, or at least an important part of his progeny. He would protect George Herriman's strip from local editors in his empire "who kept trying to remove it from their comic pages, claiming that their readers just didn't 'get it.' " But Will "got it" all too well. He sympathized with the Kat's attack on the posturings of high culture.

—Why is 'lenguage,' Igntaz? Krazy asks.
—'Language' is, that we may understand one another, answers the Mouse, full of his own etiquette.
—Then, I would say, lenguage is, that we may mis-undastend each udda.

Krazy Kat could have been Will's news editor at the *Journal*, and like Krazy, Will would have nothing to do with "polite" society. He preferred the Tenderloin. He was part of the demimonde that dined at Rector's and Delmonico's, that went to circuses and casinos, and waited backstage at the Follies for their favorite chorus girl . . . like a gallery of lovesick, adolescent boys who happened to be millionaires. Will's dream of sexuality may have been a little retarded—the gigantic, gentle predator looking for available "rosebuds"—but it was a simpler version of the same erotic myth that would fuel and fire up Manhattan in the 1920s: Louise Brooks' land of the owl and the pussycat, where nocturnal, rich, avuncular males escorted beautiful teenage "brides" of New York who had fun on their minds, not marriage. . . .

The Boy had political aspirations. He wanted to be president, and he probably would have been, if he hadn't followed his radical career of running after chorus girls and *remaining* with them. Unlike other presidential hopefuls, "he made no attempt whatsoever to marry well." He'd rather ruin himself at the Follies than sit in the White House with some former debutante at his side. Will "reminded me of a kindly child, thoroughly undisciplined and possessed of a destructive tendency that might lead him to set fire to a house in order to see the engines play water on the flames," one of his columnists at the *Journal* remarked.

In '96 or '97 he happened to spot in the chorus of a Broadway musical a pair of "bicycle girls" whose main function was to show "as much leg as possible without getting arrested," and Will immediately fell in love with the beautiful Willson sisters, Millicent (sixteen) and Anita (eighteen). He escorted them everywhere, gave Millicent her own hansom cab and her own white horse. In 1903 he decided to marry Millicent, now twenty-one, "because he could think of no other way to continue their relationship." Phoebe fought against the marriage but had to give in. Millicent might have been an ex–bicycle girl, but she had a magnificent mien. She was tall, with striking features, and "piercingly dark eyes." She would make as good a companion as Will would ever get and would present him with five sons, including a pair of twins. And in an odd twist of fate, it was Millicent who knocked at the door of high society, not Will, Millicent who devoted herself to different charities and her sons; as her causes multiplied, she became less and less of a companion to Will, who had to find other playmates. . . .

Like Meyer Wolfsheim and the Wolf himself, like Fanny Brice and Flo, he was a denizen of Broadway. He rented a suite at the Bryant Park Studios on 40th and Sixth, so he could be near the chorus girls he loved and the lights of Broadway palaces. He was an intensely private man impossible to fathom. He had many flirtations but it was a long, long time before he would fall under the influence of another dancer. Near the end of 1915, a little after Millicent gave birth to her twin boys, Will met a chorus girl who stuttered and had a slightly crooked face. "She was not a classic beauty—her nose was a bit too long, her teeth not perfect," but her stammer "only added to her charms."

The Boy began sending little gifts to Marion Davies—silver boxes and boxes of candy. He built a whirl of publicity around Marion and got her into the Follies. How could Flo have resisted his old friend, one of the Follies' most faithful fans? Besides, Will's new mistress had "a flirtatious smile" . . . and she could dance. Will would make her a movie star, and while she filmed at his Manhattan studio, Will himself would be Manhattan's most formidable creature—"ridiculed, feared, or adored [but] impossible to ignore." He'd been a Manhattan congressman, had run for mayor and lost to the wizards of Tammany Hall—he was a demagogue who envisioned himself as a radical and a reformer. Teddy Roosevelt once called him the most evil man in America, but no one, not Ziegfeld, not Madden or the Wolf, had walked the streets of Broadway and been enchanted by them like Will, he who'd scorned Park Avenue and had practically invented café society as a newspaperman and night-prowling millionaire. . . .

But in 1925 Will shut down Cosmopolitan Pictures and had a "bungalow"—it was as big as a barn—built for Marion on the

MGM lot. He wasn't a night prowler any more. He fell in love with Hollywood, "this town without history" . . . and he would become it's prime aristocrat, with his own castle at San Simeon. "He had the one great, dazzling court of the first half of the twentieth century," according to Pauline Kael. But to Louise Brooks, San Simeon was "a deadly, dull place for anyone who did not revel in opulence, who was not a member of Marion's stock company of guests." It doesn't matter whether Brooksie was right. Broadway had lost its number-one citizen to the "ranch." Louise herself rather liked Will. "Mr. Hearst was not the ogre depicted by Marion. He did not devour pretty girl guests; he loved them. At San Simeon, I had to run away from him twice—once when he came upon me drying my hair by the pool, and once when he found me looking at a rare edition of Dickens in the library—because his marked attention would result in banishment by Marion from the ranch. . . ."

But whether Marion was a dragon lady or not, she endured with Will. "I started out a g-g-gold digger and I ended up in love." And the Boy himself? Louis B. Mayer's daughter, Irene, who was able to catch him up close, saw Will as a man "whose inner self never seemed to surface." Perhaps he had no inner self. Perhaps he'd stayed the Senator's Boy all his life, and was closer to Kane than even Welles or Mank could have imagined, chasing his own childhood, even as he had "Rosebud"—Marion Davies—in his bed.

3.

Broadway never quite recovered from its absent whirlwind. How could it? Will had dominated the town the way no one, not even Ziegfeld, ever would. But Manhattan did have another magnificent owl, Otto Kahn, banker and bon vivant, among whose pussycats was Louise Brooks. Kahn had a banking house behind him, not an empire of print. He was a Jewish aristocrat, born in Germany in 1867. He had private tutors and was a prodigy at the piano, violin, and cello by the age of ten. He grew up believing that music could cure every ill. He served in a hussar regiment, and maintained a "stiff, straight-back carriage" and a hussar's waxed mustache for the rest of his life.

As a young banker in London he cavorted with Oscar Wilde, Whistler, and Lillie Langtry. He arrived in New York with a simple suitcase in 1893, joined Kuhn, Loeb, and married into the firm, taking the daughter of a senior partner as his wife. He rose at Kuhn, Loeb, becoming a senior partner himself . . . and a millionaire. He rescued the Metropolitan Opera from ruin, risked his own capital, and lured Toscanini, Caruso, Pavlova, and Diaghilev's Ballet Russe to the Met. Caruso called him "Il Ottokan." Nijinsky, the greatest of Diaghilev's great dancers and his own tempestuous "pet," astonished American audiences with impossible leaps in *Petrouchka* and *Spectre of the Rose*. Kahn signed a personal contract with Nijinsky, but couldn't prevent the madness that overwhelmed him in 1919. "Il Ottokan" was no magician of the mind.

But he could move a mountain, or have his own mountain built in Cold Spring Harbor, where he put a chateau that was modeled after the palace at Fontainebleau, with 49 fireplaces and 127 rooms and a private railroad spur that climbed up the mountain and made his castle, "Oheka" (an acronym of Otto Hermann Kahn), the highest point on Long Island's north shore. Kahn now had a Xanadu that could rival Hearst's "ranch." Robert Benchley, Dorothy Parker, and the Marx Brothers attended his weekend parties at Oheka, and were picked up by a special boat at the 26th Street pier. Kahn himself was an occasional guest at the Algonquin Round Table. He couldn't bear to sit in one place. "It's inaction, not action that kills," he claimed. Kahn "was everywhere, a small, softspoken, compact figure, tirelessly on the move. . . ."

In 1925 the little hussar was on the cover of *Time*. In 1926 he was one of the first subjects of a *New Yorker* "Profile." Otto Kahn, said the magazine, "is an element of modern life. He is fate for once smiling and having a whale of a time. . . . He gives to artists, good and bad, because he gives to the impulse of the artist."

He supported the careers of Paul Robeson, Hart Crane, and Sergei Eisenstein. He plunged into modern theatre, "indifferent to profit and loss," bringing Chekhov, Ibsen, and Shaw to New York, and O'Neill to Broadway. Yet he could also be pedantic, vain, and foolish. He admired Mussolini and wore the fascist emblem as a boutonniere. And once, while passing St. Bartholomew's with Marshall Wilder, a dwarfish vaudeville star with a hump on his back, he said: "Marshall, isn't it beautiful? It always gives me a thrill when I look at my church. You know, I used to be a Jew."

And Wilder answered him like a true vaudevillian: "You know, I used to be a hunchback."

4.

But a foolish owl was still an owl. He loved the Follies and gorgeous girls as much as he loved Caruso and Pavlova and the perversity of modern art. He was the last energetic spirit of the new Manhattan, where everyone could have a mythic evening whenever Gershwin would appear at Kahn's parties and *play*. According to one musician, Gershwin was "the only pianist I ever heard who could make a piano laugh, really laugh." And it was this improvised laughter that delighted Broadway as much as his

songs *and* the songs of Irving Berlin. Daniel Gregory Mason, a
music professor at Columbia, complained that Broadway had
been poisoned "by Jewish tastes and standards, with their Oriental extravagance, their sensual brilliance and intellectual facility
and superficiality." Mason dreamt of a return to "Anglo-Saxon
sobriety and restraint," or the whole country would drown in this
"Jewish menace."

It was rural America's last stand against the mongrelization of
the metropolis, the *orientalism* of niggers and kikes that was over-
running Manhattan, corrupting the tunes of old reliable Broadway with ragtime, jazz, and Jewish blues, with beer and half-
naked bodies . . . and George Gershwin's syncopated piano
playing. If Brooksie was Manhattan's secret bride, then George
was its bachelor prince. Born in Brooklyn in 1898, he grew up on
the Lower East Side, a street urchin with a "brooding sense of
loneliness." He left high school to become a "piano pounder" on
Tin Pan Alley. More than anything else, he "loved playing for
people." He was a rehearsal pianist for the Follies of 1918, and at
nineteen he would become a celebrity on the Big Street with a
sentimental coon song, "Swanee," that Jolson delivered in blackface at the Winter Garden. It was the sensation of *Sinbad*, Jolie's
new hit show. Soon Gershwin was writing songs and entire scores
for Georgie White. It was at the Scandals of '24 that he first met
Louise. Gershwin was racing through the score on a beat-up
piano when Louise started to flirt. "I was 17. George was 26."

She began to criticize the score, saying that the only good
song in the show was "Somebody Loves Me." Gershwin glared at
her. She glared back—and both of them "burst into laughter." He
was sailing for Paris, and asked what he might bring back for her.

"One of those long wobbly dolls in felt pajamas smoking a
cigarette. . . ."

In 1937, months before he died, he ran into Louise in a Hollywood nightclub. He was the most popular composer on the planet, while Louise was already "one of the untouchables" who couldn't land a job in Hollywood or anywhere else. Everybody was "Hi-Georging him," but he went over to Louise and asked her to dance. It was thirteen years after that brief encounter at the Scandals, and he hadn't seen her since.

The young maestro had a troubled look on his face. "I've wanted to tell you—it's been on my conscience a long time. . . ."

They stopped dancing and searched each other's eyes.

". . . I forgot to bring you the doll."

That was George's *noblesse*. He might have been robbing graves when he wrote the music for "Swanee"—not the words—but he wasn't a real grave robber, like Paul Whiteman. George knew where jazz had come from, and where it was still played. He would often accompany visiting European composers like Ravel to Harlem clubs where they could listen to "authentic jazz." His own Jewish blues captured a melancholy that was the *undersong* of white Broadway. As Samuel Chotzinoff said in the *New York World*: "He is the present, with all its audacity, impertinence, its feverish delight in its motions, its lapses into rhythmic, exotic melancholy. He writes without the smallest hint of self-consciousness."

He even fell in love with an ex–Ziegfeld Girl, Paulette Goddard, née Pauline Marion Levy, who was secretly or not so secretly married to Chaplin at the time. She was the sole person in Hollywood who intrigued him. Goddard suffered from Brooks' disease—beauty with a little too much brains. But unlike Louise, she didn't mind seeing her name on the marquee of some movie house. She began as a bit player in *Roman Scandals* (1933), was Chaplin's "muse" and co-star in *City Lights* (1936) and *The*

Great Dictator (1940), and reigned at Paramount for a little while as an authentic movie goddess. But she had a very short fling with Gershwin, who was suffering from a brain tumor and couldn't even hold a glass of water in his hand. . . .

Gershwin would play at the White House for Franklin Delano Roosevelt during the New Deal. He was a "pounder" all his life, and Broadway seemed to prosper whenever he was near: "With Gershwin back in town, it promised to be a lively, exciting season." He might show up at some rehearsal or in the middle of a party, ask for an ice cream soda or a Scotch highball—his two favorite drinks—and hold an audience captive for a couple of hours.

He had his very own "daemon"—a rhythm that was almost infallible, and more madcap, in a much quieter way, than his only rival, the Marx Brothers, who tore up the 1920s with their "fascinatin' rhythm." They did *The Cocoanuts* with Irving Berlin, and drove him crazy. Berlin had come out of vaudeville, just like them, but he didn't have their anarchic pull. Groucho & Co. "looked at the stage as a vast toy store full of pretty girls, props, lights, straight men and women, and the greatest plaything of all, a script to be tossed around and pieced together again," preferably without Irving Berlin.

Harpo became a regular at the "Gonk" (as insiders called the Algonquin Hotel), but the Gonk would have nothing to do with Groucho Marx, who was considered "Harpo's Bad Brother."

Hollywood beckoned Harpo and his Bad Brother, as it beckoned George and Ira (George's introverted older brother), and the acerbic knights of the Round Table. It was not altogether a bad thing. "New Yorkers heading for Hollywood in the 1920s were not so much betraying the theater as extending its reach," according to Ann Douglas.

Even Earl Carroll had his own pocket edition of the Vanities on Sunset Boulevard and Argyle Street. Jolson and Fanny Brice took the leap. And the Great Ziegfeld dreamt of extending *his* reach to Hollywood . . . and died there. But it wasn't an idle dream. Hollywood, throughout the 1930s, was a kind of phantom Broadway, with nightclubs that parodied "21" and the Stork, *legitimate* theatres, movie palaces, delicatessens, and a hatful of gangsters who never had the quiet flair of Owney Madden. It had musicals, like *Gold Diggers of 1933*, with Ruby Keeler, Joan Blondell, and Ginger Rogers, who sings "We're In The Money" in pig Latin and walks through an art deco Manhattan that could almost break your heart—but as Hollywood always had a time warp of ten years, these musicals were wonderful bits of nostalgia . . . and the graveyard of a Broadway that was no longer there. You could barely find a gold digger on the Main Stem in 1933. With the repeal of Prohibition, the bootlegger seemed to vanish, or slink back into narcotics and prostitution. And one had to recall how much of the social and psychic landscape the bootlegger had once inhabited—Broadway was where he was welcomed and Broadway was where he ruled, with his own particular sense of vaudeville that marked the comic dance between gangsters and Prohibition agents—like the two fearless fat men, Izzy Einstein and Moe Smith. . . .

Iz was a "magnificent clown" and a minor clerk at the post office who lived with his wife, father, and four kids in a railroad flat on the Lower East Side. He was forty years old, five foot five, 225 pounds. "Most of this poundage was around his middle, so that when he walked his noble paunch, gently wobbling, moved majestically ahead like the breast of an everfed pouter pigeon," writes Herbert Asbury in "The Noble Experiment of Izzie and Moe."

Iz decided to quit the P.O. and become a Prohibition agent—it meant more money and a wider arena in which to clown. John F. Kramer, the first Prohibition Commissioner, had talked about the "noble experiment" of ending once and for all America's consumption of alcohol. "We shall see that it is not manufactured. Not sold, nor given away, not hauled in anything on the surface of the earth or under the earth or in the air."

And Iz went along for the ride. He was ingenious from the very first day, disguising himself as—a Prohibition agent. Bootleggers didn't believe Iz and served him a drink. Iz carried his own "evidence-collector," a small funnel in his vest pocket, with a rubber tube attached to a flat little bottle inside his pants. That way he wouldn't drink all the evidence. . . .

After a few weeks out in the field, Iz got lonely for his great pal, Moe Smith, who was a slightly taller replica of himself, weighing 235. Moe had once been the manager of a fight club on Orchard Street, and now had a cigar store cut into the crack between two buildings, and Iz, who was already Prohibition Agent No. 1, convinced him to leave his cigars and come into the land of bootleg whiskey and beer barons. Together they formed a most curious and incredible partnership. Moe would play the lugubrious one, while Iz was light on his feet. Like vaudevillians on the loose, Izzy and Moe would dream up some disguise—rabbi, football player, garage mechanic, grave digger, musician with a trombone, black man in Jolson's burnt cork—and raid barbershops, drugstores, delicatessens, and Harlem warehouses, looking for whiskey. They could have been Keystone Kops carrying rubber hoses rather than guns.

Iz had become as well known as the Woolworth Building. His portrait could be found inside most gin mills and cabarets.

Newspapers followed the two fat agents religiously. They appeared on the front page almost as often as "the President and the Prince of Wales."

Iz and Moe began to "choreograph" their raids, moving about with a fleet of reporters and photographers. In one "terrifying swoop up and down Broadway," the deadly duo rendered the *coup de grace* to such celebrated restaurants as Shanley's and Jack's.

They weren't restricted to Manhattan, but covered the entire "enforcement circuit," hopping from New Orleans to St. Louis, from Atlanta to Chicago and Detroit, in one surprise raid after another.

"For more than five years the whole country laughed at the antics of Izzy and Moe," who in their own furious way had a startling success: five million confiscated bottles of booze and 4,392 arrests. But their superiors grew more and more jealous. No one at national headquarters had the same flurry of headlines. And even when Iz and Moe shunned the press and wouldn't disclose to reporters the whereabouts of their raids, these same reporters, who were so used to Izzy's habits, began to invent their own stories and embellish whatever hints they had until Iz and Moe were more mythical than ever. . . .

On November 13, 1925, the government let them go. Iz claimed that the feds wanted to relocate him to Chicago, and that he would have been homesick in the country of Al Capone, so he "fired himself." And thus ended Broadway's most illustrious vaudeville circuit. Iz and Moe were Broadway characters who could have served time in Mindy's. . . .

But they were more than that. They were the benevolent comedians of Prohibition itself—the sainted fools of an enforcement that could never really take hold. Madden and Capone probably enjoyed them as much as the rest of America did. Would Scarface have tolerated Iz and Moe if they had been genuine angels of destruction rather than fuzzy detectives?

When Iz and Moe disappeared from the scene, Prohibition would turn ugly and eat into the fabric of Broadway. Jack's and Shanley's would have closed with or without Iz and Moe. But when the feds and New York's own frantic police began to hunt down Tex and systematically attack her clubs, it was an attack on Broadway—as if the Anti-Saloon League and its watchdogs had decreed that there could no longer be any *nighttime* in New York, that the capital of delicious chaos would have to become a truncated, piecemeal affair with a lot of ragged edges and no heart at all. . . .

5.

But that nighttime capital of chaos did have one last fling in the form of a cartoon character, Betty Boop. Betty was "born" with Helen Kane, a flesh and blood singer who shocked and delighted the Big Street with her squeaky, childlike "boop-boop-a-doop" rendering of "I Wanna Be Loved by You" in a 1928 musical called *Good Boy*. Helen went to Hollywood, but she fizzled without her "boop-boop-a-doop." And then, in 1930, cartoonist Max Fleischer created Betty Boop, the "boop-boop-a-doop" girl, who was an amalgam of Helen Kane's squeaky voice and the undulant body of Clara Bow—Clara was the '20s flapper whose body just wouldn't behave. It bumped along, inventing its own curves. She was an unstable girl constantly falling out of her clothes, on and off the screen. Clara was worried about her Brooklyn accent and had terrific stage fright during the switch to talkies. She was in and out of sanitariums for the rest of her life. . . .

Betty Boop inherited Clara's famous fragility and couldn't seem to keep the clothes on her back; the sleeveless dress she wore would slither and bump down every curve until the "boop-boop-a-doop" girl was practically undressed. The men around her would grab at Betty and soon there wasn't a single part of her that was left to feel. She was much, much sexier than any live actress. . . .

Max Fleischer didn't have much use for Paul Whiteman and his brand of white jazz. Ghostly versions of Cab Calloway and Louis Armstrong would populate the cartoons and "torture" Betty with hot jazz. But in 1935, Hollywood went after Max.

It used Will Hayes, Hollywood's own "archbishop" of morals, and his little band of censoring bishops, to destroy the exuberance and *danger* of Betty Boop. Black jazz disappears, and sizzling Betty with the "boop-boop-a-doop" eyes and the big, big head, becomes a schoolteacher and a housewife with a high collar and long sleeves . . . and a minuscule head. But one has to be grateful for pre–Production Code Betty, who was as fearless and fun-loving as Zelda and Louise, and could summon up a Broadway that was bad, bad, bad. . . .

The Big Street would grow dark and dirty during the Depression. "By 1932, Broadway from Times Square to Fifty-seventh Street resembled a frontier town with its honky tonks, dance halls, and cheap bars." What did remain was a "Broadway style, including everything from neon lights and publicity hype to dress and manner and speech"—the Main Stem that Ziegfeld and Runyon and Rothstein and Tex had imagined—which had "somehow worked its way beneath our skin as a nation," and had also detached itself from a physical, palpable Broadway, and would soon be sentimentalized, since Broadway itself was no longer a "moving target," but something that limped along in more and more predictable ways. . . .

Without bootleggers, Broadway couldn't compete with East Side clubs, like El Morocco, which catered to the socially prominent and the powerful—shunned all blacks and most Jews—and served as "a conscious contrast to the more raucous, Jewish, and socially mixed Broadway nightclub."

Enter Billy Rose, the Broadway impresario who'd mingled with bootleggers and copied their mannerisms, who ran nightclubs along with Owney Madden and Larry Fay so he could put on a gangster's black hat and have his own private harem. But as soon as gangsters went out of style he got rid of them and sought protection from his pals in the FBI. He was a half-pint with a big nose who looked like W. C. Fields. The son of Russian Jews—David and Fanny Rosenberg—he was born on the Lower East Side in 1899, and supposedly slept on a table for the first six months of his life, since his parents were so poor. David was a diminutive, mournful man who peddled buttons from a cart and barely spoke a word of English, while Fanny was a little firecracker five feet tall. Billy inherited his blue eyes from her, and his endless ambition. He was a wizard at shorthand and once worked for Bernard Baruch at the War Industries Board; there was an odd fascination and a lasting friendship between the cultivated financier and the future impresario who "jumped around like a rabbit" and had a "roiling, feverish unrest." He nearly starved after the war and had to live like a little monk at a church mission on 46th Street. He became a successful songwriter but never wrote a single song on his own. He was always part of an often invisible team. As one composer said: "Billy would have drowned if he had ever had to do anything alone." His most spectacular tune was "I Met a Million Dollar Baby in a Five and Ten Cent Store."

But songwriting didn't get him near enough to Broadway—"a Niagara Falls over which silver fell." He needed Prohibition, the turmoil of Madden, Rothstein, Izzy and Moe, and in November 1924 he opened his first club, the Back Stage, on West 56th—"an upstairs place," half hidden like most speakeasies, and an immediate hit with bootleggers and showbiz people, à la Walter Winchell. It was at the Back Stage that torch singer Helen Morgan was discovered. It was Billy who invented her trademark, singing on a piano, because there wasn't enough room for customers to dance while Helen was out on the floor. Bootleggers tried to steal her away, but she was loyal to Billy and stayed with him until she opened her own club, backed by bootleggers, of course.

A. R. took an interest in the Back Stage and bought his way into the club without Billy ever knowing it. As usual, Rothstein employed a series of middlemen. He was fond of Billy, but was careful around him. "I can't trust Billy. He's halfway honest. He acts like he wants to be legitimate in an illegitimate world."

—legitimate in an illegitimate world.

This was Billy Rose's particular stamp. He *looked* like a gangster in his black hat and elevator shoes, and he would continue to talk and dress like a gangster all his life. Perhaps that's what attracted Fanny Brice to him. He was a pint-sized reincarnation of Nicky Arnstein, five feet three and a half in his "elevators." She towered over him, and Billy liked to be photographed with her while she was sitting down. He preferred *shiksas,* tall *shiksas,* showgirls, or "long stem Roses," as he liked to call them. And he was a bit of an opportunist in his courtship of Fanny Brice. She had the contacts Billy would need, the "gonnegtions." She was Madame Broadway, "someone who was in with everybody, even the Prince of Wales," and Billy, the half-pint, was "Mister Brice."

A joke about Billy and his bride swept the Street.

—Who has the biggest prick on Broadway?

—Fanny Brice.

The half-pint bristled, but what could he do? Fanny furnished him with a home and friends, like Ben Hecht, who understood the ravenous wound of Broadway, the need for constant adoration. "The celebrity is haunted by the fear of waking in the morning and, like an inverse Byron, finding himself unknown."

Hecht was actually fond of Mr. Brice, who walked "with the bounce of an overwound toy." It was another of Fanny's friends, the Jazz Mayor himself, who married the couple at City Hall on February 8, 1929. She worked to save the marriage, while the half-pint "smoulder[ed] in the shadow of Fanny." But as his fame grew, he was less and less dependent on the funny girl. He was a producer now, the "Midget Maestro of Broadway." His most popular show was the *Aquacade*, a kind of precision water ballet that featured Eleanor Holm, a beautiful Olympic backstroke champion who loved to break the rules: "I train on champagne and cigarettes." She was another of Billy's "long stem Roses." He didn't need Fanny Brice. He had a ballerina in a bathing suit. He asked for a divorce. "It's no fun being married to an electric light." Her career clashed with his. "I want my wife to be at my side." Yet in some haunted way, he would always be "Mr. Brice," the half-pint showman in Fanny's shadow. . . .

Years later, standing in front of the Ziegfeld Theatre, which was now the half-pint's domain, Fanny said: "Up there is the most evil man I have ever known." Perhaps she didn't mean it. She had a grudging admiration for Billy, the "Manhattan primitive," a self-serving force who couldn't really have any friends and was the lousiest lover in the world. Like Al Jolson, he was a locomotive driven by a hunger he never understood. But he was shrewd enough to realize the romance and adventure Ziggy had concocted on Broadway. He wanted a piece of that romance. He bought the Ziegfeld Theatre, which Joseph Urban had built for Flo, with "gargantuan swaths of color; stairs, platforms, pyramids of carpentry." Urban had grasped Ziggy's appetites and dreams, to advertize himself and the Follies through a flamboyant, Broadway style of architecture. "A beautiful building," Urban said, "is indeed the sandwich board of its owner."

Flo was dead, and that "sandwich board" belonged to Billy. But as he sat in Flo's chair, he got the shivers and began to hallucinate. He saw Flo looking down at him like some angry angel. And the angel said, "What are you doing in my chair?"

6.

Even with that angel around, Billy wasn't shy. He took advantage of bombed-out Broadway. He picked up bankrupt theatres for a song and converted them into theatre-restaurants, which offered "a drink, a dinner, and a spectacular show" for one dollar. Unlike El Morocco, Billy's theatre-restaurants were "dedicated to the interests of 'Mr. Forgotten Man.' " In 1938 he opened the Casa Mañana in the old Earl Carroll Theatre on 50th and Broadway, with statuesque showgirls called "Junos"—blonde phantoms of the Follies. His most sensational club, the Diamond Horseshoe, opened that same year, on Christmas night, with *The Turn of the Century*, a two-hour extravaganza that allowed audiences to *relive* one evening on Broadway with Diamond Jim Brady and his most constant companion, Lillian Russell, with Rector's and a barbershop quartet in the background. "You have to keep in mind that 700 people are wrestling with a five course meal. The goal is a down to earth show, with obvious audience appeal . . . no subtlety allowed," said Billy.

Billy's goal was to "domesticate the nightclub, to free it from the stigma of deviance and decadent consumerism." He longed to take Broadway out of Broadway, rob it of its flavor and wit, and leave it a kind of neutered, nostalgic circus . . . with a five-course meal.

Billy "glorif[ied] wholesomeness" rather than individual girls, like Ziggy would have done—wholesomeness rather than "dangerous love," which had been the secret song of Broadway. Billy would depict rather than provide "the intense excitement of the big city." It was like watching the world from inside an aquarium. The relationship between the audience and the performer that had once had its own lyric intensity—its own powerful *touch*—was now reduced to a sleepy handclap before dessert.

Billy had even wrestled with the architecture, stripping away "the aristocratic excess, luxury, class distinction, and exoticism [that] had produced the Depression crisis [and] left theatres dark." *Excess* belonged to Urban. But Billy's Casa Mañana "featured streamlined moderne, a style that emphasized clear lines and a smooth exterior untouched by any kind of dirt and decadence."

It was a landscape without intimacy, the Broadway nightclub as "assembly line." Billy Rose had his jumping Junos. But what a distance there was between the Casa Mañana and the Midnight Frolic, where Scott and Zelda had danced within elbows of Marion Davies. There wasn't a single "rosebud" on Billy's Broadway. . . .

The Diamond Horseshoe closed in 1951, the year Will Hearst died. Both of them had become dinosaurs: the nightclub that thrived on nostalgia and the old baron who could no longer manufacture news out of nothing and impose Krazy Kat upon his dwindling army of subscribers—the Kat died long before he did. But he had Marion, who was more and more of a lush and didn't bother hiding her bottles of gin. She stuck with the pirate, in spite of her own flirtations and his: each one paid detectives to watch the other. At one point Brooksie was caught in that web, as Marion tried to implicate her in Will's liaison with a certain chorine, Maybelle Swor. Marion grilled Louise mercilessly about Maybelle. "Through her personal spies, Marion knew more about Mr. Hearst's affair with Maybelle than I did." But like two dancing monsters, Marion and Will endured. And this silent man, who revealed so little about himself, scribbled a love poem to Marion:

> *But no beauty on earth is so*
> *fair a sight*
> *As the girl who lies by my*
> *side at night.*

Will's "beauty" began to write her memoirs.

> *I was born in 1905.*

—that would have made her nine years old when she met Will, and she couldn't have been much of a chorus girl at nine. Even if she loved to lie, she was still devoted to "Pops." As he lay dying, it was Marion who took charge. When Will was too weak to make phone calls, "Marion made them for him. She had become his gatekeeper, his listening post. . . ."

It was Broadway's best tale—romance between the owlish millionaire and the chorus girl with a crooked face—much more potent than anything a half-pint could have produced at his Casa Mañana. It would outlast Orson Welles and the brilliant satire of *Citizen Kane*. It was simple, almost outside language itself. Once upon a time, in 1915, his little whale's eyes had fallen on Marion Davies as she danced, and would never, never let go.

CODA
THEATRE THIRTEEN

I first imagined this book a few days after 9/11. I was stuck in France and felt as if my own guts had been torn with all the architecture and bodies that fell to the ground. I'd never had much affection for the Twin Towers. They were graceless monoliths from afar, and up close they were like long metallic teeth sitting on the windswept plain of some alphaville, but that alphaville was still Manhattan, was still mine. And Osama bin Laden's quest to destroy them as symbols of American might was like the dream of a barbaric bumpkin who'd never been near New York, the most welcoming city on earth.

And with Osama has come a new calculus where nothing—not history, not landmarks, not ideas, not works of art—can be taken for granted. Anything can disappear. I latched onto one particular place, Broadway, which had defined so much of New York. Its brashness, its melancholy, its rapid-fire speech. Its reverence (and exploitation) of female beauty in the hands of someone like Ziegfeld, who discovered the Follies Girl . . . and added her to his own private harem. There will never be anything quite like the Follies again. It excluded black people for the most part, cottoned to millionaires, but it was far less parochial than Greenwich Village, which did welcome blacks and worshiped failure rather than success. Edna St. Vincent Millay, or "Vincent," the first woman poet to win the Pulitzer, whose hair "was the color of fire," her skin "as pale as milk," moved to Greenwich Village in 1917 and decided that she and her sister Norma would never be shocked by the Village's unfettered language. "So we sat darning socks on Waverly Place and practiced the use of profanity as we stitched. Needle in, shit. Needle out, piss. Needle in, fuck. Needle out, cunt. Until we were easy with the words."

Vincent was very *un*Broadway. Even with all her experimentation, her love affairs with women and men, she suffered from a crippling naïveté, like the Village itself, which had its own Follies, but nothing like Flo. Little Louise Brooks had more "moxie" than Vincent would ever have. She had all the verve of the twenties about her, in her helmet of black hair; she was never "this girl poet of the new bohemia," half silly, half sublime.

The Big Street had no time for bohemias, it was changing so fast. It delighted in surfaces, textures rather than meaning. Joseph Urban built staircases, not manifestos. And Broadway lived within an exuberant whirl of energy, a signage that lit the night, and a social order that included apartment hotels and rooming houses, delicatessens and vaudeville palaces, nightclubs and cabarets, where one might meet struggling chorines, retired actresses coughing their lungs out in a room that faced a wall, Jack Johnson shadowboxing in some basement, Babe Ruth riding along in his bearskin coat, Billy Rose looking like a gangster, gangsters looking like the president of Paramount Pictures, shopgirls in their little cloche hats, veterans of the Great War still wrapped in their puttees, detectives like Johnny Broderick who once stuffed Legs Diamond into a garbage can—they were all part of a melody that thrived in the dark, that would be imitated everywhere, until no one could tell the real from the unreal. . . .

It's January 2003, and after living a whole year inside books and biographical dictionaries, I hike uptown to the Big Street from my apartment in Greenwich Village. I don't expect much. Ziegfeld's New Amsterdam, where the Follies Girl perfected her famous walk, is now the lair of the Lion King. Lindy's current incarnation on the southwest corner of 45th and Broadway, with branches on Seventh Avenue, is more like a hamburger haven than the breeding ground of Leo Lindemann's spectacular New York cheesecake, without which Fanny Brice, Al Jolson, Rothstein, Dave the Dude, and thousands of other less celebrated citizens would never have survived. I can't go inside and bear witness to such a place, this Lindy's which isn't Lindy's, and will never summon up a single ghost, even if it calls itself "a slice of history." It's a tourist trap in the land of tourist traps. A poster in the window advertizes Molly Ringwald in *Cabaret*. And it's clear what the Big Street has become: a showcase for ex–movie stars in one musical or another. Kathleen Turner as Mrs. Robinson in *The Graduate*, who will tempt audiences with a touch of nakedness that's light-years removed from the Follies, where Flo's tallest girls would stand in the background with bared breasts that never jiggled once. . . .

Broadway is no longer "an unparalleled pedestrian precinct," as Ada Louise Huxtable writes in her afterword to *Inventing Times Square*. It has become a rather tame circus that exists to suck tourists into a sanitized theatre district. Movie palaces, which had once pushed Broadway theatre onto the side streets, are now marginalized themselves. Theatre has come back to 42nd Street. But the penny arcades are gone, with their necessary bit of disorder that once defined the Big Street.

I march north on Broadway to the only tourist trap that interests me: Hershey's Chocolate Store. I'm a sucker for chocolate, particularly the bitter kind that's supposed to be good for the heart. "Hershey's Times Square," as the store announces itself, tries to give the aura of an old chocolate factory; it has miniature milk pails filled with chocolate bars and an automatic gravitational chocolate machine that can spit out an assortment of candies upon request. It even has a weathered balcony that could have been the command center of a genuine chocolate manufacturer, but there's nothing to oversee or manufacture except customers looking for tee-shirts and coffee mugs with the Hershey logo, and the world's largest chocolate bar, which weighs five pounds.

There's little else I care about on this bloodless Broadway. I head south, return to Times Square and its cluster of "legitimate" theatres. I pass Madame Tussaud's wax museum, a McDonald's with a movie marquee, an internet café, a New York Yankees Clubhouse store, selling bats and balls and bears in a Yankee uniform, and a Loew's multiplex near Ninth. Rob Marshall's *Chicago* is playing at one of the chopped-up theatres of the multiplex. I take the plunge and go inside to see it. After all, it's about the Jazz Age, even if it's Jazz Age Chicago, rather than the Big Street. The multiplex seems to be a slice of some hotel, and "Loew's Times Square" is a labyrinth inside another labyrinth, a series of caves with phantom candy counters, toilets that overflow, stairways that lead to nowhere. I almost smile, because it's only in a goddamn calamity of a movie house that I can find the randomness that was once Broadway.

I climb four flights to theatre thirteen, which is at the end of a carpeted hallway. It's the middle of the afternoon, and I practically have a private séance. I'm with two other citizens. The screen bends around us like a bow. There's a flurry of trailers, each a replica of the other, about spy handlers and their latest protégés, with predictable femmes fatales thrown into the pudding, and I wonder if all of Hollywood is run by the same mindless mogul. Not to worry. The trailers end and *Chicago* appears inside theatre thirteen, with the furor of an express train, as Edmund Wilson once described the Follies. Legs abound, long legs, as female bodies dart across the screen like so many scissors. We're in some club that could be a Chicago version of Texas Guinan's El Fey, with a pint-sized stage that's packed with dancing daughters, every single one a gold digger. With them is Velma Kelly (Catherine Zeta-Jones) in a black helmet, à la Louise. And watching her with great big eyes is Roxie Hart (Renée Zellweger), whose lover, a furniture salesman, has promised Roxie a stage career. Roxie brings him home, while her husband is at work. The salesman dawdles with her, laughs in her face, and tells Roxie that he lied about her career. Roxie kills him with her husband's gun.

She sits in jail, attended by Mama Morton (Queen Latifah), the keeper of murderers' row. The film downplays Mama's dykiness. She's just a kindhearted capitalist with a fondness for girls who happen to kill. As long as the girls feed her money, Mama doesn't complain. And she steals the show while she struts and sings "When You're Good to Mama" with a fan of feathers, and for a moment you can imagine Bessie Smith, who also sang with feathers in her fist and swung her big body around.

It's Mama who finds a lawyer for Roxie—Richard Gere as the silver-tongued Billy Flynn, who sings and dances and holds an entire court in his sway. Gere is marvelous as a middle-aged man. He isn't the pretty boy of Coppola's *Cotton Club*, Dixie Dwyer, the faux Bix Beiderbecke. He's thickened in twenty years, and the oily charm of Billy Flynn seems much more within his nature. Like the rest of the cast, he's having a hell of a time.

And then there's John C. Reilly as Roxie's hapless husband, who dresses as a clown in whiteface and sings, "Mr. Cellophane," shuffling along like Bert Williams . . . and the parallel lines are complete: *Chicago* at theatre thirteen is as close as I'll ever get to *my* Broadway. Billy Flynn could be Rothstein's lawyer, William J.

Fallon, "The Great Mouthpiece," who never lost a case until he himself was put on trial for tampering with a jury in Rothstein's behalf. Will Hearst and his newspapers were behind the crusade to send Fallon to Sing Sing. But the Mouthpiece fought back. He swore that he was the victim of a conspiracy, that Hearst was out to get him because Fallon had damaging information about his mistress, Marion, whom he wouldn't mention by name.

"I have here in court the actual birth certificates of the illegitimate children of a motion-picture actress," he sang to the jury.

There'd been rumors that Marion had secretly borne a pair of twins, "love children" to match Hearst's own legitimate pair. The rumors would plague her and Will all their lives.

The jury acquitted Fallon. He smiled and went over to one of Hearst's star reporters, Nat Ferber, whose investigation into the dealings of Rothstein and Fallon had led to the trial. "Nat," he said, loud enough for the court to hear, "I promise you I'll never bribe another juror."

Richard Gere might have sung those lines in some other film—about Rothstein and Madden and the old Lindy's, the real Lindy's, before people ever talked about guys and dolls. . . .

I leave theatre thirteen and the swollen carpets of the multiplex, with Queen Latifah and Mr. Cellophane humming inside my head.

NOTES

CHAPTER 1

Page

8. "dozens of suits": Gabler, p. 89.

8. "more jewelry than a bride": Breslin, p. 22.

9. "in his personal relationships": Walker, p. 212.

9. "cardplayers, horseplayers, bookies": Kanfer, p. 79

9. "into a crater of light": Breslin, p. 85.

10. "They do not stop": Breslin, p. 261.

12. "Runyon's world": Taylor, p. 228.

19. "extend[s] the mystique": D'Itri, p. 150.

19. "a common tradition": Taylor, p. 228.

20. "Finally after a nightcap of ice-cream sodas": Gabler, p. 348.

20. "one unable to speak": Gabler, p. 349.

21. "Winchell, the ex-hoofer": Walker, p. 150.

21. "Broadway is a street of synthetic romance": Walker, p. 199.

21. "the Grey Ghost of Broadway": Gabler, p. 173.

21. "revealed nothing of himself": Breslin, p. 279.

CHAPTER 2

Page

25. "I have not seen one real gentleman": Burns, p. 29.

26. "wild worldly" men: Kouwenhoven, p. 53.

26. "but kidnapped from their context": Koolhaas, p. 11.

26. "a startling percentage": Burns, p. 12.

26. "They all drink here": Burns, p. 14.

27. "introduced an imagined world": Alexander, p. 50.

28. "I've had nothing but chuck steak": Asbury, *The Gangs of New York*, p. 177.

28. "There is more law": Asbury, *The Gangs of New York*, p. 237.

29. "Audiences felt that each show": Knapp, p. 134.

29. "trick animals or trapeze artists": Knapp, p. 138.

29. "I loved it—miss it": Knapp, p. 146.

29. "which radiated from New York City": Knapp, p. 134.

31. "she was a tired, nervous little woman": Walker, p. 12.

31. "Mephistophelian look": Morris, p. 266.

31. "bad brown eyes": Mizejewski, p. 53.

31. "fashionable and filthy": Mizejewski, p. 44.

32. "consumed by superficiality": Robert C. Toll, quoted in Mizejewski, p. 38.

32. "illuminated griffin suspended from its facade": Lloyd Morris, p. 62.

32. "A hush fell on Rector's": Lloyd Morris, p. 266.

33. "nagging him into producing a revue": Lloyd Morris, p. 269.

33. "played to a vast cultural imagination": Mizejewski, p. 16.

34. "supposed freedom and independence": Mizejewski, p. 74.

34. "[H]e had the most penetrating eyes": Davies, p. 13.

34. "living curtain" of chorines: Mizejewski, p. 194.

35. "All there is to this Follies racket": Tynan, p. 51.

35. "but the most modern and daring": Mizejewski, p. 8.

36. "would preside over the square": Taylor, p. xxv.

36. "as sheriffs parked out in the office": Gabler, p. 67.

37. "By the twenties, *Variety*": Taylor, p. 219.

39. "a large man in a camel's hair coat": Creamer, p. 221.

40. "bigger than the President": Joe Dugan, quoted in Creamer, p. 281.

40. "I don't mind being called a prick": Creamer, p. 270.

40. "driving down Broadway": Creamer, p. 219.

40. "beautiful nonsense": Lloyd Morris, p. 238.

40. "In Charleston he swung so hard": Creamer, p. 191.

40. "Everything about him reflected sexuality": Creamer, p. 322.

41. "Maybe—maybe to be king of the world": Katcher, p. 225.

41. "He ate a hat once": Creamer, p. 221.

41. "He was the noisiest fucker in North America": Creamer, p. 221.

44. "Part fraud, part fanatic": Cashman, p. xi.

45. ride mechanical horses: Jackson, p. 273.

45. "and the city block prepared for the next performance": Koolhaas, p. 48.

46. "For many years after the holocaust": Koolhaas, p. 63.

46. "delightedly d[raws] caricatures of cubist art": Lloyd Morris, p. 304.

46. "Chorus girls, dressed in playful and glorious attire": Taylor, p. 164.

47. "mirror the theater's design": Taylor, p. 136.

47. "Signboards are so placed": Taylor, p. 236.

47. "that allowed merchants to change": Taylor, p. 235.

48. "Nobody went into Rector's to dine": Taylor, p. 162.

49. "I hobnobbed with actors": Taylor, pp. 103–104.

50. "One does not relight a dead cigarette": Golden, p. 168.

50. "I don't care at all who is President": Golden, p. 150.

50. "celebrate the present moment": Gilmartin, p. 273.

50. "seemed to glow in intensity from a distance": Leach, p. 239.

51. "concentrate and confine such activity": Leach, p. 240.

51. "Put out the lights": Golden, p. 152.

52. "with balloons for playing 'catch' ": Furia, p. 200.

53. "Within weeks, the blond midwesterner": Burns and Sanders, p. 317.

54. "And I don't want to be famous and fêted": Milford, p. 82.

56. "You had to go there, dance every night": Berliner, p. 97.

56. "presented American life": Allen, p. 81.

56. "He was dangerous and senseless": Walker, p. 73.

57. "a staggering machine of desire": Leach, p. 99.

57. "Bottles of beer appear": Odette Keun, quoted in Burns and Sanders, p. 349.

57. "It has an appetite of its own": Leach, p. 114.

57. "flowed as a central capitalist space": Leach, p. 116.

57. "America in the twenties": Brooks, p. 60.

58. "as New York's underworld entrepôt": Gilfoyle, p. 313.

59. "the first sports figure to be packaged": Burns, p. 360.

59. "literally step out of the action": Gilmartin, p. 277.

59. "It was like nothing ever seen": Burns and Sanders, p. 351.

60. "The effect was not so much": Cook, p. 249.

60. "drove nightlife underground": Erenberg, p. 159.

60. "All dressed up": Erenberg, p. 167.

62. "this formidable woman": Wilson, p. 32.

62. "Better a square foot of New York": Berliner, p. 46.

63. "She seated guest stars": Berliner, p. 93.

63. "the Ziegfeld of his profession": Goldenbeger, p. 80.

64. "a small bronze-black elephant": Farnsworth, p. 174.

CHAPTER 3

Page

67. "We had four orchestras playing in relays": Donald L. Morris, p. 47.

67. "The better hotels and restaurants": Donald L. Morris, p. 5.

68. "marked the slide of local jazz into oblivion": Donald L. Morris, p. 183.

68. "bizarre, surrealistic zig-zag patterns": Donald L. Morris, p. 162.

68. "You were no longer a highwayman": Billy Rose, quoted in Donald L. Morris, p. 118.

70. "Rothstein wants to rob people sitting down": Breslin, p. 113.

72. "the perfect Jew": Alexander, p. 54.

73. "He was a battered, colossal man": Borges, p. 54.

74. "I'm not dead": Katcher, p. 30.

75. "found himself a king without a kingdom": Asbury, *The Gangs of New York*, p. 95.

75. "He had so many interests": Katcher, p. 43.

76. "Rothstein is a man who ducks in doorways": Katcher, p. 8.

77. "a Greek tragedy that was played as a farce": Katcher, p. 139.

77. "Abe Attell did the fixing": Alexander, p. 54.

78. "folk heroes": Katcher, p. 146.

78. "had money in everybody's mouth": Kennedy, p. 253.

79. "He'd failed at that as a teen-ager": Kennedy, p. 92.

79. "a moving gob of electricity": Kennedy, p. 97.

79. "the dauphin of the town for years": Kennedy, p. 13.

79. "a frail, tubercular, little rat [who loved] to burn men's feet": Walker, p. 234.

80. "making enemies like rabbits make rabbits": Kennedy, p. 97.

80. "Did Legs take him home?": Walker, p. 236.

80. "Jack had imagined his fame all his life": Kennedy, p. 89.

81. "lust for blood and torture": Walker, p. 23.

81. "Regular as clockwork, he comes here": Katcher, p. 2.

81. "*Dear Carolyn*": Katcher, p. 317.

81. "He was a man who had no inner resources": Katcher, p. 32.

82. "had been soft and chalky since childhood": Katcher, p. 214.

82. "He removed the last of his clothes in the dark": Katcher, p. 215.

83. "I think I gambled because I loved the excitement": Katcher, p. 20.

84. "We spoke of many subjects, but mainly of love": Katcher, p. 6.

84. "I shot him right through the prick": Breslin, p. 269.

85. "caplike hairdo and the Chiclets smile": Mitgang, p. 80.

CHAPTER 4

Page

91. "whose disembodied face floated along": Fitzgerald, *The Great Gatsby*, p. 197.

93. "I was in love with a whirlwind": Milford, p. 74.

93. "In the last analysis": Milford, p. 314.

95. Gatsby is a pun on *gat*: Bruccoli, p. 208.

97. "that banty rooster out of hell": Nash, p. 262.

97. "almost the exact antithesis": Asbury, *The Gangs of New York*, p. 346.

98. "and frequently let it be known": Asbury, *The Gangs of New York*, p. 351.

99. *Thursday*—Went to a dance: Asbury, *The Gangs of New York*, p. 346–347.

99. "in full view of a dozen passengers": Nash, p. 263.

100. "and toward all his comrades": Asbury, *The Gangs of New York*, p. 297.

101. "A lesser man": Walker, p. 103.

102. "His face was small": Walker, p. 106.

102. "frail and almost forgotten man of legend": Walker, p. 104.

103. "All publicity, to Owney, was bad publicity": Walker, p. 107.

104. "During his period of ascendancy": Walker, p. 122.

104. "his largesse": Walker, p. 111.

104. "so sweet and so vicious": Watts, p. 67.

105. "His word, except among madmen and low competitors": Watts, p. 104.

105. "always on outward order": Watts, p. 123.

105. "Wildest bunch of roosters you ever saw": Watts, p. 117.

105. "He saw no reason for killing anyone": Watts, p. 123.

105. "about the best dancer in New York": Anderson, p. 175.

106. "was enveloped in bitterness and melancholy": Anderson, p. 124.

106. "entrust himself to no one but Dr. Charles Sweet": Anderson, p. 122.

107. "created out of old New York a gaudy, upside-down metropolis": Anderson, p. 104.

108. "None of Fay's Broadway friends attended his funeral": Nash, p. 162.

108. "Flattery was sweet to him—and so fatal": Fowler, p. 111.

108. "was Jimmy Walker's Versailles": Caro, p. 338.

108. "What little I know, I've learned by ear": Fowler, p. 34.

108. "to put an illuminated wristwatch": Fowler, p. 188.

109. "cabal of crooked vice-squad policemen": Caro, p. 324.

109. "He loved like a woman": Fowler, p. 164.

109. "paraded the gaming rooms": Lacey, p. 122.

110. "more or less dropped out of sight": Asbury, *The Gangs of New York*, p. 355.

112. "the toughest nigger to ever live on 125th Street": Breslin, p. 333.

112. "hauntingly borderless without his music": Douglas, p. 416.

CHAPTER 5

Page

119. "became the Coney Island of the period": Asbury, *The Gangs of New York*, p. 6.

119. "who lived into their teens": Asbury, *The Gangs of New York*, p. 14.

119. "But when he wanted to cross": Asbury, *The Gangs of New York*, p. 36.

120. "demonstrated their mingled respect": Sante, p. 235.

121. "the Hebrew conquest of New York": James, p. 132.

121. "torture-rooms of the living idiom": James, p. 139.

122. "expressing that part of the American psyche": Warshow, p. 86.

123. "They did 'Dutch' [German] dialect routines": Howe, p. 561.

123. "sang and sang and sang": Goldman, p. 123.

124. "into something emotionally richer": Howe, p. 563.

124. "the very pace at which they lived": Howe, p. 564.

125. "like a cacophony of clashing tin pans": Furia, p. 191.

125. "that enabled him to learn": Furia, p. 194.

126. "Bix was not doing with black jazz": Douglas, p. 417.

129. "great farceur": Seldes, p. 198.

130. "One Saturday afternoon": Alexander, p. 44.

130. "Nicky is a long man": Katcher, p. 170.

131. "Mastermind!": Katcher, p. 171.

134. "The way to become famous fast": Gabler, p. 500.

134. "how a human being could have so little sense": Gabler, p. 258.

134. "a hole in his soul": Gabler, p. 500.

134. "large blue eyes, a thin, almost feminine mouth": Gabler, p. 9.

134. "had left him with four inches of scar tissue around his heart": Gabler, p. 7.

135. "Vaudeville made Walter an entertainer for life": Gabler, p. 45.

135. "Nighthawk of the Roaring Forties": Gabler, p. 93.

135. "human electricity": Gabler, p. 108.

135. "We learned Broadway from her": Gabler, p. 181.

136. "newsboy": Gabler, p. 64.

136. "I call every man I don't know Fred": Berliner, p. xi.

136. "She wheedled bald, dignified millionaires": Lloyd Morris, p. 328.

136. "attracted a set of largely rootless, dissatisfied": Gabler, p. 88.

137. "a moveable feast, flitting from one nightspot to another": Gabler, p. 188.

137. "Miss Guinan blended the Social Register": Lloyd Morris, p. 227.

137. "I decided that my clientele": Gabler, p. 189.

138. "New York's New Yorkiest place": Gabler, p. 188.

139. "a man without a private life at all": Gabler, p. 345.

140. "Don't you think that Al Jolson is just like Christ?": Milford, p. 157.

140. "in religious mania": Seldes, p. 191.

141. "When Jolson enters": Freedland, p. 100.

141. "Every person has an aura about him": Goldman, p. 87.

141. "outgrew Jolson's all-powerful but limited gifts": Douglas, p. 361.

142. "In those days you must remember": Friedland, p. 52.

142. "He teased, cajoled, and thrilled": Goldman, p. 78.

142. " 'She's a chandelier' ": Skolsky, quoted in Goldman, p. 168.

143. "She was flatfooted": Goldman, p. 157.

144. "It was frightening out there": Berliner, p. 103.

144. "Where Ruby had it over the rest": Goldman, p. 156.

144. "Jolson is here in Washington": Goldman, p. 163.

145. "like a prospective bridegroom": Freedland, p. 138.

145. "who could feel awfully lonely on a honeymoon": Goldman, p. 162.

145. "She was a stubborn, somewhat sassy young woman": Goldman, p. 162.

146. "I was just as surprised as anyone": Goldman, p. 192.

146. "the prospect of having a wife": Freedland, p. 193.

146. "Al was a possessive man": Goldman, p. 229.

147. "She has neither beauty nor youth": Berliner, p. 161.

CHAPTER 6

Page

152. "The strange, unnerving, distorted trees": Seldes, p. 245.

152. "I like to hear them people talk": Alexander, p. 59.

153. "is a little too piercing at times": Seldes, pp. 154–155.

153. "I say the negro is not our salvation": Seldes, 97–98.

153. "Can it be that the Republic": Mencken, quoted in Anderson, p. 180.

154. "not simply the exclusion of color": Mizajewski, p. 9.

155. "the funniest man I ever saw": Fields, quoted in Anderson, p. 41.

155. "the slovenly, lazy, dull-witted": Anderson, p. 37.

155. "excruciatingly slow": Watts, p. 13.

156. "imitated, with variations": Douglas, p. 75.

156. "American entertainment": Douglas, p. 76.

156. "you started black and ethnic": Douglas, p. 360.

157. "an exaggerated take": Douglas, p. 365.

157. "Free of the white person's gaze": Gates, p. xxiv.

157. "the slave's trope": Gates, p. 52.

157. "the trickster's ability to talk with great innuendo": Gates, p. 14.

157. "The Monkey is not only a master of technique": Gates, p. 54.

158. "an ebullient strut": Anderson, p. 40.

158. "resurrected a practice": Watts, p. 13.

159. "a pretty and demure-looking Chicago showgirl": Anderson, p. 38.

159. "grand pianos, gold and silver watches": Anderson, p. 40.

160. "hurling bricks and bottles": Jackson, p. 113.

160. "Do you know why I didn't recognize him?": Watts, p. 14.

160. "blacks had to study whites": Douglas, p. 399.

162. "and a burlesque of Russian ballet star Nijinsky": Douglas, p. 340.

163. "Jack was so fast": Farr, p. 66.

164. "a long, lean, bullet headed, flat-chested 'coon.' ": Jakoubek, p. 34.

164. "The fight, if fight it must be called": Jakoubek, p. 53.

164. "made a noise with his fist like a lullaby": Jakoubek, p. 61.

164. "Jim Jeffries must emerge": Jakoubek, p. 63.

164. "A giant-killer who was himself a giant": Farr, p. 82.

165. "I'm afraid of killing them": Jakoubek, p. 63.

165. "Come on now, Mr. Jeff": Jakoubek, p. 113.

165. "I could never have whipped Jack Johnson at my best": Farr, p. 122.

165. "a handsome blonde divorcée": Jakoubek, p. 59.

165. "the most elaborate and expensive brothel in the world": Farr, p. 72.

165. *The white man pulls the trigger*: Jakoubek, p. 70.

166. "a few real Rembrandts": Jakoubek, p. 86.

166. "I was a bigger attraction than the king": Farr, p. 138.

166. "Etta's face in repose": Farr, p. 79.

166. "I am a white woman": Jakoubek, p. 86.

167. "Jack Johnson has hypnotic powers": Farr, p. 149.

167. "They didn't want me": Farr, p. 168.

167. "in Chicago, white girls": Farr, p. 164.

167. "wept when he saw the shackles": Farr, p. 160.

167. "debauchery . . . and crimes against nature": Jakoubek, p. 82.

167. "the world's most notorious fugitive": Farr, p. 177.

167. "My real crime": Farr, p. 182.

168. "catch punches in his gloves": Farr, p. 66.

168. "Jack Johnson, like a man on the beach": Jakoubek, p. 98.

169. "You know I laid down": Jakoubek, p. 12.

169. He even had his own butcher: Farr, p. 226.

171. "a hieroglyphic in black and gold": Douglas, p. 451.

171. "Jack fell to the floor": Farr, p. 65.

173. "After one of her stomping performances": Howe, p. 563.

175. "She was a favorite of the crowd": Walker, p. 249.

175. "tall, leggy, and light haired": Mizajewski, p. 166.

176. "The tremendous strides": Whiteman, quoted in Jablonski, p. 69.

176. "sometimes hooked onto the train": *New York Panorama*, p. 256.

176. "Jass it up": *New York Panorama*, p. 254.

176. "jazz always meant a loosened beat": Douglas, p. 354.

CHAPTER 7

Page

181. "the secret bride of New York": Brooks, p. 9.

181. "As emblematic figure of the twenties": Tynan, p. 68.

181. "I like to drink and fuck": Brooks, quoted in Douglas, p. 48.

182. "and fell in love with New York forever": Paris, 33.

182. "standing motionless in front": Paris, p. 34.

182. "wore smiles as fixed as their towering feather headdresses": Paris, p. 34.

182. "because she was so extraordinarily beautiful": Paris, p. 41.

182. "no boyfriends, no drinking, and certainly no sex": Paris, p. 39.

183. "The Follies is such fantasy": Paris, p. 51.

183. "black-bobbed teenage rage": Paris, p. 78.

183. "as a pussycat, I sat under many a king's chair": Paris, p. 175.

184. "black-haired blonde": Paris, p. 508.

184. Money wasn't the main pursuit: Paris, p. 101.

184. "I let him take me just once": Brooks, p. 15.

184. "I just wasn't equipped to spoil millionaires": Paris, p. 3.

184. "a girl in a Prince Valiant bob": Paris, p. 3.

184. "finding debutantes a threat": Paris, p. 68.

185. "smiled his charming, silver-fox smile": Paris, p. 82.

185. "a four-yard train": Paris, p. 87.

185. "I'm not a chorus girl, I'm a dancer": Paris, p. 79.

185. "looked so stunning in a black suit": Paris, p. 87.

186. "looked like a corpse": Paris, p. 87.

186. "Central Park West Voltaire": Kael, p. 19.

186. "In 1925, he was the most famous person": Ricky Leacock, quoted in Paris, p. 104.

187. "Do you know": Tynan, p. 72.

188. "Isadora Duncan danced in a storm": Paris, p. 108.

188. "a bangle from Cartier": Paris, p. 110.

188. "I learned to act by watching Martha Graham": Paris, p. 110.

188. "dance in the *Follies* by night": Paris, p. 97.

188. "She is so very Manhattan": Tynan, p. 48.

189. "Making films in New York was okay": Paris, p. 499.

189. "Love is a publicity stunt": Paris, p. 231.

189. "like a terrible dream I have": Paris, p. 499.

189. "quickly lost in the void": Paris, p. 335.

190. "to get in my bed": Paris, p. 252.

190. "He loved parties. I loved solitude": Paris, p. 244.

190. "Staring down at my name in lights": Paris, p. 469.

190. a one-page article on Marlene Dietrich: *Positif*, May 1966.

191. "From dancing and acting": Paris, p. 469.

191. "does not consist of descriptive movement": Paris, p. 541.

191. "In my dreams I am never crippled": Paris, p. 544.

191. "Your life is exactly like Lulu's": Brooks, p. 80.

191. "When I was young": Paris, p. 521.

192. "They were sitting close together": Tynan, p. 71.

192. "All in three days": Fitzgerald, *The Crack-Up*, p. 88.

192. "living the American dream": Milford, p. xiv.

193. "Fitz [is] absorbed in Z's personality": Milford, p. 103.

193. "named after a gypsy queen in a novel": Milford, p. 24.

193. "bluest eyes in Montgomery": Milford, p. 30.

193. "cut with Coke": Milford, p. 30.

193. "did what she pleased when she pleased": Milford, p. 38.

193. "Soon the little box was filled": Milford, p. 37.

193. "a clear ice green that changed color with his moods": Milford, p. 43.

194. "They even looked alike": Milford, p. 43.

194. I AM IN THE LAND OF AMBITION AND SUCCESS: Milford, p. 56.

194. "would accept being his creature": Milford, p. 63.

194. "We were the most powerful nation": *The Crack-Up*, p. 14.

194. "[S]omething had to be done": *The Crack-Up*, p. 13.

194. "New York had all the iridescence": *The Crack-Up*, p. 25.

194. "[A]t the Midnight Frolic": *The Crack-Up*, p. 28.

195. "the world of motion pictures": *The Crack-Up*, p. 28.

195. "Suddenly, as though in a dream": Milford, pp. 127–128.

195. "If she's there Fitz can't work": Milford, p. 107.

195. "the curiously savage intensity": McKaig, quoted in Milford, p. 121.

195. "There began to be a touch of the vaudeville": McKaig, quoted in Milford, p. 128.

195. "I've studied ballet": Milford, p. 133.

196. "like two children playing together": Milford, p. 179.

196. "a Pavlova, nothing less": Milford, p. 170.

196. "I worked constantly": Milford, p. 183.

196. "she was in and out of mental hospitals": Gordon, p. xvi.

197. "He couldn't stand by": Milford, p. 268.

197. "I want you to stop writing fiction": Milford, p. 328.

197. "I cherish her most extravagant hallucinations": Milford, p. 268.

197. "[t]he mistake I made": Milford, p. 384.

197. "You're so thin": Zelda Fitzgerald, p. 138.

198. "Charlie Chaplin wore a yellow polo coat": Zelda Fitzgerald, p. 48.

198. "her toes picking the floor": Zelda Fitzgerald, p. 120.

198. "a feeling for the flights of the human soul": Milford, p. 304.

199. "otherwise she'd never have made all that money": Zelda Fitzgerald, p. 293.

199. "and to soften the harsh loneliness": Zelda Fitzgerald, p. 295.

199. "hung above New York like indigo wash": Zelda Fitzgerald, p. 327.

199. "flirted because it was fun to flirt": Zelda Fitzgerald, p. 391.

199. "I believe in the flapper": Zelda Fitzgerald, p. 388.

199. "And so if our women": Zelda Fitzgerald, p. 417.

200. "wide clear eyes and free boyish laughs": Zelda Fitzgerald, p. 296.

200. "Success was the goal": Zelda Fitzgerald, p. 408.

200. "The philosophy of our time": *New York Panorama*, p. 174.

201. "to make history": Dinnerstein, p. 21.

201. "crawled into the friendly caves": Zelda Fitzgerald, p. 40.

201. "beautiful, female, mad": Gordon, p. xviii.

CHAPTER 8

Page

205. "the No. 1 whore": Paris, p. 240.

205. "It's like stumbling into Caligula": Kael, p. 105.

208. "they could bring to the screen": Kael, p. 19.

208. "every night for eight weeks": Kael, p. 101.

208. "leading men were afraid to kiss her": Kael, p. 102.

208. "took a beautiful, warm-hearted girl": Kael, p. 103.

209. "I got to like him": Nasaw, p. xv.

209. "He was little esteemed in the college": Santayana, quoted in Nasaw, p. 33.

209. "was furious at his mother": Nasaw, p. 92.

210. "a master at constructing news from nothing": Nasaw, p. 102.

210. "who kept trying to remove it": Nasaw, p. 108.

211. "he made no attempt whatsoever to marry well": Nasaw, p. 115.

211. "reminded me of a kindly child": Nasaw, p. 15.

211. "as much leg as possible without getting arrested": Nasaw, p. 114.

211. "because he could think of no other way": Nasaw, p. 165.

211. "piercingly dark eyes": Nasaw, p. 164.

212. "She was not a classic beauty": Nasaw, p. 255.

212. "a flirtatious smile": Nasaw, p. 255.

212. "ridiculed, feared, or adored": Nasaw, p. 175.

212. Teddy Roosevelt had once called him the most evil man in America: Nasaw, p. 210.

213. "this town without history": Nasaw, p. 347.

213. "He had the one great, dazzling court": Kael, p. 102.

213. "a deadly, dull place": Brooks, p. 40.

213. "Mr. Hearst was not the ogre": Brooks, p. 52.

213. "I started out a g-g-gold digger and I ended up in love": Nasaw, p. 412.

213. "whose inner self never seemed to surface": Nasaw, p. 346.

214. "stiff, straight-back carriage": Kobler, p. 11.

215. "It's inaction, not action that kills": Kobler, p. 146.

215. "is an element of modern life": Kobler, p. 155.

215. "indifferent to profit and loss": Kobler, p. 129.

215. "Marshall, isn't it beautiful": Kanfer, p. 7.

215. "the only pianist I ever heard": Jablonski, p. 100.

216. "by Jewish tastes and standards": Jablonski, p. 59.

216. "brooding sense of loneliness": Jablonski, p. 1.

216. "loved playing for people": Jablonski, p. 15.

216. "I was 17. George was 26": Paris, p. 67.

216. "burst into laughter": Paris, p. 68.

217. "authentic jazz": Jablonski, p. 154.

217. "He is the present": Jablonski, p. 106.

218. "With Gershwin back in town": Jablonski, p. 172.

218. "looked at the stage": Kanfer, p. 106.

218. "Harpo's Bad Brother": Kanfer, p. 87.

218. "New Yorkers heading for Hollywood": Douglas, p. 62.

219. "magnificent clown": Lloyd Morris, p. 322.

219. "Most of this poundage": Asbury, *Aspirin Age*, p. 36.

220. "We shall see that it is not manufactured": Asbury, *Aspirin Age*, p. 35.

220. Iz had become as well known: Asbury, *Aspirin Age*, p. 40.

221. Newspapers followed the two fat agents religiously: Asbury, *Aspirin Age*, p. 39.

221. "the President and the Prince of Wales": Asbury, *Aspirin Age*, p. 40.

221. "For more than five years": Asbury, *Aspirin Age*, p. 45.

221. "fired himself": Asbury, *Aspirin Age*, p. 48.

223. "By 1932": Erenberg, p. 169.

223. "somehow worked its way beneath our skin as a nation": Taylor, p. xi.

224. "a conscious contrast": Erenberg, p. 170.

224. "jumped around like a rabbit": Conrad, p. 79.

224. "roiling, feverish unrest": Conrad, p. 197.

224. "Billy would have drowned": Conrad, p. 50.

225. "a Niagara Falls over which silver fell": Conrad, p. 65.

225. "an upstairs place": Conrad, p. 69.

225. "I can't trust Billy": Conrad, p. 78.

225. "long stem Roses": Conrad, p. 80.

225. "someone who was in with everybody": Conrad, p. 82.

226. "The celebrity is haunted": Hecht, p. 398.

226. "with the bounce of an overwound toy": Hecht, p. 399.

226. "smoulder[ed] in the shadow of Fanny": Richard Maney, quoted in Conrad, p. 85.

226. "Midget Maestro of Broadway": Hecht, p. 399.

226. "I train on champagne and cigarettes": Conrad, p. 111.

226. "It's no fun being married": Conrad, p. 117.

226. "Up there is the most evil man I have ever known": Conrad, p. 96.

227. "gargantuan swaths of color": Gilmartin, p. 278.

227. "A beautiful building": Gilmartin, p. 281.

227. "a drink, a dinner, and a spectacular show": Erenberg, p. 173.

227. "dedicated to the interests of 'Mr. Forgotten Man' ": Erenberg, p. 173.

228. "You have to keep in mind": McNamara, p. 178.

228. "domesticate the nightclub": Erenberg, p. 174.

228. "glorif[ied] wholesomeness": Erenberg, p. 174.

228. "dangerous love": Erenberg, p. 158.

228. "the intense excitement of the big city": Erenberg, p. 175.

228. "the aristocratic excess": Erenberg, p. 173.

228. "featured streamlined moderne": Erenberg, p. 173.

228. "assembly line": Erenberg, p. 174.

229. "Through her personal spies": Paris, p. 243.

229. *But no beauty on earth is so*: Nasaw, p. 577.

230. "Marion made them for him": Nasaw, p. 595.

CODA

Page

233. "was the color of fire": Milford, *Savage Beauty*, p. xvi.

234. "So we sat darning socks": Milford, *Savage Beauty*, p. 163.

234. "this girl poet of the new bohemia": Milford, *Savage Beauty*, p. 182.

238. "I have here in court": Katcher, p. 206.

238. "I promise you I'll never bribe another juror": Katcher, p. 207.

SELECTED BIBLIOGRAPHY

AGNEW, JEAN-CHRISTOPHE, "Times Square: Secularization and Sacralization," in Taylor.

ALEXANDER, MICHAEL. *Jazz Age Jews*. Princeton: Princeton University Press, 2001.

ALLEN, FREDERIC LEWIS. *Only Yesterday: An informal History of the Nineteen-Twenties*. New York: Harper & Brothers, 1931.

ANDERSON, JARVIS. *This Was Harlem*. New York: Farrar, Straus and Giroux, 1982.

ASBURY, HERBERT. *The Gangs of New York*, 1928. Reprint. New York: Paragon House, 1990.

———. "The Noble Experiment of Izzie and Moe." In *The Aspirin Age, 1919–1941*. New York: Simon and Schuster, 1949.

BERLINER, LOUISE. *Texas Guinan: Queen of the Nightclubs*. Austin: University Of Texas Press, 1993.

BORGES, JORGE LUIS. *A Universal History of Infamy*. New York: Dutton, 1972.

BRESLIN, JIMMY. *Damon Runyon*. New York: Ticknor and Fields, 1991.

BROOKS, LOUISE. *Lulu in Hollywood*. New York: Alfred A. Knopf, 1982.

BRUCCOLI, MATTHEW J., ed. *The Great Gatsby*.

———, ed. *The Collected Writings of Zelda Fitzgerald*.

BUCKLEY, PETER G., Introductory Essay to "Boundaries of Respectability," in Taylor.

BURNS, RIC, and JAMES SANDERS. *New York: An Illustrated History*. New York: Alfred A. Knopf, 1999.

CARO, ROBERT A. *Robert Moses and the Fall of New York*. New York: Alfred A. Knopf, 1974.

CASHMAN, SEAN DENNIS. *Prohibition: The Lie of the Land*. New York: The Free Press, 1981.

CHARYN, JEROME. *Metropolis: New York as Myth, Marketplace, and Magical Land*. New York: Putnam, 1986.

CONRAD, EARL. Billy Rose: Manhattan Primitive. Cleveland, World Publishing, 1968.

COOK, DAVID A. *A History of Narrative Film* (third edition). New York: W.W. Norton, 1996.

CREAMER, ROBERT W. *Babe: The Legend Comes to Life*. New York: Simon and Schuster, 1974.

DAVIES, MARION. *The Times We Had: Life With William Randolph Hearst*, 1975. Reprint. New York: Ballantine Books, 1977.

DINNERSTEIN, DOROTHY. *The Mermaid and the Minotaur: Sexual Arrangements and Human Malaise*, 1976. Reprint. New York: Harper Colophon Books, 1977.

D'INTRI, PATRICIA WARD. *Damon Runyon*. Boston: Twayne Publishers, 1982.

DOOLEY, DENNIS. *Dashiell Hammett*. New York: Frederick Unger, 1984.

DOUGLAS, ANN. *Terrible Honesty: Mongrel Manhattan in the 1920s*. New York: Farrar, Straus and Giroux, 1995.

ERENBERG, LOUIS. "Impresarios of Broadway Nightlife," in Taylor.

FARNSWORTH, MARJORIE. *The Ziegfeld Follies*. New York: Putnam, 1956.

FARR, FINIS. *Black Champion: The Life and Times of Jack Johnson*. New York: Charles Scribner's Sons, 1964.

FITZGERALD, F. SCOTT. *The Great Gatsby*, 1925. Reprint (the authorized text). New York: Scribner Paperback Fiction, 1995.

———. *The Crack-Up*. New York: New Directions, 1945.

FITZGERALD, ZELDA. *The Collected Writings of Zelda Fitzgerald*. New York: Charles Scribner's Sons, 1991.

FOWLER, GENE. *Beau James: The Life and Times of Jimmy Walker*. New York: Viking, 1949.

FOX, RICHARD WIGHTMAN, "The Discipline of Amusement," in Taylor.

FREEDLAND, MICHAEL. *Jolson*. London: W.H. Allen, 1972.

FURIA, PHILIP, "Irving Berlin: Troubadour of Tin Pan Alley," in Taylor.

GABLER, NEAL. *Winchell: Gossip, Power and the Culture of Celebrity*, 1994. Reprint. New York: Vintage, 1995.

GATES, HENRY LOUIS, Jr. *The Signifying Monkey: A Theory of Afro-American Criticism*. New York: Oxford University Press, 1988.

GILFOYLE, TIMOTHY J., "Policing of Sexuality," in Taylor.

GILMARTIN, GREGORY F., "Joseph Urban," in Taylor.

GOLDMAN, HERBERT G. *Jolson: The Legend Comes to Life*. New York: Oxford University Press, 1988.

GOLDEN, EVE. *Anna Held and the Birth of Ziegfeld's Broadway*. Lexington: The University Press of Kentucky, 2000.

GOLDENBERGER, PAUL. *The Skyscraper*. New York: Alfred A. Knopf, 1982.

GORDON, MARY. Introduction to *The Collected Writings of Zelda Fitzgerald*.

GROSSMAN, BARBARA. *Funny Girl: The Life and Times of Fannie Brice*. Bloomington: Indiana University Press, 1991.

HAMMACK, DAVID C., "Developing for Commercial Culture," in Taylor.

HAMMETT, DASHIELL. *The Thin Man*. New York: Alfred A. Knopf, 1934.

HARRIS, NEIL, "Urban Tourism and the Commercial City," in Taylor.

HECHT, BEN. *A Child of the Century.* Reprint. New York: Donald I. Fine, 1985.

HEMINGWAY, ERNEST. *A Moveable Feast.* London: Jonathan Cape, 1964.

HOWE, IRVING. *World of Our Fathers.* New York: Harcourt Brace Jovanovich, 1975.

JABLONSKI, EDWARD. *Gershwin*, 1988. New York: Da Capo Press, 1988.

————. *Irving Berlin: American Troubadour.* New York: Henry Holt, 1999.

JACKSON, KENNETH J., ed. *The Encyclopedia of New York City.* New Haven: Yale University Press, 1995.

JAKOUBEK, ROBERT. *Jack Johnson: Heavyweight Champion.* New York: Chelsea House, 1990.

JAMES, HENRY. *The American Scene.* New York: Harper & Brothers, 1907.

KAEL, PAULINE. "Raising Kane." In *The Citizen Kane Book*, 1971. Reprint. New York: Bantam Books, 1974.

KANFER, STEFAN. *Groucho: The Life and Times of Julius Henry Marx.* New York: Alfred A. Knopf, 2000.

KATCHER, LEO. *The Big Bankroll: The Life and Times of Arnold Rothstein*, 1959. Reprint. New York: Da Capo Press, 1994.

KENNEDY, WILLIAM. *Legs*, 1975. Reprint. New York: Penguin Books, 1983.

KNAPP, MARGARET, Introductory Essay to "Entertainment and Commerce," in Taylor.

KOBLER, JOHN. *Otto the Magnificent: The Life of Otto Kahn.* New York: Charles Scribner's Sons, 1988.

KOOLHASS, REM. *Delirious New York*. New York: Oxford
University Press, 1978.

KOUENHOVEN, JOHN A. *The Columbia Historical Portrait of
New York*. New York: Harper & Row, Icon Editions, 1972.

LACEY, ROBERT. *Little Man: Meyer Lansky and the Gangster's
Life*. Boston: Little Brown, 1991.

LEACH, WILLIAM, "Brokers and the New Corporate, Indus-
trial Order," in Taylor.

———. Introductory Essay to "Commercial Aesthetics," in Taylor.

LEINWAND, GERALD. *1927: High Tide of the 1920s*. New
York: Four Walls Eight Windows, 2001.

McNAMARA, BROOKS, "The Entertainment District at the
End of the 1930s," in Taylor.

MILFORD, NANCY. *Savage Beauty: The Life of Edna St. Vincent Millay*. New York: Random House, 2001.

———. *Zelda*, 1970. Reprint. New York: Avon Books, 1971.

MITGANG, HERBERT. *Jimmy Walker, Franklin Roosevelt, and
the Last Great Battle of the Jazz Age*. New York: Free Press,
2000.

MIZEJEWSKI, LINDA. *Ziegfeld Girl: Image and Icon in Culture
and Cinema*. Durham: Duke University Press, 1989.

MORRIS, DONALD L. *Wait Until Dark: JAZZ and the Underworld, 1880–1940*. Bowling Green: Bowling Green University Press, 1980.

MORRIS, LLOYD. *Incredible New York*. New York: Random
House, 1951.

NASH, ROBERT JAY. *World Encyclopedia of Organized Crime*.
New York: Paragon House, 1992.

NASAW, DAVID. *The Chief: The Life of William Randolph
Hearst*. Boston: Houghton Mifflin, 2000.

New York Panorama. New York: Pantheon Books, 1984.

PARIS, BARRY. Louise Brooks. New York, Alfred A. Knopf, 1989.

ROSENBLUM, CONSTANCE. *Gold Digger: The Outrageous Life and Times of Peggy Hopkins Joyce*. New York: Metropolitan Books, 2000.

ROTHMAN, SHEILA M. *Women's Proper Place: A History of Changing Ideals and Practices, 1870 to the Present*. New York: Basic Books, 1978.

RUNYON, DAMON. *Guys And Dolls*. Philadelphia: Lippincott, 1935.

SAFIRE, WILLIAM, "Redefining the 'rope-a-dope' strategy." *International Herald Tribune*, October 14, 2002. Reprinted from the *New York Times*.

SANTE, LUC. *Low Life*, 1991. Reprint. New York: Vintage, 1992.

SCHULBERG, BUDD. *Moving Pictures: Memories of a Hollywood Prince*. London: Souvenir Press, 1982.

SELDES, GILBERT. *The 7 Lively Arts*. New York: Harper & Brothers, 1924.

SNYDER, ROBERT W., "Vaudeville and the Transformation of Popular Culture," in Taylor.

TAYLOR, WILLIAM R., ed. *Inventing Times Square*. New York: Russell Sage Foundation, 1991

———. "Broadway: The Place That Words Built," in Taylor.

TYNAN, KENNETH. "The Girl in the Black Helmet." *The New Yorker*, June 11, 1979.

WALKER, STANLEY. *The Night Club Era*. New York: Frederick A. Stokes, 1933.

WARSHOW, ROBERT. *The Immediate Experience*. Garden City: Anchor Books, 1964.

WATTS, JILL. *Mae West: An Icon in Black and White.* New York: Oxford University Press, 2000.

WEST, NATHANAEL. *The Complete Works.* New York: Farrar, Straus & Cudahy, 1957.

WILSON, EDMUND. *The Twenties.* New York: Farrar, Straus and Giroux, 1975.

———. *The American Earthquake.* New York: Farrar, Straus and Giroux, 1971.

WPA Guide to New York City, The. 1939. Reprint. New York: Pantheon Books, 1982.

INDEX

A. R. *See* Rothstein, Arnold "A. R." "The Brain" "Wolf"
Adams, John, 25
Aeolian Hall, 176
African-Americans. *See* blacks
Alexander's Ragtime Band (movie), 127–29, 132
"Alexander's Ragtime Band" (song), 48, 126
Algonquin Hotel "Gonk," 218
Algonquin Round Table, 67, 141, 208, 214–15
Ali, Muhammad, 172
all-black shows and revues
  In Dahomey, 161
  Dixie to Broadway, 175
  near-white chorus girls in, 57–58, 67, 103, 123
  Shuffle Along, 152–54
Allen, Lee, 39
Ameche, Don, 127–29
American Notes, 119
Amsterdam theater, 49, 234
Anderson, Dave, 172
Anderson, Jervis, 170
Ansonia Hotel, 39
Anti-Saloon League. *See* Prohibition
anti-Semitism, 72, 121, 154, 216, 224
Apocalypse Now, 110
Aquacade, 226
arcades, 170, 235
Armory Show of modern art, 46
Armstrong, Louis, 177
Arnstein, Nicky
  ineptitude as criminal, 131
  love of Brice for, 129–30

manners and refinement, 74, 130
portrayal in *Funny Girl,* 133
work with Rothstein, 74–75
Asbury, Herbert, 110, 119, 219
Attell, Abe, 76–77

Baby Snooks, 124, 131–33
Back Stage club, 225
Baline, Israel. *See* Berlin, Irving
Bambino. *See* Ruth, Babe
Baruch, Bernard, 224
Bayes, Nora, 173
Beau James. *See* Walker, Jimmy
Beiderbecke, Bix, 42, 112, 126
Benchley, Robert, 141
Benjamin, Walter, 146–47
Berlin, Irving
  Alexander's Ragtime Band (movie), 127–29, 132
  "Alexander's Ragtime Band" (song), 48, 126
  boyhood and early musical jobs, 124–25
  compared to Beiderbecke, 126
  elopement with Mackay, 58
  rise from Jewish ghetto, 121–22
  success, 125–26
  "white rag" music, 126
  work with the Marx Brothers, 218
  work with Ziegfeld Follies, 52
Bernays, Edward, 49
Betty Boop, 222–23
Beverly Wilshire, 190
bigotry. *See* racism
Big Street. *See* Broadway
Billingsley, Sherman, 137–38
Black Bohemia, 48, 159–60

287